Praise for *Insurgent Muse*

"The spirit of the legendary Woman's Building lives on in this unflinchingly brave and tender memoir. Terry Wolverton's *Insurgent Muse* is witty, heart-rending, superbly honest and deeply moving, providing an acute social analysis of a young life and a memorable era of feminism that fueled so much art and so many epiphanies. The great work of the Woman's Building deserves this book." — Lucy Lippard, author of *The Pink Glass Swan: Selected Feminist Essays on Art*

"Written by one of the chief carpenters, *Insurgent Muse* is a history, personal and political, of a building and its spirits in residence. A wonderful mixture of personal memoir, performance art history, the sea changes in feminism, a novelist's narrative, lesbian soap opera, and Los Angeles lore, Wolverton's work is informed, honest, hilarious and excruciating. It is particularly valuable for the claim it stakes to a West Coast history, both of lesbian culture and feminist art." —Catherine Lord, professor of studio art at UC Irvine

"In a memoir, I expect a personal journey and hope for more. Terry Wolverton's *Insurgent Muse* delights me with an individual, collective, institutional, and historical text. My friend and colleague for over two decades, Wolverton can always be counted on to write with integrity, commitment, and charm." — Arlene Raven, award-winning art historian and cofounder of the Woman's Building

"The Woman's Building was magical, like the Hollywood sign and the Santa Monica pier. It was physical proof that the future was indeed here, now, and we were it. *Insurgent Muse* is a singular rite of passage that is simultaneously a collective coming of age. Wolverton is a passionate and accomplished writer." —Kate Braverman, author of *Lithium for Medea*

"Terry Wolverton's amazing *Insurgent Muse* is a smart, funny, sexy and deeply honest tribute to the extraordinary community of women artists whose creativity and fierce living rocked the world from an old building in downtown L.A. Part engaging memoir and part trenchant social history, Wolverton tells a story that is remarkably moving and inspiring. *Insurgent Muse* is a triumph." — Tim Miller, solo performer and author of *Shirts and Skins* and *Body Blows*

"Wolverton's memoir chronicles her 'coming of age' as a lesbian feminist writer and performance artist at the historic L.A. Woman's Building. It's a story of utopian ideals, passionate politics and the struggle to survive the changing political landscapes of America." — Harmony Hammond, artist and author of *Lesbian Art in America: A Contemporary History*

"Is any individual life a representative life? Terry Wolverton's seems to be in so many ways. Her searingly honest memoir tells what it was like to be a woman, an artist, a lesbian during those heady, storm and stress decades of the 1970s and '80s. It's all here — the multi-lover dyko dramas, the intersection of personal and political, the Coming Out and Recovery and remembering sexual abuse movements, the rise and fall of a women's cultural center, the Woman's Building in L.A. Wolverton has a poet's sense of the complexities of the interior life and an eye witness's intimacy with that era. Anyone wanting to know what it was like to be a woman, an artist, a lesbian at the end of the last American century will find this book indispensable." — Rebecca Brown, author of *The Terrible Girls* and *The Dogs*

INSURGENT MUSE
LIFE AND ART AT THE WOMAN'S BUILDING

by TERRY WOLVERTON

CITY LIGHTS
SAN FRANCISCO

Cover photographs © Maria Karras
Cover graphic by Sheila de Bretteville
Cover design by Rex Ray
Book design by Elaine Katzenberger
Typography by Harvest Graphics

All photos © the individual photographers
(Note: Every reasonable effort was made to contact each photographer and to secure her permission, though we were not successful in all cases. We hope that the credit given herein will serve to honor all those whose work is represented here.)

Grateful acknowledgment is due to Sue Maberry for her help with accessing images from the Woman's Building Slide Archive, which is housed at the Otis College of Art and Design Library.

Library of Congress Cataloging-in-Publication Data

Wolverton, Terry.
    Insurgent muse : life and art at the Woman's Building / by Terry Wolverton.
       p.   cm.
    ISBN 0-87286-403-0
    1. Feminism and the arts—California—Los Angeles—History—20th century.
  2. Woman's Building (Los Angeles, Calif.)—History. 3. Wolverton, Terry.
  4. Lesbians—California—Los Angeles—Biography. I. Title.
    NX180.F4 W636 2002
    704'.042'0979494—dc21   2002019773

Visit our web site: www.citylights.com

CITY LIGHTS BOOKS are edited by Lawrence Ferlinghetti and Nancy J. Peters and published at the City Lights Bookstore, 261 Columbus Avenue, San Francisco, CA 94133

Acknowledgments

Thanks to Robert Drake and Elaine Katzenberger for their belief in the vision of this book when there was little more of it than a vision, and especially to Elaine for her insightful guidance in its realization. Gratitude and praise to all my students in One Page At a Time, especially Cara Chow, Jeanne Cordova, Tim Grant, Marcella Greening, Anita Guerrero, Matt Knight, Ellen Lazares, Trish Nickels, and David Vernon. Deep appreciation also to Jacqueline de Angelis, Julia Gibson, and Noelle Sickels, for their many years of friendship and literary sisterhood. I am further indebted to Matt, Julia, Pat Alderete, Cynthia Bond, Sasha Marcus, and Lisa Nemzo for the many writing dates over the course of years it took to develop this book. And to Gwin Wheatley, for her tireless efforts to help extend its reach. The truth is, I am blessed to have an abundant community of friends, students, colleagues, practitioners, and readers who support me in the creation of my work. Although you are too many to list here, please know that each of you is precious in my heart.

To Judy, Sheila, and Arlene
who lit the torch, then passed it

to Deena
who took me seriously as a writer

and to my students
who remind me why the vision is important still

No one ever told us we had to study our lives . . .
from "Transcendental Etude,"
The Dream of a Common Language
by Adrienne Rich

Contents

Introduction

Feminist art raises consciousness,
invites dialogue, and transforms culture.
—Arlene Raven, art historian and
Woman's Building cofounder

LAST SPRING, WHILE ATTENDING A WRITING CONFERENCE IN THE DESERT, I had occasion to share a table over lunch with a woman I'd never met before. Perhaps ten years my senior, she confided that she was back in school pursuing her doctorate. Her dissertation, she divulged, would be about representations of Eve in the work of contemporary writers and artists.

"I have a poem with Eve in it," I couldn't help but offer, and she insisted I send it to her.

Like me, she was a feminist, and it was through this door that we entered to find common ground. Our conversation was deep and intimate, rapid-fire, ideas and revelations spilling over themselves in our fervor to express them. Amid the sea of writers and academics at the conference, we were delighted to have found each other. Truth is, for that hour or so over salad and sandwich, I think we fell a little in love with each other. I don't mean that in the romantic sense. I was reminded of the early years of Second Wave feminism, the seventies, when women were becoming conscious of our own power and vibrancy, and when we'd meet another who was engaged in that same process, we couldn't help but fall in love because she was a reflection of our own possibilities.

So I was startled when, near the end of our meal, my table companion lamented, with great sorrow and weariness, that the women's movement had been "a failure."

"How can you say that?" I asked, incredulous.

"Well, so much of what we fought for didn't come to pass," she explained.

"But so much has! Don't you remember what it was like before?" I pleaded with her. "In the 1960s, would you have imagined that you could get your Ph.D.? Could we have regarded Eve as anything other than the source of original sin? We have to measure our success from where we've come, not by how far we have to go!"

Breathless, I made myself stop; I was in danger of spontaneous combustion. Yet here we were: two women writers engaged in passionate discourse about ideas we held dearest: our work, our inspiration, our identities as women. Without the women's movement, and for myself, specifically without the feminist art movement, I knew, we would not have been there.

~

TO UNDERSTAND THE ORIGINS of the feminist art movement in the United States, one must look to the foment of the 1960s and early '70s, the swarm of rebellion and leaps in consciousness that redefined American culture. In 1955 a seamstress named Rosa Parks refused to give up her seat on a Montgomery, Alabama, bus and thus gave rise to the civil rights movement, which ignited a host of struggles for social liberation waged by women, Chicanos, Native Americans, gays and lesbians, and others. These movements not only demanded more equitable distribution of power and resources, but raised profound questions about the meaning assigned to these identities and the cultural representations of these groups.

Opposition to U.S. involvement in Vietnam stoked an unprecedented youth movement which, in addition to the politics of protest, embraced "sex, drugs, and rock 'n' roll." This fueled a thriving counterculture determined to forge alternatives to the economic, social, and moral structures of the mainstream.

Within the art world, too, there began to be a challenge to the hegemony of formalism that had dominated the 1950s and '60s, in which any concern for content in art was disregarded or disdained. Questions of cultural identity incited a push for the democratization of art, a demand for greater inclusiveness with regard to both who could make images and who had access to them.

The feminist art movement in California began in 1970, a year that saw the protest by women artists of the "Art and Technology" exhibit at the Los Angeles County Museum of Art (LACMA) in which not one woman artist was included. Further research uncovered the statistic that of eighty-one one-person shows at LACMA in a ten-year period, only one presented the work of a woman artist. That same year, artist Judy Chicago established the Feminist Art Program at California State University, Fresno. These two events serve to illustrate the dual concerns of the feminist art movement: the push for better inclusion of women in the mainstream art world and the utter redefinition of art and culture within a feminist context.

The Woman's Building, on which this book centers, attempted to walk the line between these two positions, calling itself "a public center for women's culture." Founded in 1973 in Los Angeles by Judy Chicago, graphic designer Sheila Levrant de Bretteville, and art historian Arlene Raven, the Woman's Building offered opportunities for women in the fields of creative writing, graphic design, the printing arts, performance art, video, and visual arts. "Public center" signified the wish to make a place for women artists in the mainstream, while "women's culture" revealed more subversive intentions. Women live in a different culture than men, was the claim, bounded not only by social position and opportunity but also by differing concerns, values, and worldviews. In 1973, when the Building was founded, we were arrogant enough to try to codify those differences, blithely secure in the assumption we could speak for all women. The late 1970s and especially the 1980s would foreground pervasive differences among women — including race, class, and sexual orientation — and the pitfalls of essentialism.

The initial vision of the three founders, all of whom had been on the faculty of California Institute of the Arts, was to create an alternative program for women's art education, the Feminist Studio Workshop (FSW). But de Bretteville, especially, did not want to replicate another ivory tower, and sought to align this new school with the burgeoning women's movement in Los Angeles. Out of this expansive vision was formed the Woman's Building,[1] a public center that could house the school as well as other feminist organizations and businesses. When it opened in 1973, the Woman's Building was home to three galleries dedicated to women's art — Womanspace, Grandview, and 707. Sisterhood Bookstore sold feminist and nonsexist literature and music. Three women's theater groups — the L.A. Feminist Theater, the Women's Improvisational Theater, and the Women's Performance Project — staged productions in the auditorium. Other tenants included an office of the National Organization for Women (NOW), a coffeehouse, and Womantours, a feminist travel agency.

Still, its principal program was the Feminist Studio Workshop. At a time when the mainstream art world was primarily concerned with forms and surfaces, the Feminist Studio Workshop offered a wholly different set of questions: "What is it you want to say as an artist, and to whom do you wish to say it?" Participants were encouraged to create work inspired by their life experience. Critiques were focused not on what was "wrong" with

---

[1] The Woman's Building in Los Angeles was named for another structure built in 1893 by architect Sophia Hayden for the Columbian Exposition in Chicago. That building, which was demolished after the exposition, exhibited arts and cultural works by women and included a mural by Mary Cassatt.

the work, but on what message the work was communicating, and how that might be accomplished most effectively.

Between 1973 and 1981, women from across the country and from around the world moved to Los Angeles to participate in the two-year program of the FSW. Some of these women went on to become established artists in their own right; a number of them also became responsible for the operations of the Woman's Building.

The FSW closed its doors in 1981, victim of economic shifts and the sea change in social attitudes that followed the election of President Ronald Reagan. Still, the Woman's Building continued until 1991 to offer opportunities for artmaking, exhibition, and education for women artists.

I spent thirteen years—from 1976 to 1989—at the Woman's Building, beginning as a student in the FSW, then becoming a teacher, program director, exhibiting artist, publicist, typesetter, newsletter editor, grantwriter, board member, development director, and eventually, executive director. I washed dishes and painted walls, sorted bulk mailings, and hauled enough folding chairs for a few lifetimes. Although I was not there at the founding, I did experience some of those brazen, heady days of the 1970s when we were convinced we would change the world. I lived through the years of backlash, when we struggled to maintain our values in the face of economic hardship and a hostile political climate. I was witness to its eventual demise, the final succumbing—as with all utopian experiments—to inevitable change that rendered, if not its vision, then the manifestation of its vision obsolete. And I mourned it for years after, inconsolable, the way one grieves for a lost mother.

I met literally hundreds of remarkable women in each of the incredible years I spent at the Woman's Building. Most of them do not appear in these pages, but I beg them not to think that it's because they were insignificant to me. Similarly, huge projects, groundbreaking exhibitions, and innovative events abounded at the Building; they cannot all be included in this book. Someone will no doubt read and exclaim, "How could she leave that out? It was the most important thing!" Rather than attempt a comprehensive history, I've chosen to focus on the activities with which I was most directly involved and that best illustrate certain premises I want to highlight here.

No single history can ever do justice to the phenomenon that was the Woman's Building, and I ask the reader to understand that what appears in these pages is but one version out of thousands.

For those thousands of women, the Woman's Building provided an unparalleled opportunity: to experience oneself as both woman *and* artist, and to explore the potential significance of those intertwined identities in a context in which the value of such investigation was understood. Without this context, one is left to face alone the oppression any artist confronts—indifference, hostility, suspicion, self-doubt. Add to this the baggage of sexism, the inclination to question whether a woman is entitled to express herself at all, and in which ways, and to whom, and about what, and with what reward.

The Woman's Building provided a community in which a woman was encouraged not only to speak, but to find her authentic voice and cultivate an audience eager to hear it. Keeping alive that vision that it may seed future endeavors of its kind—in other forms, at other times and places—is the purpose of this book.

The Woman's Building, 1727 North Spring Street, Los Angeles. (Photo by Anne Gauldin, courtesy of the Woman's Building Slide Archive)

Requiem
1995

A chair is still a chair,
even when there's no one sitting there
but a room is not a house
and a house is not a home
when there's no one there . . .
—from "A House Is Not a Home,"
lyrics by Hal David, music by Burt Bacharach

IN THE EARLY MORNING, THE AIR ALREADY STICKY WITH SUMMER HEAT, A pearly yellow light seeps over this part of town, the forgotten backyard of the city, where the river is bedded in concrete and railroad cars roll by on rusted tracks. It's a scarred industrial pocket, grubbing in the shadow of downtown's gleaming spires, an area snubbed by developers for decades. It used to be called "Dogtown" by the local gangs until the animal shelter closed a few years back, the victim of budget cutbacks. To the south and west stretch the streets of Chinatown, their bustling commerce, their tacky allure. To the north and east, Latinos set down roots in Boyle Heights, struggling to maintain their traditions while chasing the American dream. Hidden just behind a hill, nestled in Chavez Ravine, Dodger Stadium looks down on this graffiti-streaked collection of crumbling warehouses and desolate railroad yards.

This particular terrain is claimed by no one; even the homeless scarcely venture this far north, except for the hoboes who leap from the boxcars to build their fires beneath the concrete bridge that spans the cement-lined L.A. River.

Yet on this morning, as my car traverses the bridge, the summer heat pressing down like a giant hand, this neighborhood is as familiar to me as breath, filling my head like the scent of garlic rising from the Asian food warehouses, blending with the odor of exhaust. For years this obscure section of decrepit streets and aging structures was the starred capital on my personal map of Los Angeles, its grit settled into pores, its din pounding in ears like the beat of my own heart.

At the end of the bridge I brake reflexively, hands ready to guide the steering wheel to the right, into the pot-holed, dead-end Aurora Street, being careful to watch for the random eighteen-wheeler that might happen to be exiting. But unlike the thirteen years of mornings when I made that turn, dodged the big rig, negotiated a parking place beside the metal dumpster, today I want to drive on by, accelerating past the three-story red brick building that had for so long been the center of my universe. Built in the 1920s by the Standard Oil Company, this red brick building was known from 1975 until 1991 as the Woman's Building, a public center for women's culture.

A painted strip around the building once proclaimed the name, but now it's painted over, a flat gray. So I stomp the accelerator, speeding past the blur of brick as if fleeing from a ghost. But not quite fast enough, for time unravels anyway; I am caught up. North Spring Street curls into a ribbon, blacktop twisting back upon itself, knotting inside me, dragging me into the past.

$\sim$

THE WOMAN'S BUILDING. A public center for women's culture. In that terse descriptor spins a universe of ideas, of history: the way you, as a woman, searched in vain to find yourself reflected in the mirrors of culture. What did you find? Dull-eyed beauties whose gaze evaded yours; mounds of flesh arranged like bowls of voluptuous fruit; evil temptresses, corrupters of men. More often, you found nothing at all, a curious silence. Culture proved to be a funhouse mirror, distorting and diminishing, a surface into which you walked and then disappeared.

Still you kept searching until one day your eyes caught the glimmer of refracted light, a spark in the night sky, and like all such luminosities it drew you, lured you all the way across the continent to its very edge, Los Angeles. That spark lodged in your imagination where it burned for years. Where it smolders still.

The Woman's Building. What other city but Los Angeles could have given birth to such an edifice? City of extremes, pressed against the brink of the Pacific, the endpoint of our restless explorations. City of dreams, where multitudes flock to reinvent themselves, to live out their personal myth. City that has slipped from the yoke of tradition, eluded the burden of history. City that levels and starts anew.

You came here to do that too, left behind the constricted fictions of the Midwest, its constipated possibilities, the cold, the drab, the predictable gaze that would not see you in your full dimensions. You came to put the fragments of your life together, following that spark, to re-knit the woman to the artist, the body to the brain, the spirit.

It was a journey worthy of Ulysses, a mythic voyage: departing wizened expectations, resigning from the family, the clan, abandoning the marble fist of culture that had closed against you, traveling two thousand miles to arrive at the home of women's culture, founded in the city of dreams. What could you have expected? Gleaming columns, a vast expanse of lawn, carved fountains spouting sparkling streams of water that glimmered in the afternoon sun? Anything, perhaps, except this neglected red brick building in a dour industrial district, an iron gate across the door bolted with a padlock.

In one way the site was perfect, no accident at all, a seamless representation of women's place in culture: a once-grand, now run-down structure on a remote street in an obscure part of town where toil goes unrecognized, pushed against the margins of a river choked in concrete; hard to find, down on its luck, a derelict part of town. It was anger at this circumstance that had struck the spark, anger that provided the fuel. That, and the ether of imagination.

And imagination is keener than broken glass, tougher than pavement, wider than the smog-filled vistas you can see from the top of the bridge. The truth is, there was not one, but *two* Woman's Buildings: the one that squatted modestly beside the railroad tracks and the one that blazed, like an idealized lover, inside your brain. Entering the first, you inhabited the second, the parallel home of women's culture, the one with wide hallways and open courtyards on a sunny, tree-lined street, a city landmark wherein every woman's act gained its deserved significance.

Women all over the world knew this second Woman's Building, women in Tokyo, in Mexico City, in Amsterdam, women who'd never set foot on North Spring Street still walked the vast rooms of this other Woman's Building, seized it as their Mecca, their "room of one's own."

You could never understand when others failed to see this second Woman's Building, so brightly did it shine for you. Walking newcomers through the edifice on North Spring Street, you'd puzzle at their dismayed glances, their diffident enthusiasm, and wonder at their failure of imagination. For you it was never a question — you dwelt in both buildings, each as real to you as the scent of your own skin. Huddling in winter in the unheated corridors of the first, you warmed yourself by the glorious fire in the second. And sometimes, when the art was brilliant and the rooms were full of women who were happy to be there together and the words were spoken from the deepest place in the heart, those twin images would blur, begin to swim together, two architectures becoming one.

∼

NO ONE COULD ever describe the Woman's Building. It would require a language of multiple dimensions, of texture, a language that could encompass the passage of time as well as contradictory points of view. Perhaps no language could accomplish it. Perhaps only music would be capable of sounding those myriad notes — the harmonies, the dissonance, syncopation, counterpoint — to arrive at a composition of the whole.

Like the blind men in the parable, groping sightless at the surface of their elephant, each woman's grasp of the institution was fragmentary, partial and particular. The Woman's Building was a place. An institution. A gathering of women. It was an eighteen-year experiment. It was a collision of history and politics and art. It was poetry, painting, performance. It was the one night you went there for a dance, and it was the thirteen years you spent trying to keep it ablaze.

It was the day you showed up with hennaed hair only to find that five other women had hennaed their hair the night before too. It was the rope straining in your hands as you hoisted the ten-foot-tall sculpture of a naked female figure onto the roof of the building, from which vantage point the entire city was her domain. It was a field of crosses planted on the lawn of city hall by women dressed in nuns' habits the colors of the rainbow, in protest of nuclear arms. It was a wall made of bottles, a tree of dolls' heads. A circle of women who stared unflinching into the video lens and told the stories of their sexual abuse.

It was the dope you smoked on the fire escape, the Friday nights you stayed late trying to figure out how to pay the bills. It was the first book you self-published on the antique printing press; it was the consciousness-raising group you hated.

Language splinters under the complexity, the immensity, the tens, perhaps hundreds of thousands of women whose imaginations and emotions and lives touched and were touched by the Woman's Building. All their stories, their dreams. And it was the art that was made within its walls, yes, but also the art that was made by some woman in some little town, work that came into being because she'd heard that the Woman's Building dared to exist.

The Woman's Building offered up a spark, and this was the message in its glow: that you, a woman, could be an artist too, and that your woman's life — whatever its particulars — could kindle your art, and that in turn, the act of making art would ignite that life, and finally, that a community of women, engaged in the twin acts of making art and making a new life, would transform the mirrors of culture into windows through which you all would fly, like sparks, into the night sky.

An extravagant promise, perhaps. But imagining the promise made it possible, and that possibility stretched like a roof over your head, marking the territory, giving you a place to stand. No edifice of bricks and mortar could contain all women — the kaleidoscope of political persuasions, sexual identities, cultures, and personalities — and that was certainly true of the humble warehouse on North Spring Street. Still those eaves spread like wings and their breadth provided context and therefore meaning for what you did, for who you were.

~

AND WHO ARE YOU NOW, as you sit in your idling car, unable to drive away from a decaying building, just a husk, a shell, the façade left behind once the living thing has fled? A woman, yes, an artist still, but these are now mere details, decontextualized, robbed of their particular significance. Four years since you last entered those glass doors, and still you are inconsolable. Graffiti covers the walls and the sky that stretches above is empty but for the brown cotton of smog.

Perhaps at one time you disdained the body, thought the physical architecture was of no consequence, believed that the building itself didn't matter — the walls, the scarred floors, the girders connecting one story to the next. Just square footage, a pile of red bricks. But now, as you find no key to fit the padlocked entry, you know the ache of homelessness, the despair of exile. Now you come to understand that this building was intrinsically the foundation for the second — that grander, gleaming manse of your imagination — their visions dependent on one another, joined at the heart. Now that this building is vacated, its twin has all but disappeared and with it, that vast embracing context that gave meaning to your every act, vanished like a spark in an airless room, like a dream in the pitiless light of day.

Feminist Studio Workshop students and Woman's Building staff hoist Kate Millet's Naked Lady *sculpture to the roof of the Woman's Building, 1978. (Photo by Mary McNally, courtesy of the Woman's Building Slide Archive)*

Resurrection
1976

But suicides have a special language.
Like carpenters they want to know which tools.
They never ask why build.
—Anne Sexton,
from "Wanting to Die," in *The Complete Poems*

THIS STORY BEGINS WITH RESURRECTION: HOW I SWAM UP FROM THE DARK oblivion of overdose into the unwelcome light of a new morning. How its pale rays leaked in through dirty windows, stinging my dilated pupils.

I was bleary from the residue of Dalmane that still spun in my bloodstream, but not dead, despite my most determined efforts. I woke in the wood-paneled bedroom of the house trailer that belonged to Pat, the woman who had, until a week earlier, been my lover. The room was not unfamiliar; I'd spent many nights with her in this bed. Pat was not the first woman to make love with me, but she was the first to do so more than twice — my first real lesbian relationship. We'd been together almost seven months, but our bond had been unraveling for six of them.

This morning, though, July 12, 1976, I was alone in the bed, my body not curled as in sleep, but a stiff, stone corpse in the center of the mattress. I was still dressed in the gauzy, flowered shirt and loose pants I'd worn the day before. An old quilt had been stretched over my body, tucked neatly under my chin, as if to tidy the mess of me.

Through the thin walls of the trailer I could hear Pat banging around in the kitchen, probably brewing coffee. Pat was a wiry woman whose gestures were always nervous and impatient, but hearing them this morning I imagined they were even more so: the problem of what to do about me was making her late for work. She was talking to someone; I couldn't distinguish her words but her Pennsylvania twang was unmistakable, blunt and gruff from the years she'd spent in the army. It carried down the hallway, wafting like smoke from the menthol cigarettes she was always trying to quit.

I'd met Pat the first week I moved to Grand Rapids, Michigan, in September 1975. I'd come to enroll at Thomas Jefferson College, an experimental school where students majored in things like "construction of bamboo flutes" and invented their own classes. It was my third institution of higher learning in as many years, and I'd hoped the lack of formal structure at this school might calm the restiveness I'd exhibited at the previous two.

Once I'd settled into my apartment, I searched the phone book and found a listing for "Feminist Center." One of my problems with college was its seeming separation from real life, and I was eager to meet the women's community in this new city. I showed up at the next Sunday night meeting.

For a midsized midwestern city, Grand Rapids turned out to have an unexpectedly large population of lesbians, but it was still a small enough community that, especially in the nonmonogamous seventies, nearly everyone had slept with nearly everyone else. New arrivals like myself tended to generate a lot of interest. At that first meeting I met Pat and her lover Carol, a tall, brawny woman who'd grown up in Grand Rapids and who did line repairs for Michigan Bell. Carol took a strong liking to me; she'd come by my apartment during the week to smoke joints on her lunch break, pulling up in her Michigan Bell truck, her utility belt slung low on her hips. Pat was small; her short hair was bleached blond and she drove a Jeep. I liked her best for her mercurial mind. They broke up when Pat and I got together. That's how Pat described it, "getting together," as though it were a meeting over coffee.

From where I lay on the bed I could smell the coffee percolating in its electric pot. I could barely make out the voice that responded to Pat's, its tone more subdued, calmer, a music of reassurance, a cello to Pat's frantic clarinet. From this quality I deduced that it belonged to Suzanne, who had also, until a week ago, been my lover. Who was now Pat's new lover.

When I met Suzanne, she was working at the Shell Car Wash, at the time a popular job for working-class dykes in Grand Rapids. But she also wrote poetry, as I did. She was one of the few women I'd met in the community who seemed to have a deep feeling for art, and she promised me that "Someday, we'll be famous lovers, like Stein and Toklas." She wore her light brown hair long, parted in the center, and she moved her short, compact body with a distinct gait, as if it were covered in a thick suit of armor.

It had been the sudden and wholly unexpected announcement, one week earlier, that my two lovers had decided to embark the next day on a week's vacation, signifying that they had already been or soon would be "getting together," that had moved me to steal the bottle of Dalmane from Suzanne's medicine chest. This was easy enough to accomplish: I just told her roommates that I'd left a lid of marijuana in her room. I'd grabbed the Dalmane at random from an assortment of brown bottles lining the glass shelves of the bathroom cabinet.

It had been seeing the two of them together, laughing over a Sunday breakfast of pancakes and eggs at the Copper Kettle — the day after returning from their trip and neither one had called me — that moved me to swallow all the pills in the brown bottle, washed down with glasses of burgundy. Then I called Mary.

I'd met Mary waitressing during in my first year of college at the University of Detroit. She'd been an art student at Wayne State, and we'd stayed friends during the year I moved to Canada to attend the University of Toronto, and the next year, when I dropped out of school and was living back at home, waitressing full time. Mary had a tiny body, delicate features, and bright, intelligent eyes; the overall effect was birdlike. She was not a lesbian, but after a nasty breakup with her boyfriend she'd surprised me by agreeing to my suggestion that she accompany me on my move to Grand Rapids.

The day I swallowed the bottle of Dalmane and most of the burgundy, I called her at the Chinese restaurant where she waitressed. I asked her to look after Ruby, my calico cat.

I expected to lie then on my small bed in the close July heat of my attic apartment where mice ran through the walls all night. I expected to gaze out the third-story window, and watch the hazy sky through a shifting pattern of leaves until my eyes closed and I became no more than the wind stirring green trees.

I did not expect Mary to leave work in the middle of her shift, to pedal her bicycle up the cobblestones of Cherry Street to try to save me. I didn't expect to hear the distant chime of the doorbell, to struggle to stand and make my stumbling way down the narrow stairs, past the doughy young man who masturbated all day in the open doorway, to drift down the hall, swing wide the front door, to find Pat standing there, demanding, "Damn, woman, what the hell did you do now?"

A woman of the 1970s feels abandoned by her two lovers, who get together to form their own romantic partnership. This is routine lesbian drama, and I must have recognized it even at the time. Catalyst, not cause. The truth is that at the age of twenty-one, I saw my life funneling, its confines narrowing to a space too tight to inhabit, possibilities closing down. At twenty-one I saw a train of failures following me everywhere, like a string of tin cans tied to my tail, rattling with every step: my dreams of an acting career, my college education, the challenge of making a living, the prospect of finding anyone to love me.

I'd been depressed since the onset of winter; it snowed for forty days in a row that year I lived in Grand Rapids. I remember sitting in a diner with Mary one sleeting February afternoon. We were broke that winter, and frequently ate popcorn for dinner; our "lunch" that day was coffee, with cream for added nutrients. I'd been staring out the window at a monochrome landscape—gray sky, gray buildings, gray slush—reciting, as I'd been doing for weeks, my litany of despair.

"My whole life is crumbling before my eyes, and I can't stand it! Pat doesn't care about me—y'know what she told me last night? She was supposed to come over and spend the night with me, but then she calls and says, 'I can't come 'cause I don't want to leave Phaedra alone.' I mean, her fucking dog's more important to her than I am! Then she says, 'Well, you can come out here if you want,' but like she couldn't care less if I did or not. So I did, I drove all the way out to the trailer park, and when I get there she tells me she's 'tired' and falls right to sleep. I cried my eyes out all night!

"And school—I don't know what I'm gonna do! I'm supposed to be working on this one-woman show, right? I'm doing that for my credits instead of taking classes this semester, but I can't make myself work on it. Every time I try, I just freeze up! If I drop out of this school, I'll never graduate. And I can't stand the idea of spending the rest of my life scooping salad dressing in a hair net and waitress shoes!"

Inevitably, though, the chain of complaint would link to the most acute source of my distress: my inability to launch myself into the world as an artist. This was not (just) about ego or careerism. The arts had been my life raft in my youth, carrying me through the swamp of loneliness and boredom of being the only child of working-class parents whose primary pastimes, aside from jobs they despised, were drinking and fighting with one another. In school I took classes in art and music, sang in the glee club, and tried out for every staged performance. I had a fifth-grade teacher who allowed me to write poems instead of book reports. And although it would not have occurred to my mother to take me to museums or concerts or

13

plays, she did allow me unrestricted access to any volume in the public library. There were times I read a book a day, but never less than one a week. I read *Jane Eyre* and *To Kill a Mockingbird* right alongside *Tobacco Road*. Books were doors into parallel worlds, and I strode through as many as I could. My involvement with the arts had made it seem possible that I could create a different kind of existence than the one my parents cursed.

In high school I studied acting, even winning an award for my Desdemona in a state competition. If I'd been braver, I might have gone straight to New York after graduation, but my mother, who'd quit college to get married, had drilled into me the importance of getting a degree. "You don't want to end up a secretary like me," she'd warned since I was in diapers.

At each of the colleges I attended, I'd spurned her wish for me to study something that would help me support myself, instead taking classes in theater, writing, ceramics, and art history. The "stars" of these classes, the ones who got praise from the instructors, whose work was held up to the rest of us as "bold" and "innovative," were always men. The arts were still my life raft, but the seas were hostile to my feminism, my lesbianism. I feared these identities would have to be cast overboard if I were to stay afloat.

Now, though, I found myself in a lesbian feminist community whose main interests were softball, drinking at the Three Sons, and the romantic intrigues that were a staple, it seemed, of lesbian life. "They don't care about my one-woman show," I complained to Mary that afternoon in the diner, "they just want to know if I can rebuild my engine or catch a pop fly. When I try to talk about my poems, their eyes glaze over."

Maybe she'd gotten her fill of my whining. That day Mary handed me a fortune, a narrow strip of white paper like the ones baked into cookies at the Chinese restaurant, made specially for me. Its hand-lettered message read: "The will feeds on enormous vistas; deprived of them, it collapses."

With its hybrid influences of Calvinism and Republican politics, Grand Rapids was not a place to seek expanded horizons. In this city that boasted of being "the birthplace of Gerald R. Ford," I felt my life spiraling down, a trajectory of doom from which neither drugs nor sex nor radical politics could save me.

But this too is an incomplete explanation. At twenty-one I was no stranger to suicide's allure. It was my lucky charm, my ace in the hole, my fallback strategy, my last hope. I was ten when I'd first experimented with ingesting large doses of aspirin, a dozen at a time, a small pillbox full in a single swallow. They made my ears ring, left a sour ache in the pit of my stomach. I wasn't sure how many it would take to kill me, but I was drawn to dance on that edge.

I'd do it at school, a semipublic act calculated to impress my friends. I'd announce my intention in furtive notes passed desk-to-desk in homeroom: "After school I'm going to take all the pills I have in my purse." A performative statement.

I needed a grand gesture to illustrate the nameless thing that gripped me like a fierce, cruel hand, threatening to squeeze the breath out of me. I couldn't see it, and at ten had no way to understand it — was I inside its grasp or were the pitiless fingers clenched inside of me? Either way I felt trapped. So I overdosed on Bayer, and I pounded my head against the trees that lined the green residential streets on which we walked home from school. As a small crowd of kids looked on, I would lean my weight against the trunk and rhythmically bang my head against bark. Softly at first, then harder, until the ache in my skull displaced that other, more pervasive pain, until I was emptied out, the constriction temporarily relieved.

I was a ten-year-old who loved to read, who was good at school, who sang in glee club, and had a crush on Mr. Sommers, my gay art teacher. I was a ten-year-old who'd been beaten by my father as an infant. I was a ten-year-old who was tall for my age, who already wore a bra, who was chased on the playground by boys trying to grab at my breasts. I was a ten-year-old who'd been taught at age five to play with my stepfather's penis. A ten-year-old who dreamed of being a writer. I was a ten-year-old who could mix a perfect martini, dry and on the rocks. Who was often alone late into the night, soul music on the Detroit radio station my only company, waiting for my mother and stepfather to come home.

I was thirteen when I first carved horizontal lines across the insides of my wrists. In my memory it was a Tuesday night, and I sat on my purple bedspread slicing open the tender, bluish skin with a razor blade. The sting of it was horrible, and I wondered how anyone withstood it long enough to cut sufficiently deep. It was clear I was not going to die of my wounds, not that night, but there was a certain relief I found in slitting open the tight container of my body, letting some of the insides out. I was watching the blood bead out of the shallow slashes when my mother walked in. I had no lock on my bedroom door, and knocking was not a courtesy in which my parents believed.

"What are you doing?" she demanded. Her eyes glowed dark in a face gone white and dangerous. She wore her bathrobe wrapped across her chest like armor, her hairdo protected by a helmet of tissue paper around her head. When she sat beside me on the bed, I could see she was afraid. I'd had ample experience in soothing my mother's fears, becoming the reassuring parent to her frightened child. I knew the tone of voice to take, calm and low with a singsong lilt, the way one coaxes a toddler back to sleep after a nightmare. The particular words didn't matter. What mattered was that the words erased the gesture, dissolved the blade, and hid the dripping blood; the words gave her permission to forget what her eyes had seen, to empty her brain and so find relief. This was what I gave her and she gratefully accepted. We never talked of it again.

I was thirteen when I started drinking, stealing from my parents' stash. If they noticed, they never said anything. By fifteen I had a fake ID and could buy whatever I wanted. The bored owner of the liquor store around the corner from my high school didn't care, and I looked years older than my birthdate. Drinking brought a kind of relief; it dulled, if temporarily, the force of the thing's hold on me. It gave me permission to forget all my eyes had seen, made it easier to live inside my skin.

I awoke on that Monday morning, July 12, 1976, eighteen hours after I had swallowed a full bottle of Dalmane. Dalmane is a derivative of benzodiazepine; it's prescribed for anxiety, insomnia, muscle tension, and convulsions. The symptoms from which I sought its relief were these: profound hopelessness, unbearable pain.

I have not retained any memory of those eighteen lost hours. The other people involved were, perhaps understandably, reluctant to talk to me about that lapse of time. Still, I can imagine they went to considerable trouble: transporting my inert body out of the house, getting me to the hospital in time, convincing the emergency room staff that the overdose was accidental, so I wouldn't be locked up.

This last was especially generous, and couldn't have been an easy task. Still, these women would have seen it as their mission as good radical lesbians not to deliver me into the hands of the patriarchy, the medical/psychiatric establishment. I was very lucky. But on that Monday in 1976 I wasn't grateful for their kindness or their care. I was furious at their thwarting my wish to die.

Nor was I resigned to my life sentence. Despite the chemical overload my poor neurons were carrying, my brain was alert, conniving to finish what I'd started. Although Pat's job with the state of Michigan required minimal effort, I knew she was obligated to at least put in an appearance at her office. This would take her away from the trailer for a while — thirty minutes each way to Muskegon and back, at least an hour at her desk, I figured — leaving me in the care of Suzanne. I was counting on her to be a more sympathetic and less vigilant guardian.

I heard the sounds of Pat leaving for work, a few murmured instructions to Suzanne, the whistled call to Phaedra, her Alaskan malamute, who always accompanied her to the office. The screen door slammed, her engine revved, and then the trailer was quiet. I rose from the bed.

The vertical position seemed an entirely new challenge to my body, as if I'd suddenly commanded it to walk on the ceiling. I swayed on rubbery knees, or was it my brain that was spinning? The paneled walls were essential to my progress down the short hallway, and I collapsed into a dining room chair as if I'd just landed after a space mission during which I'd been weightless for three weeks.

Suzanne said, not unkindly, "You should stay in bed," but I ignored her. I reached for the wall phone and, aiming a finger at the blurred numbers on the dial, called my manager at the department store restaurant where I waitressed. I was sick, I told him, wouldn't be in today. This he accepted without argument. What about tomorrow, he wanted to know, and I promised I'd call if it were going to be a problem.

There is, of course, a contradiction here. A woman who plans to kill herself before the end of the day doesn't worry about losing her job. So even in this moment, sick with overdose and bent on accomplishing my death, another part of me was also functioning: the survivor, the one determined to live. Two impulses coexisted in the shell of my body, but they weren't talking to each other.

The second call I placed was to my mother. This came from some deep instinct, its logic buried somewhere between the heavily doped up folds of my brain. What she might have thought about hearing from her daughter at ten o'clock on a Monday morning—a groggy voice on a crackly line saying, "I want you to know I'm all right," when she had no reason to believe that anything was wrong—is unknown to me. Like so much else, we've never discussed it.

This was during a period of time, though, when my mother frequently found herself engaged with me in bizarre interactions. There had been, in the fall of 1974, the telephoned announcement that I had to quit college. It had been weeks since I'd been able to go to classes; most days I spent in my rented room, smoking dope and listening to Joni Mitchell and crying. She encouraged me to move back home.

During that long winter when I'd lived again under my parents' roof, there had been the time she'd come home from work and found me barricaded under my old purple bedspread, mumbling to her that I was "too tired" to talk, when in fact I was too high on psilocybin to hold up my end of a conversation. There'd been the Saturday night she and my stepfather had come home late from the bar, and she and I sat up and talked until the sky grew light—she fueled by hours of martinis, me by the mescaline snapping through my internal wiring—our communication perfectly in sync.

And only a few months earlier, there'd been the call from a pay phone beside the freeway that connects Grand Rapids to Detroit. The day before, I'd accidentally whacked off a good chunk of my thumb on a pottery-grinding wheel in the campus ceramics studio. Since I hadn't signed up for the college health insurance plan, the medical office would not treat me. I bandaged the hand as best I could and went off to Lake Michigan with my friend Mary, where we dropped acid and watched the lake thaw on that early spring afternoon. That night I'd needed alcohol and pot to come down from the LSD; the next day I embarked on a scheduled visit to Detroit. It was usually an easy drive in my Pontiac Tempest, with Aretha or Earth Wind & Fire blasting from the eight-track, but on this day a combination of chemical overload, sleeplessness, and physical shock from my injury caused the pavement to stretch interminably before me into a sky that dropped low against my vision. I had to pull off at a rest stop, and I called my mother to say, "I don't think I can get there." I remember trying to explain to her that I could no longer move forward on that devouring highway, that I couldn't conceive of turning around and driving back to Grand Rapids, and surely couldn't imagine remaining there at the rest stop. I believed that my molecules might dissolve right there, beside the redwood picnic tables and rustic bathrooms and the recreational vehicles. My mother asked no questions, and if she was panicked about her only daughter's mental state, she did not betray this. "Take your time," she advised me, "I'm home all day. When you get here, we'll go to lunch." It reminded me of when I was a little girl, tormented with insomnia. The more I couldn't sleep, the more anxious I became. "If you can't sleep," she'd say to me, "then, just rest." In this way, she guided me home.

On this morning too, she asked no questions. I don't believe she understood the true circumstances of my call, nor did I intend her to. As determined as I was to make the call, it did not sway me from my ultimate purpose, and once I hung up, I returned to it.

I knew Pat kept a gun; she'd once taken me out to shoot at tin cans in a field, early on in our relationship when she was still trying to interest me in what she loved: guns, motorcycles, malamutes. I searched for that gun, trying to be surreptitious as I opened cupboards and drawers in every room of the trailer.

"What are you looking for?" I hadn't even heard Suzanne come into the bedroom.

I was too dull-headed to think up a convincing lie, but cunning enough in my mission to realize that Suzanne might be swayed to my point of view. I figured a woman with that many pills in her medicine chest was certainly no stranger to despair.

"Pat's .38," I murmured, without looking her in the eyes. I made a show of growing more industrious in my search, rummaging through the top shelf of the closet with increasingly frantic gestures.

Suzanne came over to me then and grabbed my arms, leading me back to the bed. She was at least six inches shorter than I, but her hands possessed unexpected strength. I remembered a night when a man had wandered into a meeting at the Feminist Center. Whether he was there by accident or with hostile intent we weren't sure, but he was huge and hulking, over six feet tall, close to three hundred pounds, and even the toughest women were startled by his sudden intrusion. I remembered Suzanne had risen, all five feet of her, and walked over to him, taking his hand as if he were a child, then simply leading him to the door.

"I don't want you to die," she said to me.

"It would be so much better for everyone," I countered. I launched into my familiar litany of hopelessness, rattling off my string of failures: in love, at school, in art.

She did her best to refute them, one by one, but her arguments were hollow. I knew she too was miserable; how could she persuade me that things would get better when she didn't believe it herself?

"I don't want you to die," she said again, but I could see a shadow of doubt edging into her marbled eyes.

Before I could win my case, though, Pat's jeep pulled into the carport beside the trailer, and Phaedra scratched at the screen door to be let in. Suzanne and Pat had a whispered consultation and Pat left again, perhaps to dispatch the gun to a safer location. When she returned she would barely speak to me; she had no patience for emotional theatrics. How many times had I heard her say, "Things come and they go," and of course by "things" she meant lovers. She was furious with my suffering.

Soon after her return I locked myself in the bathroom of the trailer and began slicing up my wrists with a razor blade I conveniently found in a drawer. I was able to cut more deeply than I had at thirteen, deeply enough to stain my clothing with wide streaks of blood.

The two of them broke the flimsy latch on the hollow door and got the straightedge away from me. I demanded to be taken home. Neither Pat nor Suzanne thought this was a good idea, but they were exhausted and eager to be rid of me as well. I used this to my advantage; I made myself unendurable, yelling "Let me go, you can't make me stay here," pretty much nonstop until they gave in. Suzanne agreed to drive me back to my apartment.

The deal I'd made was that I'd go home and stay put, but once there, I found I could not remain in the hot, dingy apartment that smelled of mice. I wanted to find my friend Kit, with whom I imagined I was newly in love. So I got into my Tempest, still stoned on the Dalmane that would take weeks to leave my system, and drove to Fulton Park, where the dykes had a game of softball going, just as they did every Monday night of summer.

The softball field was at one end of the park; I left my car at the other end and stumbled down the soft green lawn that led to the diamond. I think I walked right onto the softball field, stopping the play, or perhaps Kit left her position in right field to intercept me.

"Hello, Wolverton," she grinned, as if it were a normal encounter, as if I were not wearing blood-streaked clothes, a gauzy shirt too feminine for the androgynous Grand Rapids style, as if my long hair were not uncombed, my pupils dilated to fill the iris.

Kit was tall and lean, with black hair and dark eyes fringed with thick lashes. Her skin was still tanned from living in Africa, where she'd served two years in the Peace Corps. She'd grown up in Kentucky, and her soft drawl was sweet as a caress.

I wanted her comfort, but also, just as when I was ten years old with a tin of Bayer aspirin in my purse, I wanted witnesses. If the schoolyard suicide announcements had the quality of sideshow, this was opera: the soprano enacting her death while the whole team looked on. But the lesbian community of Grand Rapids didn't want theatrics; they didn't want display or passion or excess. Kit was not cruel, but she was embarrassed.

"I think you should go home," she told me, "and I'll come by and see you tomorrow." It was a promise she would not keep. I did as I was told. As I drove away, the game resumed.

By that time the sky had darkened and I returned once more to my attic, where Ruby greeted me with her soft mew. I lay on my narrow bed and watched the stars through my third-story window. It wasn't that I had decided to live; it's just that I had exhausted my momentum for dying. I lay like a cloth sack, rumpled and limp, emptied out, my ears ringing deep inside my head.

The next morning I was back at my waitress job at the Greenery, wearing my uniform of white ruffled blouse and Easter green jumper. Coffee cups rattled in their saucers as I carried them across the dining room. I told the pay clerk that the bandages on my wrists had come from falling off a bicycle.

It was weeks before my ears stopped ringing. During that time I stopped eating altogether, living on grapefruit juice and black coffee. The next time I went home to see my mother, I was a size 7, I who only months earlier had worn a size 13. A snapshot from that visit shows a too-thin woman, neck rising scrawny out of a loosely draped shirt, posing carefully as if her bones were brittle.

The lesbians in Grand Rapids had pretty much washed their hands of me; clearly, I was trouble. A few showed kindness: Carol stopped by one evening after work to see how I was doing. A woman named Stormy, perhaps due to her own propensity for emotional excess, cooked dinner for me one night; she too had wrestled with madness and she too had been exiled from the community. And I had a brief, unhappy affair with Kit.

None of it mattered, though, because I was leaving. The week after swallowing the bottle of Dalmane, I made the decision to move to Los Angeles, to enroll in the Feminist Studio Workshop at the Woman's Building. I had read about the Woman's Building in the *New Women's Survival Sourcebook* during that long, dreary winter when it never stopped snowing. The idea of it was like a beacon—a place where the identities of "woman" and "artist" were not a contradiction in terms, where feminism and culture were not incompatible concepts. The Woman's Building had glimmered in my imagination, but its light faded in my fog of misery; I had not been able to envision myself transported to the Pacific Coast, the very edge of possibility.

Now, though, if I was not going to die I knew that edge was where I had to live. It was time to reach for those "enormous vistas" prescribed by Mary's hand-printed fortune. I grew fierce with purpose; I started asking for double shifts at work, volunteering to work for any waitress who wanted a day off. Every night I came home with my apron bulging with coins that I painstakingly rolled and put away in a ceramic jar. In this way, the survivor in me overcame the one who was so determined to end her life.

Still, whenever I tell this story, I never talk about a suicide "attempt." Instead I say this: at the age of twenty-one I committed suicide, that the effort was successful, that a part of me was killed off and something else reborn. The young woman who arrived in Los Angeles at midnight on October 2, 1976, clutching a carrier with the heavily sedated Ruby, was not the same one who had swallowed the bottle of Dalmane when her two girlfriends went on vacation together. When people wonder at the meaning the Woman's Building continues to have for me, they must consider that my story there began with resurrection, and I came to it mucky and tender and quivering as any newborn.

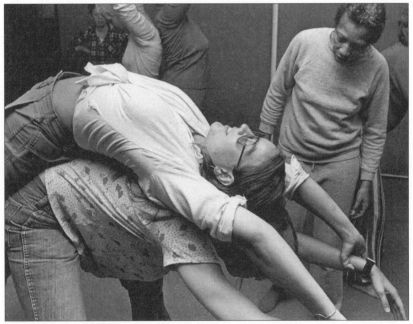

Observed by E. Kitch Childs (right) Wolverton stretches out in self-defense class at Sagaris, 1975. (Photo by Laima Druskis)

Feminist Education
1976–1977

*The focus of feminist education at the FSW
is to assist women in developing their strength,
leadership, expertise, and creativity; to help
them make a transition from victimized, powerless
outsider to effective, powerful participator in
reshaping the world according to feminist values.*
—Ruth Iskin, "Feminist Education at the Feminist
Studio Workshop," in *Learning Our Way*

I WAS STILL IN HIGH SCHOOL WHEN JUDY CHICAGO FOUNDED THE FIRST feminist art program in the country at California State University at Fresno in 1970. That spring, at Kent State University, National Guardsmen had shot and killed four students protesting the Vietnam War. The Beatles were breaking up. At sixteen, I was studying acting and directing, stage-craft and modern dance in the performing arts department of Cass Technical High. Inarguably the best school in Detroit, Cass boasted Lily Tomlin and Diana Ross among its most illustrious alumnae. My dreams were of a brilliant career on the New York stage.

Even in high school I had an avid interest in the women's liberation movement that had begun to ignite across the country. Like a newborn who craves the breast long before she has the language for it, I was already a feminist, just waiting for the word to give me a way to think about it. I could not know, though, the way that word would detonate in me, rearrange my molecules, how it would redefine my past and alter the course of my future.

That first year, Judy Chicago's visionary Feminist Art Program[2] drew fifteen women students, many of whom were new to both feminism and artmaking. Still, it was from the work of this initial group of participants that many of the core principles of feminist art education evolved. These concepts would guide Chicago and her colleagues when they established the Feminist Studio Workshop in Los Angeles three years later.

It was in the Fresno program that women first employed the process of consciousness-raising[3] in the classroom, both to understand more deeply their position as women and to generate material for their art. This strategy flew in the face of the art establishment; in 1970, women's experience was considered trivial and frivolous, unsuitable as subject matter for creative work. Indeed, since the end of World War II, narrative content had become taboo in the New York art world; formalist concerns dominated the critical discourse. Serious art was, by definition, the province of men, and if a woman hoped to pass into this hallowed terrain, she could only do so by making herself as much like a man as possible. The rare female art student who called attention to her gender by daring to create a work about menstruation, marriage, motherhood, or household drudgery could fully expect to be criticized or mocked by her male instructors.

In order to create an environment in which women could explore their lives through art, participants in the Fresno program insisted upon a sep-

---

[2] I am indebted to Faith Wilding's *By Our Own Hands* for this history of the early feminist art movement in California.

[3] Consciousness-raising, or C-R, is a communication process in which women sit in a circle and each takes equal time to speak, uninterrupted, about her experience while the others listen attentively. C-R sessions are usually directed to a specific topic, such as body image, mothers, etc. The practice allows an individual to validate her experiences and to probe their meanings; it also encourages women to see the commonality of their experiences, to realize that some problems have social, not personal, causes. The slogan "The personal is political" is rooted in the C-R process. It is crucial to remember that in the early days of feminism, most women rarely considered the events of their lives to be worth mentioning, to have any significance at all. C-R was adapted by North American feminists from a practice called "speaking bitterness," used by women in revolutionary China.

arate classroom environment for female art students, one in which women could create the context and control what happened there. Such separation would provide not only protection from corrosive or undermining feedback, but also allow women to bond with one another and to define for themselves their paths as artists. Additionally, the women of the Fresno program asserted the importance of female role models, both in being instructed by women and in studying the long-buried history of women's art. Finally, Chicago and her students openly challenged the notion of art as a work of individual genius by engaging in collaborative creations.

In 1971, Judy Chicago moved the Fresno program to California Institute of the Arts (Cal Arts). With the school still under construction, the twenty-five students of the Feminist Art Program launched a large-scale, site-based, collaborative project, "Womanhouse," spearheaded by Chicago and her colleague, artist Miriam Schapiro. Working together, they transformed the rooms of a slated-for-demolition Hollywood mansion into art environments that eloquently protested the domestic servitude of women's lives. In *Breast Kitchen,* for example, the all-pink walls and ceiling were affixed with fried eggs—sunny side up—that gradually morphed into women's breasts, a trenchant comment on women's role as nurturers. *Fear Bathroom,* contained a plaster figure of a woman in the tub, frozen up to the neck in cement, and addressed the state of confinement and paralysis felt by women. *Linen Closet* displayed the torso of a female mannequin segmented by the closet shelves. This latter image was reproduced in *Time* magazine, which ran a story on the project; it galvanized me, and I sped around for the next week, showing the magazine to everyone at school. "Womanhouse" was, without question, the most publicly visible work of feminist art to date.

Art historian Arlene Raven had joined the faculty of the Cal Arts Feminist Art Program, and graphic designer Sheila Levrant de Bretteville established the Women's Design Program at Cal Arts as well. In conversations with Chicago, they shared their frustrations about working within a male-dominated institution. Separate classes for feminist students could only be so effective, they observed; what went on in those classrooms was too easily dwarfed by the larger context. They would routinely spend their class sessions building up the confidence of women students, encouraging them to take risks, only to see those same students' work disparaged or dismissed by male instructors.

In 1972, I entered the BFA program in theater at the University of Detroit. Having received awards and encouragement at Cass Tech, I was unprepared for the indifference and hostility with which I was met in this college program. My instructors were all men, and I couldn't help but notice that the women who managed to nab the few roles that were available to actresses were both conventionally pretty and submissive to authority. My close-cropped hair, six-inch platform shoes, and tendency to talk back to the director received scant appreciation. Part of me saw this for the sexism it was, but another part internalized my failure: *maybe they were right, maybe my work just wasn't any good.* Eighteen is a tender age for anyone, but especially in the life of a developing artist. One is still learning one's craft, finding one's voice, developing a fragile confidence, and is deeply susceptible to the opinions of others. The failure of these instructors at the University of Detroit to embrace and validate me as an artist was a wound I would carry for years.

It was this kind of injury that the proponents of feminist art education were determined to prevent. In 1973, Chicago, de Bretteville, and Raven made the decision to leave Cal Arts to found an independent school for women in the arts, a place where students could explore a feminist vision of their work and gain authority and power within that vision. The Feminist Studio Workshop (FSW) opened in September. Initial class sessions were held in de Bretteville's living room, but by the end of November the FSW was installed in the building that had once housed the old Chiounard Art Institute on Grandview Boulevard.

That same fall, I transferred to the University of Toronto. My disappointment over the reelection of Richard Nixon in 1972 (the first election in which I'd been eligible to vote) and the defeat of the Michigan abortion rights initiative for which I'd campaigned made me resolve to leave the country. "I just can't stay here!" I'd declare dramatically to whomever would listen.

U of T had a women's studies program, and I took as many classes as I dared, though it was not an approved major. The program was solidly based in Marxist-Feminism; my teachers tended to shapeless sweaters in muted tones, bowl haircuts, and Roots shoes. With my frosted hair and green nail polish, short skirts and glam-rock satins, I was a conspicuous anomaly, but I gradually earned a grudging respect for my feminist fervor and analytic ability.

Although the content of these classes was radical, teaching methods were traditional: lecture/discussion, assigned reading and written reports. In truth, I found classes like "Labor History of Canadian Women" a little dry, but they did provide relief from the active misogyny of the theater department. I'd been cast in a production in which the notion of high art included scenes in which a woman was raped and thrown from a moving train. The director spent several rehearsals trying to figure out how best to hurl the actress offstage with a convincing *thump,* so that the audience might worry that she had actually sustained injury (thus "blurring the line between art and life," he'd pontificate).

It was in Toronto that I began to explore my interest in feminist theater, teaming up with two other women — Lucy Winer and Jude Angione, both American expatriates like myself — to create a production called *But Something Was Wrong with the Princess.* It was an amalgam of presentation styles and content — pageantry, agit-prop, monologues. Some of it we wrote ourselves, other parts were appropriated from other feminist texts. We sang a song called "I'm Tired of Fuckers Fucking Over Me."[4]

---

[4] By Bev Grant.

In that production we created a scene with a woman on a carnival float, like the queen of the Rose Parade. She wore gigantic false breasts and a huge smiling lipsticked mouth. But at the climax she stepped from her float, removed her fake breasts, wiped her mouth, and declaimed, "I am a lesbian, and I am proud." Not understanding why, I clamored to play that part, and thus began my coming-out process.

Out in Los Angeles, the vision of the FSW was taking shape. As a young design student, Sheila de Bretteville had been fascinated with the Bauhaus movement and, later, by utopian experiments in Italy and Scandinavia that used principles of architecture and design to construct new models of community, new structure for social relations. The FSW was intended to be a community for its participants, and de Bretteville argued that their new school should not be isolated from the life of the burgeoning feminist community in Los Angeles. The Woman's Building was born of this intention and became the hub of a rare synthesis between cultural, political, social, and entrepreneurial strands of feminist Los Angeles.

I dropped out of the University of Toronto in the late fall of 1974, and spent a bitter winter back in Detroit waitressing, feeling isolated both as feminist and artist. I took classes in ceramics at the local art association and attempted to stay connected to the feminist movement through books and newspapers.

In the spring of 1975, the Woman's Building hosted a series of ground-breaking conferences on feminist design, performance, film and video, ceramics, and writing. Hundreds of women gathered to listen as Kate Millett, Meridel Le Seuer, and others spoke about the new directions feminists were forging in the arts.

That same spring, I saw a headline in the *Detroit Free Press,* "Feminist College in the Works." Women from the faculty of Goddard College in Vermont were seeking to create "an independent institute for the study of feminist political theory." Their pilot effort would be two five-week sessions that summer. I applied for and was admitted to the first. The impressive faculty included authors Rita Mae Brown and Bertha Harris, editor/theoretician Charlotte Bunch, and philosopher Mary Daly. One hundred and twenty women came from across the United States; approximately 80 percent of them were lesbians, not including those who would convert — temporarily or permanently — before the session was over. Not yet twenty-one, I was among the youngest of the participants, declared but not yet initiated in my sexual preference. I wandered through most of the five weeks in a state of stoned overwhelm.

I had expected that the classes — on topics like "Strategies and Organization," "Socialist Feminism," and "Leadership" — would provoke vigorous discussion of issues, but I hadn't imagined the level of personal contentiousness that would divide us. Scarcely a day went by without fresh controversy: mothers were upset that daycare wasn't provided around the clock; daycare workers felt both underpaid and underappreciated. Some women were incensed by the exclusion of boy children; others challenged the rule excluding dogs from the dorms, since one member of the organizing collective had her dog with her. Lesbians protested their invisibility, and working-class women protested what they saw as the elitist structure of Sagaris.

Each woman who came seemed to carry a different expectation of what this institution was supposed to be. Some saw it as an extended conference for political networking; others sought academic rigor. Still others viewed it as a boot camp for activists, a launching pad for the inevitable feminist revolution, while many seemed content to kick back and enjoy their time at "lesbian summer camp." And some women believed they were creating a women's world, or as close to it as we could get without leaving the planet. There seemed to be the expectation that a female world would be perfect, magically cleansed of the schisms of race and class, sexism and homophobia, as if by eliminating men we would purge all discord, as if women did not also carry the seeds of oppression.

I held myself aloof from the intrigue. Part of me felt too inexperienced to understand the nuances of the growing conflict, but another part just felt distaste for it. I couldn't fathom the heated pitch of the criticisms; what had anyone done to inspire such venom? One class, Psychology of Oppression, taught by E. Kitch Childs, presented tools by which to understand the dynamic at work, our collective refusal to invest one of our own with authority.

The organizing collective of Sagaris was gradually crumbling under a constant stream of accusation that grew ever more personal. One woman was trashed for being heterosexual; another was suspect because she'd grown up with money. Still another was criticized because her lover was also on the collective. Women complained that the collective members were overly educated, elitist, that they dared to take a salary — modest as I'm sure it was — for their work. Near the end of the session, one particularly vitriolic community meeting dragged on past midnight. I didn't attend, stayed in my room reading. I was sick of the squabbling. The gossip that buzzed through the cafeteria next morning was that the collective had walked out of the meeting, refusing to hear any more, and this fueled the belief that they were inflexible, unwilling to share power. For months afterward, the pages of the feminist press would be filled with charges and countercharges, passionately worded indictments and defenses.

On the other side of the continent, the Woman's Building moved to a new location in the fall of 1975; some, but not all, of its original tenants came along. FSW students were predominant among the small army of women who hammered sheetrock and sanded floors, renovating the new building for its grand opening. Actress Lily Tomlin and feminist singer Holly Near headlined the gala opening event.

After Sagaris, I enrolled in Thomas Jefferson College (TJC), a small experimental school outside of Grand Rapids, Michigan. At TJC, students could construct their own majors, design their own curricula, or pursue independent study. TJC also housed a program called Women, World, and Wonder.

The Women's Studies program at the University of Toronto had emphasized history and scholarship; Sagaris had focused on political theory and activism. In contrast, the Women, World, and Wonder program was rooted in spirituality, ecology, and art. It offered a model of "seasonal education" to align students with the cycles of nature. Fall was the time to gather resources for the coming winter—a place to live, a support system; winter—in this place of extreme cold and voluminous snow—was given over to study, introspection, and inner journeying. Spring was the time of reconnecting with community, and summer was devoted to "wo-manifestation," bringing forth the fruits of our labor. Self-exploration and personal development were encouraged as a vital part of the educational process.

Not that I was personally prepared to engage in such an inner journey; my defenses were solid as a fortress. Feminism had allowed me to externalize the things that had happened to me; what I suffered from, I maintained, were social problems with political solutions. I wasn't yet prepared to dive beneath the skin, probe hidden wounds. I preferred to light another joint, down a shot of tequila or a glass of ouzo, crank up the stereo, and "dance my way out of my constrictions."[5]

In that fall of 1975 at TJC, I designed an independent study to form a feminist theater troupe and easily attracted five collaborators[6] to create *Indecent Acts*. The piece was a compilation of writing by participants and excerpts from published writers. Since Sagaris, I'd adopted an increasingly separatist stance and I decided I wanted *Indecent Acts* to be performed for an audience of women only.

My faculty adviser warned me that the college would oppose this, so I proposed an academic experiment: we would offer one performance for women only and a second show for a mixed audience. I agreed to survey both audiences and write a paper comparing the responses. The dean approved this plan.

---

[5] Lyric from "One Nation Under a Groove" by G. Clinton, G. Shider, and Walter Morrison, 1978.
[6] Pat MacKenzie, Mary Musinski, Jo Ellen Pasman, Peg Preble, and Rachael Stark.

On the day of the performance I was alerted that the college lawyers had advised the dean to disallow the women-only event, claiming it constituted sex discrimination. Campus police were mobilized to ensure that the performance did not take place. In those halcyon days of the revolutionary early seventies, the police — even rent-a-cops — were viewed as symbols of repressive state authority; I took this gesture by the college as a declaration of war.

My first priority, though, was the performance, which I determined to move off-campus to the Feminist Center in downtown Grand Rapids. The women's community sprang into action: some organized a phone tree to announce the change of location; others spent the day transforming the center's drab office space into an impromptu performance arena — hanging clip-on lights, scattering pillows for seating, draping the windows with bedspreads. Still others drove to campus to shuttle women students who did not have cars.

The performance was standing room only, but the artistry was overshadowed by the political drama. Furious at what I saw as the attempt to censor my work, I canceled the mixed audience performance the next night. It was years before I understood that in making that decision I'd participated in self-erasure and deprived other women of the opportunity to experience the work and its message.

I no longer believed TJC was a supportive environment in which to produce my work, its hippie-liberal veneer stripped clean to reveal its reactionary soul. Nor did I feel at home in the lesbian community in Grand Rapids, whose members considered art frivolous, a luxury. I was told, "When the revolution comes, you'll only be fit to entertain the troops." My sojourn in western Michigan was full of romantic upheavals as well. Every door seemed to slam shut before me, and I spiraled toward that bottle of Dalmane, washed down with burgundy wine.

When I did not die, it was the Woman's Building's vision of feminist art and community that drew me to sell most of my possessions, including my '67 Tempest, and move to Los Angeles where I knew no one, to link my story to the story of the Woman's Building.

~

MY PLANE ARRIVED at midnight on October 2, 1976. I stumbled through the terminal at LAX, dazed and weary from the flight and from the days of tearful good-byes that had preceded it. Clutching the carrier in which my calico, Ruby, lay in a drugged stupor, I looked around for the greeter I'd been promised in a letter from the faculty.

Waiting for me at the gate were two women, both students in the FSW themselves. Kathleen, in a Hawaiian shirt, was in her second year; she had the deep tan and relaxed posture I would later come to associate with the women who lived in Venice, "the beach dykes." Donna, a shorthaired blonde, had just driven from Texas a day earlier. I was extremely relieved to see them and moved by their generosity, coming to the airport in the middle of the night to welcome a new immigrant. This was my introduction to the spirit of the FSW community.

They piled me, my luggage, and my freaked-out cat into Kathleen's VW bug. "Do you think we could stop and see the ocean?" I asked them, and they readily agreed, especially when I lit a joint and passed it around. The Pacific was luminous under a full moon as I stood on the sand and tried to absorb the fact that I was now in California. It was impossible to comprehend. I let the smoke flood my lungs; it soothed my nerves and brightened my mood. Then Kathleen deposited both Donna and myself at the studio of Suzanne Lacy, who taught performance at the FSW; she'd offered her workspace, an unconverted warehouse off an alley in Venice, as a crash pad to newly arrived students. There we hunkered down on cots in the raw space.

Donna had a car, and the next morning she suggested we set out to find the Woman's Building. I was stupefied by having just uprooted my entire life, by the long flight and late night; the immensity of my decision was just starting to dawn on me. All of a sudden I felt stranded and helpless. I was grateful to this blonde stranger with a Texas accent for setting the agenda; otherwise, I might have spent the day immobilized, unable to leave the warehouse.

In the Midwest I'd just departed it had already begun to be fall, the nights grown chilly, leaves turning to flame. My first day in Los Angeles saw the thermometer soar past one hundred degrees; the city was enshrouded in a third-stage smog alert, air literally dun-colored. The glaze of disorientation that enveloped me as we set out in Donna's un-airconditioned Toyota gave way to genuine distress once we entered the maze of freeways and traffic. The noise of cars and horns and radios, the smell of exhaust, grit embedded in the sweat of my skin—every sense felt over-stimulated. Even the light was merciless, careening off shiny hoods of cars, windows of buildings, pavement, trapping me in its white glare.

When the Woman's Building moved from Grandview in 1975, it had relocated to a forsaken corner of industrial downtown, on the far fringe of Chinatown. The new Woman's Building was a challenge to locate even for road-savvy Angelenos. Donna and I spent almost an hour being lost— finding ourselves inexplicably on a freeway I couldn't seem to locate on the map, then caught in a labyrinth of downtown streets that appeared to pay no heed to the dictates of north and south, west and east.

At last we found North Spring Street. I was stunned by the desolate character of the neighborhood: the squat industrial buildings, the barren railroad yards, the hobos under the bridge. There were no retail outlets, no cafés, no foot traffic to speak of. Still, I was relieved to finally spy the three-story red brick structure at number 1727, our destination. I leapt eagerly from the car before Donna had turned off the engine, and raced to the front door, ready to be welcomed into my new home. Instead, I found the security gates drawn, their crisscross pattern of iron like stubborn, folded arms. The door was padlocked.

"Oh no," Donna said, as she read a sign announcing the hours of operation. "Closed Monday."

I was furious, and actually rattled the bars as if my will alone might part them. "They knew we were coming," I fumed.

They knew we had journeyed all this way. I'd left everyone I'd known, everything familiar to me, to come to this ugly, sprawling city where the air was brown and the hazy light assaulted my eyes. I had no car, no job, no place to live, only a little money, no friends. I'd bet everything on this institution, and now the doors were barred to me.

I was getting my first lesson from the Woman's Building: self-reliance. Like many women, feminist or not, I still expected others to take care of me. I had leapt from a precipice into the unknown, and I wanted solid arms to catch me, cushion the impact of my fall, coddle me until I learned to walk on this new ground. "You have two legs and two feet," was what I'd hear at the Woman's Building. Oh, it made me mad to be reminded of my own power! "You can walk and run on your own. Perhaps you can even learn to fly."

Donna was calmer than I about this setback. She'd bought a newspaper and suggested we use the rest of the day to look for apartments. It was a practical idea, but we knew nothing of the neighborhoods in Los Angeles, could barely manage to navigate between one listing and the next, let alone determine which of them might be safe or desirable. I could barely think for the heat and my disorientation. At one point we were driving on Sunset near downtown, and I saw a "For Rent" sign in front of a courtyard of squat stucco houses set into the hillside. Donna stopped as I asked her to; I got out and climbed a steep set of crumbling concrete steps and entered what seemed like another country. The dirt hillside was littered with debris, garbage, scraps of wood, and discarded clothing. Each tiny stucco unit was in need of repair—roofs with holes, windows without panes, portals without doors. A few skinny dogs flopped listless in the dust; even the grubby, half-dressed children seemed torpid. Stout men in undershirts stopped to stare; a few women came to stand in doorways to gawk at the interloper.

I regarded this scene with the pure ignorance of a tourist. "This is how people live in Los Angeles," I thought. In Grand Rapids, I'd rented a room in a house designed by Frank Lloyd Wright, had made my bed in a window seat with leaded panes on three sides through which I could watch the sky all night. Had I traded such splendor for this?

By the time Donna and I made it back to Venice I was sick with heat, smog, and despair. Kathleen had invited us, along with some other women from the FSW, to dinner at her Venice apartment, just a few blocks from the ocean. After she gave her permission for me to make a collect call, I walked the blue princess phone into the bathroom and dialed the 616 area code for Grand Rapids. I was calling Pat, my ex-girlfriend.

"I want to come home," I wailed. "I hate it here."

As I went on to describe my day, Pat listened, sympathetic. Had she argued with me, I might well have stubbornly gotten on a plane the next morning. Instead she said, in her familiar Pennsylvania twang, "Look, if you want to come back here, we'll take up a collection and bring you home."

If I could have hugged her right then, I would have. She was willing to rescue me.

"But you worked so hard to get there," she continued. "You might as well go ahead and have a week's vacation and enjoy yourself out there. See the sights, sit on the beach, rest up. Then if you want to come home, you can."

I could see the logic of her suggestion. Okay, I thought, a week's vacation, then I'm out of here. I hung up the phone, reassured. Kathleen offered me the chance to have a bath in her tub, to wash off the grime and discouragement of the day. She lit a candle, poured lavender oil into the tub. As I soaked in steaming water, the moon rose over the ocean and shone through the open window, and I felt just a bit of myself return to me.

~

WITHIN A FEW DAYS I had found a place to live, not with Donna, but with Jan and Erika, two other new arrivals to the FSW. Jan was a hippie from

Berkeley who drove a silver VW van and worked as a bookkeeper; she talked nonstop and had a steady supply of good pot. Erika was a true tomboy, the butchest straight woman I'd ever met, with blunt-cut blonde hair that framed a freckled boyish face. She'd come from New Mexico in her International Scout with Lilac, her beautiful but neurotic Afghan hound. Jan hated Lilac, but needed three people to swing the rent on the third floor of a ramshackle house in the hills of Echo Park. I was cheered by the morning glories that twined the railing of the rickety stairs and my room that was mostly windows. A few streets over, a rooster crowed at dawn, a sound I'd never expected to hear in Los Angeles. The following week the FSW convened, and all thoughts of returning to Grand Rapids receded from my brain.

At my first meeting of the FSW, forty women crowded into a room on the second floor of the Woman's Building. We perched on folding chairs or sprawled on the wood floor. Two-thirds of us were new to the two-year program; the rest were continuing into their second year.

Most of us were in our twenties, although a couple of women were in their forties. We wore jeans or army fatigues; a few were in vintage dresses. Only a couple of women appeared nonbohemian in slacks and pressed shirts. We sported odd haircuts, more than two earrings, silver women's symbols or crescent moons on chains around our necks. We wore sandals or work boots, had unshaved legs and armpits. Our clothes were brightly colored. Almost no one wore makeup. All but two of us were white. The distribution of lesbian- to heterosexual-identified women was probably about equal, although each group believed themselves to be outnumbered by the other.

I looked around the room, sizing up my sister students. I determined quickly that none of them appeared to be a potential sexual partner, and this produced a pang of disappointment. Then I scanned for possible allies, women who seemed smart and hip and offbeat. I'd shared a joint a few nights earlier with two women who'd moved down from San Francisco—

Jerri and Nancy—and they'd seemed fun and interesting. I'd chatted a little with Maurine, a dark, intense poet from Seattle; we'd talked about being
working-class women, the inherent contradiction that going to art school
represented for someone of our backgrounds. We went around the circle,
and each woman introduced herself. Most were coming from college or from
art school, a large number of them from outside of California. A few were
housewives, and one or two were professional women who had to work the
FSW around their jobs. For the most part, I felt a sense of letdown, and
wondered how I could hope to find community within this group.

In all likelihood, I was no different from many of the women who came
to be part of the Woman's Building, dragging lifetimes of damage like battered suitcases: our parents who valued our brothers more, our brothers
who raped us, our rapes at the hands of strangers, the strange voices in our
heads, our heads full of secrets and shame, our shameful women's lives.

The contented are seldom drawn to revolution, rarely summoned by
utopia's siren song. It was the women with those suitcases stuffed with
damage who were the backbone of the women's movement; we gravitated
to feminism as a balm for our pain, an outlet for our fury. Later, we would
joke that women saw the Woman's Building as the Big Tit in the Sky—a
place to come and suck—but how could there ever be enough milk to satisfy the hunger in our bellies, our balled fists?

Thousands of miles from home, confronted suddenly with the prospect
of exposing myself to strangers, I made the snap decision that most of the
other women in the program were losers. The woman who cried at every
meeting; the one who looked like a 1950s movie star, the kind destined to
die early and tragically; the hulking woman who was wall-eyed from psy-
chotropic medication—their damage was only too apparent, and I hated
them for it. I assumed that my own wounds were well hidden under my
funky shoplifted thrift store clothes, my Motown dance steps, and Motor
City attitude. I didn't realize that I reeked of damage, an odor that clung
to me like the smell of pot smoke, evident to everyone but myself.

I didn't ask myself why, among a group of forty women artists, the very company for which I'd claimed to be longing, I could find so few with whom to identify or bond. It was easier to judge them than to risk vulnerability. Sitting on the second floor of the old brick building perched on a deserted margin of downtown, sitting in the community room in a circle large enough to press against each of the four walls, slumped in rigid folding chairs or sprawled on pillows on the splintered wood floor, I judged them. That one with the whiny voice was too neurotic. That one talked too much and never said anything smart. That one had a stupid haircut that made her ears stick out. That one dressed too conservatively. That tiny woman who looked like a bird never spoke a word. The woman with the shadows under her eyes was always complaining. That one with the perfectly straight teeth — obviously class privileged. That one with all the jewelry — she wanted everyone's approval. That one with the shaved legs slept with men. All appeared lacking in the finely honed defenses that armored me, the only thing I trusted.

Later that morning, the faculty made their introductions. Sheila de Bretteville, who taught graphic design, was the only one of the original founders present.[7] Tall and thin, with a beautifully sculpted face, she exuded a distinctive sense of style. Her voice had never lost its Brooklyn accent and she talked at rapid speed, as if her mouth couldn't contain all the thoughts produced by her keen intellect. Ruth Iskin was also tall, a fleshy woman with striking dark hair and eyes. One of the second-year students whispered to me that Ruth had done a stint in the Israeli army and, indeed, her clipped accent could seem commanding and abrupt. An art historian, she would be leading the critique workshop.

Although I'd slept in her workspace, I hadn't met Suzanne Lacy, the performance art instructor, until that morning. Suzanne had been a student in

---

[7] Judy Chicago had left the FSW in 1974 to work on her monumental collaborative project, *The Dinner Party*. Arlene Raven was on a yearlong sabbatical in 1976–1977.

Judy Chicago's original Feminist Art Program in Fresno. A thin blonde with a compact frame, she exuded high energy and a brusque, no-nonsense manner. Helen Alm Roth was also slight of frame, and spoke in a thin, high voice. She would be teaching printing arts.

The fifth member of the FSW faculty was Deena Metzger, the writing instructor. She did not appear that first day, deepening my sense of disappointment. She would be teaching her class from her home "in the Valley," and although I had no clue as to where "the Valley" might be located, I began to worry about how I would get there without a car.

Once more my anxiety surfaced. With which of these teachers would I be able to bond? Whom could I trust? Which would be able to see me? None of them had identified herself as a lesbian. Fear began a slow trickle down my spine. What if I had chosen wrong in coming here?

After lunch, the program of the FSW was explained to us. Weekly classes would be offered in graphics, performance, writing, and fine printing and book arts. Although there was no visual artist currently on the faculty, Ruth would be available to work with students producing visual art. One could take as many or as few of these classes as her schedule allowed. We could also sign up for classes offered through the Woman's Building Extension Program, which had been created to involve women from the community who were not enrolled in the FSW. We were further expected to participate in a consciousness-raising group, in Ruth's critique workshop, and in weekly FSW community meetings, which would involve not only discussion of program issues but guest speakers, film screenings, and other kinds of presentations. Finally, there were available to us the many events sponsored by the Woman's Building, including gallery openings, concerts and performances, dances, lectures, and readings.

It was a cornucopia; one might have been busy every day and night of the week. Although I couldn't begin to absorb all the possibilities, I felt an excitement stirring, a sense of promise, despite my alienation from the group.

∼

THE PRINCIPLES CARVED OUT by Judy Chicago and those first students at Fresno were still intact: we were in a female-centered environment and our role models were women artists, both those on faculty and the many who came to the Woman's Building to exhibit or lecture or read their work. We were encouraged to make work about our experiences as women, and we were expected to engage in consciousness-raising sessions. Each of us was, in fact, assigned to a C-R group that met weekly; we were given topics — violence, sex, money, work — to explore. I hated my group; it contained none of the women to whom I'd been drawn initially, and I couldn't find a way to bond with those who were there. One of them was a hulking blonde who seemed to be certifiably mentally ill; her very presence produced tension in me, and the level of her distress when she spoke was overwhelming to the rest of the group, precluding any meaningful interaction. I thought she needed care far beyond what a feminist art program could provide, and I resented that the faculty had not screened more carefully and now our group was expected to deal with her. After a few meetings, I stopped showing up for C-R sessions.

As the weeks unfolded, other dissatisfactions crystallized. I couldn't get over the fact that, with Arlene Raven on sabbatical, there were no other lesbians on the faculty. I harbored a mistrust of heterosexual women: I believed that through their allegiance to men, straight women had the power to hurt lesbians. This had been true with my mother; this had been true with Lyn, the first woman with whom I'd fallen in love. I'd had one close heterosexual friend who stopped speaking to me after I came out to her, another who'd reneged on a long-planned travel excursion because she'd acquired a boyfriend. I feared that nonlesbian women in the FSW would prove capable of the same treachery.

Over time, I would develop a deep appreciation for these women, so fully immersed in feminism while still trying to maintain their relationships with men. My own feminist education was inextricably tied to my journey as a lesbian, the effort to claim territory for myself beyond the boundaries of heterosexual definitions of womanhood. What must it have been like for Sheila or Suzanne or Deena to live in both worlds, traverse this border every day and night?

Throughout that first year at the FSW, I was impatient with what I perceived as a dearth of feminist theory guiding the program, its instructors, and the student body. Having been to Sagaris, I kept asking: Where was the rooting out of sexism? Where was the trenchant analysis of race and class, where the vision of reshaping society? Where was the activism? Focusing on "our experience as women" was not the same as forging a blueprint for a feminist future.

To be fair, the absence of dogmatism did create a climate in which I felt freer to be decorative and feminine. Wearing a skirt produced no scowls; no one looked askance at lipstick. I showed up one Monday at the FSW having hennaed my hair; to my amazement, five other women had hennaed their hair the same weekend. It was as if we'd all gotten our periods at the same time. "Clit heads," someone joked.

In fact, the performance art orientation of the program encouraged women to explore alternative personae, to reinvent our presentations of ourselves. One woman took a job as a taxi dancer as research for a planned performance; another dressed as Cinderella and left a trail of shoes in her wake. In my second year at the FSW, Nancy Fried worked to open a thrift store to generate income for the Woman's Building. Its kick-off event was a fashion show in which the woman in a slinky nightgown from the twenties was applauded as fervently as the one decked out in top hat and tails. This was a welcome relief from the pressure to conform I'd felt in other lesbian communities, the not-so-subtle message that I needed to "butch up" to be taken seriously.

There was a sense, though, during that year in the FSW, that the good times had already happened. "Womanhouse," though only five years earlier, was but a memory, its very building demolished. The first site of the Woman's Building was now occupied by a Korean church. All the effort and energy of renovating the Spring Street building, working toward the grand opening, had also dissipated. One could see the faculty and previous students racking their brains to figure out a way to re-create the experience for us. They were trying to replicate an earlier journey of discovery, but of course that terrain had already been explored; we would need to find our own. I would later learn that the faculty was embattled as well; during my entire first year they held no staff meetings, but this was not disclosed to students as we were being exhorted to build community.

These misgivings dawned gradually. During my first weeks in the FSW, I went to every activity I could. No one in my working-class family had ever prepared me to imagine that I might go to art school. Now that I was here, I saw myself standing before an enormous banquet table laden with sumptuous dishes and I was ravenous to sample it all. I ingratiated myself with some women who were planning to carpool to Deena's writing class in Studio City. I signed up for Suzanne's performance art workshop and Sheila's typography class, though I wasn't entirely certain what typography was. I even enrolled in a drawing class through the extension program, although I'd never evidenced the slightest talent for the visual arts. I bought a large sketchpad and a box of pastels and began making drawings, mostly wild bursts of color or crudely rendered female figures with big hair, the kind scrawled on notebook covers during seventh-grade algebra. I knew nothing of form or perspective, of line or shading.

Nor do I still, because I dropped out of that drawing class after my second week. Since it wasn't an FSW offering, I couldn't count on getting a ride home, and it seemed risky to take the bus at night, transferring at Sixth and Hill, downtown deserted after dark. I was lost in Sheila's typography class; I'd never given any thought to design, to why things looked the way they did. I couldn't tell a serif from a sans serif, let alone be able to calculate the x-height of a letter. My dilemma in Suzanne's class was the opposite; I'd spent years studying theater, and the performance art class just seemed like a bunch of adult women playing dress-up, exploring their fantasy lives, indulging themselves. Where was the craft, I wanted to know; where was the discipline? It seemed too much like "therapy," which I disdained because it threatened me.

The lessons of life began to lure me out of the classroom. Los Angeles offered the largest feminist community I'd ever encountered; perhaps I'd find more commonality there than in the confines of the FSW. A few weeks after I'd arrived in Los Angeles, I took a job in the Lesbian Resources office of the Gay Community Services Center.[8] My boss, Cheryl Swannack, was a short powerhouse of a woman who had graduated from the FSW a year earlier. She was a visual artist, she told me, and this claim was supported by her distinctive personal style: hot pink jeans, multiple earrings, and five-inch platform sneakers. I was thrilled to be working in a gay agency, and for someone who was both a feminist and an artist.

Not only did Cheryl employ me, she also took it on as her personal mission to show me around the city and introduce me to the feminist and lesbian communities. A landmark exhibition, "Women Artists 1550–1950"[9] was about to open at the L.A. County Museum of Art in December 1976, and it seemed as if every gallery in town was mounting a show of women artists. Cheryl squired me to all of them, tossing off gossip and anecdotes about everyone we saw. She appeared to know all of the major figures in the women's community—"Colleen runs the Women's Saloon"; "Oh, that's Simone from Sisterhood Bookstore"; "Jeanne edits the *Lesbian Tide*"—and I felt lucky to have the chance to meet many of them.

We went dancing at women's bars and browsing in the feminist bookstores. Cheryl revealed the secrets of some of her favorite places to shop for vintage clothing and unusual jewelry. From the passenger seat of her fuschia VW bug, I was treated to the "Neon Tour" of Los Angeles. Many of these

---

[8] Now called the L.A. Gay and Lesbian Center.
[9] Curated by Ann Sutherland Harris and Linda Nochlin, this was the first-ever major survey of women artists.

excursions were conducted on work time—a condition we justified to one another by saying we needed to stay abreast of the city's lesbian resources.

What I was initially oblivious to was the fact that Cheryl was courting me. When she made her intentions known to me—in a memo that she gave me to type at work—I was hesitant about getting involved with my boss. But this was the seventies; within feminism in particular and the counterculture in general we saw it as our mission to dismantle hierarchies, blur boundaries, obscure the power differences between people. Cheryl was bright and funny; I appreciated her sophistication and love of the arts. And she had been generous with me, bringing glamour and stimulation to what might have otherwise been a lonely life in this new city.

One early evening after work, we were in her studio. We began to kiss and ended up making love in her pink waterbed. Next morning she made me a steaming bath in her enormous clawfoot tub—she had lived for a while in Japan and was accustomed to very hot temperatures—and I drowned my misgivings in that scalding water.

Being Cheryl's girlfriend further changed my relationship to the FSW. My four-day-a-week job already kept me from much of the daily life of the school, and I continued to let my dissatisfactions with the program distance me. Because Cheryl had already been through the Workshop, I felt as if I, too, had moved somehow beyond it.

Within the program I gained some borrowed status through my association with her. Cheryl was not only an alumna but had taken a leadership role while at the Woman's Building. She was a woman of strong opinions and high energy and was respected as someone who got things done.

She had also engaged in a semiclandestine affair with Arlene Raven while Cheryl was a student and Arlene was her teacher in the FSW. I had only a shadowy sense—gleaned from gossip and oblique references—of the ripples this caused; Arlene was living with another woman at the time, and the heterosexual faculty were scandalized that Arlene would become involved with a student. Whether Arlene's sabbatical was related to this episode or not, I didn't know, but I did know that since their affair had ended the previous spring, Cheryl had felt exiled from the Building.

~

THE ONE FSW CLASS I did continue to attend was Deena Metzger's writing workshop. Deena was slightly older than the other FSW faculty, perhaps in her early forties when I first met her in the fall of 1976; she had raised two sons who were nearly adult. Hers was a feminism born of humanism; not for her the separatist politics and male-bashing that were in the vanguard at the time. She held a deep commitment to liberation struggles and progressive politics; she had fought her own battle with academic censorship in the late sixties, and had visited Allende's Chile before the coup. She was also rooted in spirituality and mysticism; as an artist, as a political being, as a woman, she cultivated the sacred in everyday life. Small black eyes radiated from her tanned face. Her compact body was usually adorned in colorful, hand-woven garments from Central and South America. An aura of wisdom radiated from her, and even back then she seemed to embody the archetype of the Crone.

Her approach to writing was different than anything I'd previously encountered; she wanted her students to escape the dictates of rational thought, set ourselves loose in the lush wilderness of the imagination. Our purpose, she suggested, was not merely to record the known, but to court the unknown. She encouraged us to write gibberish, reveal our secrets, tell lies, lose our way.

In one exercise, we lay on the polished wood floor of her living room with our eyes closed as she guided us into a meditative state. "Before you lies a path," she instructed, and inside the darkness of my eyelids I saw a dirt road spread before me.

"Walk along the path, and just notice what you see." Pale green lawns to either side, the occasional young tree.

"Soon you will encounter someone on the path," she continued. "Just accept whomever it is who appears." And old woman walked toward me, her face as gnarled as her form. Her clothes were black.

"This is your spirit guide," Deena crooned. I was disappointed. I'd hoped for someone more flamboyant, less severe.

"Ask this person a question, and then listen for the answer."

At age twenty-two, my probing question was this: "Will I be famous?"

The answer echoed inside my head: *You will be known.* It would take me years to appreciate that the latter was infinitely preferable to the former.

Deena insisted that the way to achieve the best product in writing was to pay careful attention to the process. "Treat writing as a sacred activity," she exhorted her students, "Give it ritual and magic." Our writing should be about discovery, should take us beyond our own paltry knowing into deeper understanding, revelation. This notion of writing as an inner journey began to change my work. What I couldn't yet do in my life, I began to attempt on the page.

It was Deena, too, who would take me aside a year later, after I'd started teaching classes and writing the Woman's Building newsletter and co-directing the Lesbian Art Project. "You will never be the kind of writer you want to be," she cautioned me, "if you keep giving yourself away to the community. They will take everything and always ask for more." Her black eyes bore into mine. "A writer must be selfish, must keep everything for her own work." I felt the gravity of her words, the intensity with which she pressed my hand as she spoke them. It wasn't that I disbelieved her; it was only that I wanted to be the exception to the rule. I needed that community, was willing to feed it pieces of myself unendingly in order that I might feel nurtured by it. I wanted to do it all.

~

IN EARLY SPRING OF 1977, Arlene Raven took a break from her sabbatical to do a one-day workshop at the Woman's Building, presenting her art historical research on lesbian art. I attended for a number of reasons: hunger for lesbian visibility in the FSW, genuine interest in the topic, and curiosity about the woman who'd broken Cheryl's heart. Arlene was in her early thirties, attractive in an understated way that she made no effort to enhance. Slender, she had dark hair curling past her shoulders, fine features on her small face. I was impressed with the serious analysis she brought to the images she projected onto the screen, works by Romaine Brooks and Rosa Bonheur, and I found myself wanting to wow her too.

Lesbian artists from L.A. had been invited to share and/or talk about their work as well, primarily visual artists, but I stood up and read a poem. If it registered with Arlene, she gave no evidence of it. Two months later Arlene hosted a follow-up gathering at her home and announced that she was embarking on a project to study lesbian art. She was, she said, looking for women to collaborate with her.

A tingle of energy surrounded me as I heard these words, a path opened before me, and I was filled with light. In that moment I understood that my entire journey to California, that whole disgruntled year in the FSW, had been about bringing me to this point: I would work with Arlene on the Lesbian Art Project. The obvious complication of working with the ex-lover of the woman I was seeing made no difference to me. Even if I'd known that Cheryl and I would separate a month later, that she and Arlene would rekindle their relationship, and that I would be drawn into a treacherous high-wire act of trying to be a working partner with my ex's lover, it still wouldn't have mattered. I believed I was meant to do this work.

I don't know whether my decision to work with Arlene hastened my breakup with Cheryl. We were on a path of disintegration, our interactions increasingly corrosive. The attention she'd once lavished on me had cooled to criticism and neglect, and I, for my part, slid easily into the role of the persecuted. I had no experience, and really no model, for how to participate in a real relationship. We had to let go, although my work with Arlene would force us into continued and uncomfortable proximity for the next few years.

I didn't know it then, but I was on the verge of transformation. Come fall, I would help to launch the Lesbian Art Project. I would be hired by the Woman's Building to produce its newsletter. I would engage in a different relationship with the FSW, taking responsibility to change many of the aspects of the program I'd criticized. I would become a teacher.

In that summer of 1977, I couldn't see what lay ahead. All that sustained me during that time of dissolution was my excitement about the Lesbian Art Project and the publication of my first book, *Blue Moon*.

I'd come to the FSW the previous fall with a dream of self-publishing a collection of poetry and prose. Deena's writing workshop helped me to hone the text and gave me encouragement to follow through on my intention. I'd grown up in a world—working class, industrial Midwest—in which every spark of initiative was met with the reasons it would fail. "You might get hurt." "How do you think you're going to support yourself?" "Don't be crazy." Caution and fear were guiding principles; people clung to their limitations as a hedge against disappointment. But at the Woman's Building we were exhorted to risk, to "go for it," to follow the path of inspiration, pursue our dreams.

Access to the Woman's Building printing presses and my almost accidental acquisition of basic graphic design skills made it possible to bring my words into print. I typeset the text myself. Under the guidance of Sheila de Bretteville, I ordered paper samples, made a dummy copy of the book, and located a bindery to assemble the pages. Nancy Fried volunteered to test her newfound letterpress skills by printing the cover. Meridee Mandio, a second-year student, agreed to print the inside pages on the Building's ancient, cranky offset press. Friends contributed illustrations and cheered me on. I was experiencing the FSW philosophy in action: a community of women eager to support one of its members to produce her art. Not only did my sister students want me to accomplish what I'd set out to do, their energy and vision pushed me to take the project further than I might have on my own.

Nancy further offered the spacious patio of her rented Craftsman home for a publication party—an event it would not have occurred to me to plan. "No, no, you've got to have a party," she insisted, "This is a great moment in your life: your first book!" How can I begin to describe the impact of knowing that someone else—a group of someones—cared about my artistic work? In my family there'd been consternation that pursuing this dream would leave me disappointed and destitute. In college theater programs there'd been competition, a kind of vicious doubt, an expectation of failure. Among the lesbians in Grand Rapids there'd been at best an amused tolerance at my frivolous pursuit of art. But here my ambitions were applauded, celebrated.

A sculptor, Nancy set about decorating for the party with great enthusiasm, creating a canopy of flowers that overhung the backyard. To whatever she did, she brought an air of exquisite style that was not about spending a lot of money but about lavishing her attention on it. She organized other FSW students to bring refreshments, platters of cookies and fruit, an elegant repast. In late July, fifty women gathered on the patio to celebrate the publication of *Blue Moon*. They *ooh'd* and *ahh'd* as I read poems about ravens and Snow White, madness and Marilyn Monroe, my search for the blue moon. They clapped and cheered and danced with me when I was done.

I'd been so judgmental, so aloof from them all year. Yet they forgave my complaints and defensiveness, overlooked my damage. For the moment they were happy to revel in another woman's artistic accomplishment, claim me as part of their community.

There is a photograph of me from that afternoon. I wear a yellow linen dress printed with red hibiscus, its long skirt bias-cut. I am dancing with Katja Beisanz, a choreographer, who wears a long gown of vintage lace. Our hands cling to each other's forearms, skirts swirling over our bare feet. We have thrown our heads back in abandon. We are spinning in the afternoon light, twirling past dizziness, spinning and laughing, creating our own vortex.

And from its center I was birthed into the family of feminist art.

Wolverton dances with Katja Beisanz (right) at the publication party for Blue Moon, *1977. (Photo by E.K. Waller)*

(l. to r.) Wolverton, Brook Hallock, Catherine Stifter (hidden), Nancy Angelo and Cheri Gaulke accuse Leslie Belt (center) of politically incorrect behavior in "An Oral Herstory of Lesbianism," 1979. (Photo by Jo Goodwin)

Lesbian Art: A Partial Inventory
1977–1980

Every woman who ever loved a woman
you ought to stand up and call her name.
Mother, sister, daughter, lover . . .
—Bernice Johnson Reagon,
from "Every Woman"

Summer 1977

Two black-and-white photographs, 8"x10" glossies shot by a professional; the companion images portray a group of five women posing in a garden. We are the Natalie Barney Collective,[10] five women from the Feminist Studio Workshop[11] who have come together to conduct the Lesbian Art Project, an endeavor consisting of equal parts art historical research, community building, activism, group therapy, heavy partying, and the kind of life-as-art performance sensibility inherited from the Fluxus artists and so prevalent in southern California art of the 1970s. A labor of love that will define the next two years of my life.

   The companion photos are a study in contrast, the subjects' attire, stances,

---

[10] Named after the expatriate writer who lived in Paris in the 1920s and gathered about her a community of artistic and independent women, many of them lesbians, which was known for its celebratory and iconoclastic spirit.

[11] A sixth member, Kathleen Burg, did not attend the photo shoot that day.

The Natalie Barney Collective butches up: (l. to r.) Maya Sterling, Sharon Immergluck, Arlene Raven, Nancy Fried, Terry Wolverton, 1977. (Photo by E.K. Waller)

and attitude wildly variant from one image to the next. In the first shot, we scowl into the lens, each of our unrouged mouths a thin, strict line. On the far right, I stand, dressed in a pinstripe business suit—trousers, vest, jacket slung jauntily over my shoulder—a tie, a fedora on my head. I lean against a stone wall with studied insouciance. Just below, Nancy Fried perches on a low step, fist on her hip. She is the only one of us in a dress, a long antique gown, but it's worn with the implacable air of a dowager empress, a manner that suggests no softness. Beside her stands a trio of women in black: Arlene Raven, founder of the Lesbian Art Project; Sharon Immergluck, debonair in top hat and tails, black bow tie against a white shirt; and finally, Maya Sterling, her posture commanding, confrontative. A black velvet shirt hangs open to the waist, baring the stripe of skin between her breasts.

This is our collective depiction of "butch."

In the second image, we have transformed ourselves into "femme." The picture is sunlit, a shag of palm leaves in the background. We are clustered together, two of us seated, our lips parted, smiling. We are all in dresses; many of us hold elaborate fans from Nancy's collection. My gown is chiffon, Arlene's is lace. Nancy is in satin, her cleavage visible. Maya and Sharon are in simpler dresses; Maya now sports Sharon's top hat, awry on her mass of curls.

Arlene had imagined the Lesbian Art Project as an organized effort to further her investigation of a lesbian sensibility in art. The rest of us— current and former FSW students drawn by her invitation to participate— have concocted a project far beyond Arlene's original intention to research the work of Romaine Brooks and other historical and contemporary lesbian artists. We are after nothing less than an exploration of the meaning(s) of "lesbian,"—an ambition consistent with Arlene's approach to art history—and the manifestation of a culture in which those meanings can be expressed and amplified.

We envision the Lesbian Art Project (LAP) as a context in which our own artwork can be produced and understood; I for one am already devising a performance project about a female future that I will produce under LAP's auspices.

Femme version of the Natalie Barney Collective of the Lesbian Art Project: (seated, l. to r.) Nancy Fried, Arlene Raven, (standing, l. to r.) Maya Sterling, Sharon Immergluck, Terry Wolverton, 1977. (Photo by E.K. Waller)

We imagine the Lesbian Art Project as a springboard from which to launch a reinvention of the lesbian community. Nancy and I concoct lavish events we will create and host. "Beautiful, elegant events," Nancy muses with a dreamy expression, conjuring the lush environments she will, with her sculptor's sensibility, fashion.

"Events that aren't boring and depressing to attend," I agree, grimacing at the memory of dark-lit lesbian bars, patrons camouflaged in flannel shirts and jeans, hard eyes and tight shoulders, the cramped and constricted body language of self-hatred.

"Events to which I could wear this!" Sharon beams, pirouetting in top hat and tails on the flagstone path of the garden. It is clear that we will not be content to merely *study* the aesthetics of lesbians; we are determined to wield our influence over them as well.

The Natalie Barney Collective is in the process of designing an educational program through which aspects of lesbian culture and experience can be examined. "There's not another context in which you can learn anything positive about lesbians," Arlene asserts, and in 1977, this is virtually true.

We're planning a gay/straight dialogue, at Sharon's suggestion, "So the heterosexual women in the FSW don't freak out." A therapist as well as a writer, Sharon is always attentive to group dynamics.

"And we need to network with other lesbian artists across the country and around the world," Maya's eyes glitter, anticipating an excuse to travel.

"And we have to get lots of media coverage," I remind them, "to contradict all those horrible stereotypes about lesbians."

"Right," Maya quips, "like that we're butch or femme!" We cackle with laughter until the photographer says, "Could you please hold still?" and we pose for another shot.

It is 1977, and feminist lesbians don't officially believe in butch and femme. Feminist cant has labeled role-playing as "heterosexist," and declared "androgyny" the sought-after standard. If butch and femme are talked about at all, it is in a historical context, as a quaint custom left over from the 1950s, the bad old days of the closet, when lesbians didn't know any better than to mimic what men and women do together. Like every generation, we unthinkingly disrespect the generation that has come before.

The members of the Natalie Barney Collective believe we are being saucy and bold in daring to depict ourselves in these ancient roles, defying not only the conventions of heterosexual culture but also flouting the current standards of correctness within the lesbian community. In our thrift-store finery, a kind of hippie elegance, we push the butch/femme stereotypes until they warp and bend, make them into material for art. There is about this photo shoot, as about all of LAP's activities, a determined element of crackpot.[12]

---

[12] A former professor of mine at Thomas Jefferson College, the feminist philosopher Linda Smith, has reminded us that during the process of alchemical transformation, as one substance is transmuted into another, the pot cracks. The old container is insufficient to house the new substance. Thus a "crackpot" may be someone undergoing just such a transformation of the self.

It is with a fervent sense of mission that I've immersed myself in the Lesbian Art Project, the first time since coming to the Woman's Building that I've felt confirmed in my decision to do so, the first time I've seen a clear focus for my considerable energies. The juxtaposition of "lesbian" and "artist" makes possible the integration of two central parts of my identity, creates more ground on which to stand. Thus named, I feel less crazy, less queer.[13]

At one of our earliest LAP meetings, Arlene had observed that, as a collective, we would need to use our own lives as a basis for this investigation, our own experiences as lesbians as the foundation of our theory. We accepted this premise, already well trained as feminists that "the personal is political." In 1977, we don't yet fully realize that our theory will be limited and circumscribed by the fact that we are six white women in our twenties and thirties. And we don't fully comprehend that looking at our lesbian experience through a magnifying glass will bring us face to face with the pain of our lesbian oppression.

Are any of us equipped to undertake this? Are we sufficiently honest with ourselves, do we have enough trust in one another? Are we capable of reading the content of our interactions at the same moment we are engaging in them? And if so, how does such studied observation alter the content of our behaviors?

On this sunny July afternoon in the garden behind Nancy's house, we don't know the answers to these questions, or even that such inquiries await us. We're not thinking about butch and femme, where each of us might fit on that spectrum of identity. We leave unspoken the fact that some of us look ill at ease in our dresses, others of us appear less convincingly butch.

---

[13] Within LAP, we explored and reclaimed the term "queer," more than ten years in advance of the political activists who in the nineties would call themselves Queer Nation. "Queer," which had been used for decades to revile gays and lesbians, was an accurate reflection of the alienation we felt within heterosexist society, and the way we often internalized that alienation, the feeling of not belonging.

We are playing dress-up, posing for pictures, engaging in performativity. Laughing and mugging for the camera, we are smoking joints, enjoying the California sunshine, grooving on being outrageous lesbians. We believe that in this way — our outright rejection of second-class status for lesbians, our refusal to accept anything less than a marvelous quality of life — the Natalie Barney Collective will change the world.

Fall 1977

Proposed logo for the Lesbian Art Project, designed by Bia Lowe, 1977.

A single sheet of thick paper, the prototype of a poster created by graphic designer Bia Lowe to represent the Lesbian Art Project. Never reproduced, it's a one-of-a-kind artwork.

At the top of the page is the project's acronym: LAP. Below these letters are two line drawings scissored from children's workbooks, stacked one atop the other. The illustration style suggests the early 1960s, the seat of nostalgia for my generation, a time when the world seemed hopeful and prosperous.

The top cutout depicts a woman seated. The viewer is aware of the bend in her hips, the drape of her dress over her thighs, the slight concavity of the dip between her thighs, a certain inviting space. Her lap.

Beneath this image, in the other cutout, a cat tongues milk from a bowl.

Within this juxtaposition, there is tension between the simple domesticity of the scenes, which bespeak comfort, even innocence, and the inescapable erotic inference created by their apposition: the lesbian, after all, is the one who laps at the lap.

The urge to render innocence to lesbian sexuality is not only character-istic of Lowe's work of the time. The organizers and students of LAP sought out the work of lesbian artists across the country; we read these images as both mirror and blueprint, a reflection of our culture as it was and a guide to what we wished it to become. Many lesbian artists in the 1970s set out to remythologize lesbianism, to redeem it from the images of depravity and evil that were common in both pornographic depiction and religious interpretation, to make it "good."

HER SHE KISSES HER

HerSheKissesHer by Clsuf. (Photo by Nancy Greene)

Thus, the "HERSHEKISSESHER" multiple by the artist Clsuf dupli-cates the signature wrapping of a Hershey's Kiss (what could be more inno-cent than a candy kiss?)—the same strip of white paper, the same blue type, playing with the language of the confectionery's brand name to sug-gest a different kind of sweetness. Or the bread dough sculptures of Nancy Fried (such a homey, nonthreatening medium!), capturing scenes of domestic lesbian life—two women in the bath, one nude woman giving another a foot massage—and painted with the exquisite detail of a Fabergé egg. Or the solarized photos of artist Tee Corinne, explicit as they are in the portrayal of lesbian sexual practice, create a rosy glow, almost a halo, around their subjects that confers a benediction on their acts.

What is common to all of these images is their intention to disarm the viewer, to make the strange familiar, even soothing. A subsequent genera-tion of lesbians in the 1980s and '90s will come to challenge this strategy, charging that it robs lesbianism of its power to shock and inflame. This generation will glorify "bad girls," bringing a punk sensibility, a calculated strategy of transgression, to the depiction of lesbian imagery. But in the 1970s, to merely raise the issue of lesbianism is incendiary, and perhaps this more gentle assertion of lesbian sexuality serves to desensitize the art world, pave the way for the more confrontational work that is to come.

Fall 1977

WILL YOU HELP?

E.K. Waller's photo created the centerpiece for "Will You Help?", an offset poster soliciting donations for The Store, a thrift store at the Woman's Building, 1977.

Seven women stare out from the poster; all eyes confront the viewer. We are posed — some seated, some standing — in a desolate corner of the Woman's Building: bare walls, ragged floor, poor lighting. We range in age from our twenties to our forties, our bodies tall or short, corpulent or thin, large breasted or small. We are all naked. In bold type, a headline demands, "WILL YOU HELP?" Smaller text goes on to specify, "We need: jeans, t-shirts, furniture, jewelry, plants, old postcards, toys, tuxedos, sunglasses, mirrors, birdbaths, shoes, scarves, umbrella stands, Christmas tree lights, beads, buttons, carpets or rugs, frames, dishes, dresses, costumes, pillows, dress dummies, leather jackets, pink flamingos . . ."

It is a poster soliciting donations for a new thrift store conceived by Nancy Fried and Valerie Angers as a fund-raising strategy for the Woman's Building. While not strictly a Lesbian Art Project endeavor, The Store is fueled by the vision and energy of many lesbians (all but one of the women in the photograph identifies as such, or did so at that time) and is launched with the outrageous spirit to which LAP is dedicated.

Over the summer of 1977, a campaign to pass the country's first anti-gay rights ordinance has been waged and won in Dade County, Florida, with Anita Bryant as its celebrity spokesperson. In the fall, conservative California state senator John Briggs introduces a bill that would ban gay teachers in public schools. Rather than retreat in the face of these threats, the gay and lesbian communities are galvanized into founding a political movement, raising millions of dollars, being vocal about our cause in the media, and demanding accountability from elected officials.

The women of the Natalie Barney Collective, too, respond with flagrant defiance of those who would deny our right to exist. More than ever we are committed to being visible as lesbians in our personal and professional lives. We channel the fear and vulnerability we feel into increasingly raucous displays of lesbian sensibility, determined to celebrate ourselves.

The Store's opening is observed with a fashion show organized by LAP. Originally conceived as an opportunity to model the wares of the thrift shop, the occasion morphs into performance art as we give vent to personas that express our gender identities. Sharon returns in top hat and tails to act as mistress of ceremonies; Bia sports elegant pajamas and robe; Holiday Jackson wears a glamorous fifties cocktail dress with a stuffed parrot on her shoulder. Madcap, with a ferocious undertone: *I am woman, hear me roar, dahling.*

The hostile political climate lends urgency to our Feminist/Lesbian Dialogue within the community of the FSW, the first time, according to Arlene, that this type of discussion has been formally held. Such events are always fraught: everyone feeling a little defensive, fearful of being made to feel like the Other, or even resentful of having to declare themselves. Lesbians historically carry this feeling of queerness and isolation from their experiences of oppression within heterosexist society, but at the Woman's Building, straight women also feel like a beleaguered minority, believing themselves judged as lesser feminists for being involved with men. LAP's dialogue does not resolve these issues, but does allow them to be aired, to become discussible, and further serves to create more visibility and presence for lesbian students in the FSW, something for which I had longed my first year there.

In addition to weekly planning meetings, LAP sponsors two additional public events this fall: one is an exhibit of Nancy Fried's bread dough sculptures. The opening reception is followed by a "Sizzling Disco" to intensify the spirit of festivity we wish to foster. The other is the first in a series of Lesbian Create•Hers Salons, highlighting significant creative work of lesbians. Our inaugural salon features architect Noel Phyllis Birkby.[14] We also launch monthly worksharing groups in which lesbian artists can present their work to others for feedback and dialogue, and consciousness-raising groups around specifically lesbian topics within the FSW. And we plan a full roster of activities for the coming winter.

The first season of the Lesbian Art Project is an enormous success, as lesbians flock to our events. So, too, the "WILL YOU HELP?" poster is a hit; donations pour in from across the country to establish The Store. Aside from its marketing function, though, the piece is also noteworthy as an art image: although nude, the women portrayed are not objectified, not sexualized, not coy. Each of us stares directly at the viewer without self-consciousness or apology. Even as we appeal for help, naked to the public eye, we do so not out of vulnerability or neediness. We have stripped ourselves of the trappings of identity handed down to us; we are starting from scratch, ready to re-clothe ourselves in another guise, poised to invent ourselves anew.

Winter 1978

They might be petroglyphs or runes, an ancient language of symbols. The six crudely rendered ideograms are my attempt to articulate a new vision of lesbian community, to define the roles apparent and necessary to further the work of the group.

---

[14] Later salons featured performance artist and filmmaker Barbara Hammer, witch/playwright/activist Zusanna Budapest, and artist and mythmaker Jere Van Syoc.

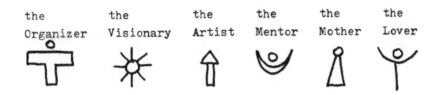

| the Organizer | the Visionary | the Artist | the Mentor | the Mother | the Lover |

Arlene Raven and I sit in my light-filled apartment in the hills of Echo Park. She and I are now the sole directors of the Lesbian Art Project. After a summer of feverish planning and a fall of breakneck producing, the Natalie Barney Collective has imploded and burned out.

It's more than exhaustion that has caused the group's dissolution. The tasks we have set—to hold ourselves up as public icons of an idealized lesbian culture, to interrogate our own conduct and motives as they are unfolding, and to reveal our findings to one another—bring us face to face with our core fears and personal weaknesses.

When one of us sends home a coming-out letter and is disowned by her family in response, we must each confront our alienation and estrangement from our families of origin. When two others end their relationship as lovers, we each find ourselves probing our own fears of trust, our reluctance to bond with another woman. When Arlene resumes her love relationship with Cheryl, from whom I have recently parted with bad feelings, we are each required to consider how community can thrive despite fissures of jealousy and resentment.

To focus on lesbianism as a state of being could not help but evoke our own internalized homophobia, the fear and hatred of our own and others' queerness. To embrace that queerness is to embrace isolation, marginalization, exile. Committed as we are to living our vision—a world in which lesbians are celebrated, luxuriant, unrestrained—we discover our insides wired for self-loathing, scorn, shame.

The tension between the world we dream of and the one in which we live creates skirmishes and misunderstandings, ruptures long-standing friendships and burgeoning intimacies. It has sorely tested everyone's commitment and accountability to the work.

Nancy has expressed her intention to stay connected to LAP as an artist, but withdrawn from all administrative work. Sharon, Maya, and Kathleen have distanced themselves from the project. I can't imagine stopping the work we have begun; my identity as a lesbian artist is central to my being at this time and in LAP I've found both mission and purpose.

Throughout the summer and fall, the collective had focused on how the Lesbian Art Project might serve the community. In shifting to a partnership structure, Arlene and I have prioritized those activities that will most satisfy ourselves. "Women always think we have to be self-sacrificing," Arlene reminds me, "but that's the same old patriarchal model—and who needs it?" And she gives her signature dismissive laugh—"Ha!"—a throaty half-cackle, one beat, as if withdrawn abruptly.

Gone are the plans for aggressive grant writing to support salaried positions. Gone is the far-reaching media campaign. Gone is anything that requires a high level of administration. The Natalie Barney Collective had, Arlene and I decide, been seduced by a male notion of institution building—the bigger the better, impact measured by numbers served. We will instead trust that our work—on whatever scale—will create a shift in consciousness that transmits itself from woman to woman, a revolution from the inside out.

In letting go of our worldly ambitions, I ask myself now, were we truly forging a female model, one that assumed our influence would be psychic, cellular, would work its way through an underground network of women's wisdom? Or were we unwittingly participating in our own marginalization, ensuring that our efforts would be buried, lost to history? Were we redefining power or giving up on it?

More than two decades later, I see a lesbian community that has more visibility, and that expects much more for itself. Lesbian lives are depicted on TV, and explicit images of lesbian art hang in the collections of major museums. Young lesbian artists don't hesitate to flaunt their sexuality and politics. These circumstances exist in part because LAP existed. But few if any of these young artists has even heard about the Lesbian Art Project. Did our decision to work outside of mainstream culture ensure our erasure?

In the winter of 1978, what Arlene and I have retained of our plan for LAP are the art projects, some social and community events, Arlene's research on the life and work of painter Romaine Brooks and her contemporaries, and the planning for a Program of Sapphic Education. This vision is inspired by the Greek poet's school at Mytilene. The program is conceptualized as a one-year, one-time-only project; neither Arlene nor I wants to create an institution the maintenance of which will be our responsibility.

We've adopted a model of seasonal education first developed by artist Jere Van Syoc and philosopher Linda Smith in the Women, World, and Wonder program at Thomas Jefferson College, wherein the activities of learning are geared to the mood or meaning of the time of year. Autumn is a time for gathering, the development of community, and for this season we've envisioned eight one-day workshops on Sunday afternoons; these are held at Arlene and Cheryl's home to create the atmosphere of a salon and provide a sense of safety and privacy. Arlene and I alternate or share responsibility to teach these workshops on subjects like "Lesbian Relationships," "The Lesbian Body," and "I Dream in Female/Lesbian Consciousness as Non-Ordinary Reality."

Winter is the time for study and contemplation, focusing and conceptualizing. During these months we will offer a series of in-depth, eight- to ten-week classes, including "Lesbian Art History," "Lesbian Writing," "Feminist Neology," "Feminist Astrology," and the workshop portion of the development of a new performance project, *An Oral Herstory of Lesbianism.*

Spring is the time for blossoming, and into this season is scheduled the performance of *An Oral Herstory of Lesbianism,* which will involve a large sampling of participants in LAP. Summer is envisioned as a time for travel, making connections with other lesbians across the country, expanding the impact of our work.

We intend our Program of Sapphic Education to not only inspire art-making, but to build lesbian consciousness and community, and the six symbols are my attempt to identify the archetypal functions required to fulfill this vision.

"The Organizer" posits a small circle, perched like a human head atop a thick, broad-shouldered "T"; any resemblance to the cross of crucifixion is strictly a Freudian slip. Within the Lesbian Art Project, I am the organizer, the one who figures out schedules and budgets, who plans events, types the press releases. The one who worries.

Like the sun, "The Visionary" radiates from a central circle, illuminating previously unlit areas of consciousness. Arlene is the visionary, purveyor of brilliance.

"The Artist" is a pure arrow of intention, direction, activity. Cheryl seems most like this symbol to me with her tenacity, her will to do. Still, there are many artists in the LAP constellation: Bia Lowe, graphic designer and writer; I admire the refined sophistication and philosophical thinking she brings to her work. Nancy Fried, a ball of fierce energy whose sculptures will one day sell in New York galleries. When she came to the Woman's Building, the same year I did, she didn't think she was an artist, but she has blossomed with the attention and encouragement she's received. Clsuf, née Claudia Samson, former member of Rhode Island Feminist Theater, is now working in graphics and other ephemeral art, including food as art. And Jere Van Syoc, creator of windmills and altarpieces — multimedia interactive sculpture — and mythmaker. Jere had been my instructor at Thomas Jefferson College in Grand Rapids, Michigan, and has come to Los Angeles as an LAP artist in residence in 1978.

Both Visionary and Artist seem like exalted positions compared to mine; I harbor a secret dread that my tombstone will read, "She was a great organizer," my own creativity buried under layers of competence and responsibility, my own brilliance unrecognized, forgotten.

Arlene is also "The Mentor," depicted as an upturned crescent cradling a smaller circle. Although she acknowledges this as her role, she is adamant that the mentorship be mutual, she and I each learning from the other. It is our declared feminist lesbian principle to unseat the hierarchy that has been traditionally inherent in the mentor/student role, but I secretly worry that this egalitarianism has no basis in reality. Other than my organizing skills, my ability to manifest ideas into practical applications, I cannot see what I might bring to her, although she insists she is inspired by my decidedly alternative vision, my metaphysical bent, and my fierce commitment to lesbianism. It will be many years later, years of being a teacher and mentor myself, before I will fully understand her determination to stave off the isolation of that role, to subvert the objectification and projections that one receives when one is a "mentor."

None of us wants to be "The Mother," this role so despised, so disempowered under patriarchy, although in truth we all want one. The glyph is an isosceles triangle supporting a small circle at its tip. As lesbians, we all feel like motherless girls, want to be taken care of, not tend to someone else. As teachers in the Program of Sapphic Education, Arlene and I are seen in this role, and not infrequently our students project onto us their disappointed expectations of their own mothers. We chafe against it.

We all want to be "The Lover," consider it an expression of our destiny as lesbians. The symbol resembles a young tree, fresh branches stretching in an inviting embrace. The unwritten history of the lesbian movement reveals how much energy is built on the energy of lovers, with presses and bookstores, coffeehouses and theater companies, political campaigns and art projects all fueled by sexual energy between women.

This energy, gone sour, has at times undermined those same endeavors, led to their dissolution. There is, in our core group, spoken and unspoken tension. We are lovers and former lovers, former teachers and students, friends and estranged friends, women with spoken and unspoken attractions, spoken and unspoken enmities.

Such details are the weft of the fabric of LAP. Our activities flow from the energy of these connections, our theories born from the attempts to wrestle with our difficulties and define our relative positions. Bereft of meaningful relationships with our biological families, we attempt to create an alternative family, a utopian community, born of our visions and dreams. The symbols and the roles they illustrate are my attempt to build a structure and find my place within it.

Winter 1978

A heart-shaped pillow sheathed in pink lamé. One of the dozens that festooned the Woman's Building performance space for LAP's "Dyke of Your Dreams Day" dance, our own saucy retort to the rituals of Saint Valentine. Though we disdain the culture of heterosexuality, we still feel free to steal whatever seems useful and transform it as we see fit.

Nancy Fried designed those pillows, then enlisted Sue Maberry to sew them. An FSW student who was just starting her coming-out process, Sue was more than glad to whip up three dozen stuffed pillow hearts if it meant getting to hang out with the women of LAP.

Nancy has also corralled a group of us to join her at the Woman's Building the day before the dance to help with installation. This first meant reclining our bodies onto long strips of midnight blue photo backdrop paper onto which our outlines were traced in gold glitter. That was followed by hours spent on ladders suspending everything from the eighteen-foot ceiling—lamé hearts hung like plump moons, the glittered panels with their diving female forms lining the perimeter of the dance floor. And twinkle lights, blinking their tiny beams across the stretch of space. This is a far cry from the wood-paneled, darkly lit bars that are the customary habitués of lesbian socializing. We go to this effort because we believe lesbians deserve a beautiful environment for valentine courtship.

The next night, this space is filled with over three hundred women flirting with their bodies to Natalie Cole's "Sophisticated Lady," the Pointer Sisters, and Gloria Gaynor's "I Will Survive"—the most female-affirmative disco we can assemble. Clsuf serves nonalcoholic beverages under a sign that reads, "Lick•Hers," both advertisement and invitation.

And I, too, am on that dance floor, in a floor-length black crepe dress from the forties—wide shoulders, narrow waist. I am shaking my hips, spinning around as flashes of glitter and pink lamé spark across my vision. Like the other women of LAP, I am tired of lesbian oppression, and tonight I want to be fabulous, transported, to dance homophobia into oblivion.

Spring 1978

The button has shiny silver print on a black background. "OVO," it reads in neon script. A made-up word. Feminists of the period are always altering language; we alter the spelling of "wimmin" to take the "men" out, we rename the study of the past "herstory," and some adopt new last names to subvert patrimony. The power to name is the power to confer meaning.

"OVO" button by Clsuf, created for FEMINA: An IntraSpace Voyage, *1978. (Photo by Twolip Art)*

The button is part of the ephemera of *FEMINA: an IntraSpace Voyage*, the collaborative performance project I have originated as part of LAP. *FEMINA* is about a group of women who find life on Earth unbearable, and who make the decision to journey together to another planet. Cheryl has joked that my next performance must be titled *Butchina*.

The buttons were made by Clsuf. The term itself was invented by the play's codirector, Ann Shannon, who also defined the word's multiple meanings. We were sitting in the brick-red Val's Café on the third floor of the Woman's Building one early evening before rehearsal, and she spelled it out on a scrap of notebook paper.

"OVO, see, it's used as a greeting, like 'hello.' But it's also an expression of approval, like 'Bravo!'" Ann bobbed her curly wedge of hair and gazed intently at me to see if I was following.

"So, like, 'Great rehearsal, women, OVO!'" I demonstrated, and she beamed.

"But, look," she continued, "it's a pictograph, too—see how it looks like the female reproductive system?" She turned the page around in case I might fail to catch the resemblance.

"*And,* it's also a *map* of our journey to Femina, see?" she pressed on. "How we start out in one space," she traces the first circle, "catapult through time and space," her pen slashes the V, "and end up in another dimension altogether!" she drew the final O, circling several times until the pen bled through the paper.

These were the years of *Star Wars*, of *Close Encounters of the Third Kind*. It made me mad—why did only men get to project their visions of future? I considered myself a witch, believed it when Z. Budapest[15] insisted that "thought forms become material." If women didn't get busy imagining our destiny, I feared we would find ourselves stuck once more in someone else's vision of the future.

The women who were drawn to the creation of *FEMINA* were desperate to reinvent ourselves, to find a world in which our values were reflected, our strengths validated, a world wherein we did not feel crazy. The performance was a metaphor for the vision of LAP—the rejection of the world we'd been handed, the undertaking to build a new context, and to construct new selves untainted by oppression. Bonding with other women, summoning our inner power, were the engines that would take us there. The scary journey from one self to another. The alchemy of transformation.

---

[15] Zusanna Budapest is a former actress and practicing witch who, through her writings and public speaking, did much to popularize the notion of witchcraft as an ancient female art, the practice of which had led to great punishment for women during the Inquisition and subsequently. Interest in the Craft was widespread within cultural feminism of the 1970s, in part as an effort to redefine the notion of power and to claim it for women.

Summer 1978

The talking bead. A clay cylinder, less than an inch long, flecked with brushstrokes of black paint in an African pattern, the bisque of the clay darkened by the oils of my skin. I wear it on a strap of leather bound with a knot at my throat; I never take it off. Over the years the press of my larynx has worn an indent in its side. Arlene teases that this bead holds all my secrets, all the words I never say.

We are in my apartment for our weekly LAP meeting. Arlene sits in the bentwood rocker; I perch in a floral upholstered chair given to me by a friend. Between us is a table made from an upended wooden crate that I retrieved from the sidewalk in Toronto's Chinatown, elegantly draped with a lace runner crocheted by my great-grandmother. The lace is spotted with dripped candle wax, scorched with roach burns, cinders fallen from the countless joints passed back and forth across this table.

One of the most critical parts of Arlene's and my work together on the Lesbian Art Project is the examination of our working relationship. The 1970s definition of "lesbian," at least among feminist lesbians, stretched to include any bond between women; neither erotic arousal nor genital contact was required. Although Arlene and I are not lovers, by this definition we are having a "lesbian relationship," and we are determined to study its every nuance for clues to further understand such connections. What we ask of ourselves is intimacy without sexuality, a willingness to open to one another in all ways but the physical.

This exploration lends our meetings—at her house or mine—a sweaty, claustrophobic, hallucinatory quality that is further enhanced by the dope we smoke at every gathering. We brew strong coffee, light candles—we share a more than casual interest in witchcraft—pass a joint back and forth, and descend into a watery underworld of the psyche.

We both gravitate to the practice of magic—many cultural feminists in the seventies embraced witchcraft as an ancient form of women's power and healing. It is common for us to begin our meetings with a tarot spread, studying the imagery of the cards for clues to our interaction. We burn candles—green for healing, red for passion, purple for inspiration—and light incense. We tell one another our dreams. The practice of magic is not so different from the practice of art, with its aim to manifest what exists only in the mind, its close reading of symbols, the insistence on a realm beyond the literal. My encounters with Arlene take place in that unmapped territory, outside the ordinary boundaries of space and time as we attempt to plumb taboo subjects—sexual abuse, madness, isolation.

The intimacy of these meetings is fervid, an exploration of secrets, of dark corners of the self we have not previously revealed, an attempt to acknowledge emotions and perceptions that the outer world neither sees nor validates. We try to push ourselves to trust enough to make this journey together, to rely on one another to lead the way into this terrain, to guide us out again.

I am terrified by these sessions, but at age twenty-four I lack the inner awareness to even recognize my own fear. When I was a child, my parents' battles drowned out the canned laughter of the television on a nightly basis, and I have spent so many years afraid that I cannot even identify it, nor all that remains closed inside me in response to it.

I can't even see, at this point in my life, how much I fear my own authenticity, even as I hunger for it. I have rejected all of the received identities—my mother's daughter, the heterosexual woman, the would-be professional striving for the middle class—in search of that authentic self, yet there remain doors inside me I can't pry open, or that, when I try, slam shut and seal more tightly than before.

And there is much to fear between Arlene and myself. Arlene is nearly ten years older, the instructor and founder of the institution where I am a student, a credentialed professional in a mainstream art world in which I believe I can never be powerful. We are attempting to create a working partnership, which requires that I simultaneously acknowledge her mentorship and perform as her equal. Each role is challenging for me; on the one hand, I have little respect for or trust in authority, and on the other, it is a constant struggle to believe I bring qualities of equal value to our partnership.

Scarier yet, Arlene is Cheryl's lover. Cheryl is a forceful personality, and although I am well aware of her capacity for charm and the intelligence and resourcefulness that initially drew me, since our breakup she has come to seem a kind of nemesis for me. I am still unnerved by how I allowed her to dominate our relationship, how spineless and enervated I felt by the end of it. Though I'd never admit it, I'm afraid of Cheryl. My work with Arlene pulls me closer to Cheryl's orb, makes our interaction inevitable.

I don't trust Arlene with regard to this issue. My mother never did protect me from my stepfather's rage, his sexual advances, and I have no faith that Arlene will prove a more reliable shield. This issue is undiscussable between us; how can I speak badly about her lover, especially since her lover was once mine? How can I talk about trust with someone I do not trust?

At the age of twenty-four I have no foundation for the kind of honesty that Arlene and I ask of ourselves. In my family, lying and denial were the balms we used to soothe our festering wounds: no one had been hit, drinking was not a problem in the family, incest was not occurring under our roof. Where would I have learned trust?

Arlene is as afraid as I am, but I only see that in retrospect. She is taking a risk to love, to reveal herself to someone who may not be fully able to receive her. She tries to tell me about her terror, but because I won't admit my own, I can't allow hers to become real to me. Instead, we light another joint and precariously step across the high wire of yet another topic. Today Arlene suggests we talk about the sexual energy between us. I am frozen. I think about my current girlfriend, and I think about Cheryl. If Cheryl knew about this conversation, she would be furious. And can I be certain that Arlene will not tell her?

I'm not aware of feeling any sexual energy between us, any physical desire for her. Is this something about which I'm in denial? My incest history has created some dislocation of my erotic impulses. My sexuality is often performative; I can't always identify authentic erotic desires. My draw to Arlene is profound, but has always seemed to be about her brain and her vision, the opportunity she has created for me. But I feel that she wants and expects something more, although I'm not completely clear what "more" might be. Still, I don't want to insult or disappoint her.

Does she feel more? Is she coming on to me? The room shrinks, its walls narrow, and my vision dims.

I drink the dregs of coffee grounds, sharp and bitter on my tongue. I sputter something, "If I . . . uh . . . did feel . . . you know . . . anything, I . . . uh . . . wouldn't want to, you know . . . do anything about it . . . because of . . . uh . . . you know . . . our girlfriends. . . ." I have stopped breathing.

She registers — what? amusement? hurt? — in her black eyes. "There are lots of reasons why this is frightening," she acknowledges. To my ears, she sounds so calm, her voice unbroken, her tone even. "Including that our lovers would be threatened. It would also be too emotionally intense."

It would? I don't know, but she is pointing a way out, and I am more than happy to concur. "And it might get in the way of our work," I add. Each reason is another step away from this nerve-racking possibility, and with every step I feel my lungs ease their constriction.

"Under patriarchy, there's so much pain around women's sexuality," Arlene continues, steering us into the safety of the theoretical. Her hands lightly rub the tops of her thighs, clad in green army surplus pants. "You were molested. I was raped. And the powerful taboo against women's intimacy, for which women have been killed."

So we construct a theory to lead us away from the source of threat. We envision a "sexual" energy abstracted from the body, consummated in our work together, expressed through the media of art and magic. And I am only too eager to embrace this theory.

There is a lull. Perhaps the meeting is over for today. Then she asks me, "Do you feel more unloved or unloving?"

I cannot know the motivation behind her question, but I assume it expresses her disappointment in me. Given my history, there is only one answer I can offer. "Unloved," I answer, and think I read in the grimace at one corner of her mouth that she believes the opposite.

She wants something else from me, I understand this much, but am uncertain of what it is or how to offer it. I don't know whether I have it in me to give.

Then I have an impulse that becomes action before it is even a thought. My fingers are at my neck; they grasp the rawhide band that circles there. They make a clumsy stab at loosening the knot, but sweat and time have melded the coiled strands into a solid mass. I say nothing to Arlene, but step over to my altar, pluck up the knife that rests there next to a hunk of crystal. I slip the blade between the band of leather and the delicate skin of my throat and pull. The blade slices, rawhide swings free; the bead tumbles into my palm.

I feel it, light in the hollow of my hand, yet it seems to fairly pulse. I remember shoplifting it from a bead store in Ann Arbor when I was nineteen. This clay bead has nestled against my larynx for four years, absorbing the vibration of every sound that emanated from me and every sound that I choked back.

I return to the living room, my chair across from Arlene. "I have something for you," I tell her, and place the bead in her hand. She stares at my throat, the white line, untanned, that cinctures my neck, and then down at the talking bead.

She smiles and is pleased.

Winter 1979

The poster is a photograph of a poster tacked to a telephone pole on a palm-lined city street. With its block typography stacked in rows, this poster mimics the style of hundreds of placards that adorn lampposts and telephone poles all over town, in bright yellow or with rainbow backgrounds announcing dances and musical events—"RAUL RUBIO Y SU COMBO."

Offset poster for the Family of Women Dance, *designed by Bia Lowe, 1979.*

This poster, designed by Bia Lowe, announces the "Family of Women Dance," sponsored by LAP. Family is a frequent topic within the Lesbian Art Project. Many of us feel estranged from our families of origin, but we hunger to belong to a unit. So we declare ourselves a family of women, will into being a mythical network of friends and lovers and ex-lovers bonded with all the ferocity of blood.

But there are problems. Some of us have ties, problematic as they might be, to our biological families, and this creates a conflict of allegiances. When, for example, my girlfriend wants to spend Thanksgiving with her mom and brothers, I feel deserted; the family of women dissolves into empty words. Will the bond between us always be secondary to the ties of blood, of history?

Too, the field of psychology has not yet offered up the model of the dysfunctional family. We assume our family problems are either political — the fault of patriarchy — or personal — our parents are just fucked up. We have yet to understand the roles we play within the family dynamic — the good child or the scapegoat, the responsible one or the troublemaker or the child who disappears — or that we are doomed to replicate those dynamics within our own utopia. I don't comprehend how Arlene and Cheryl have come to represent my mother and stepfather to me, how viewing them this way makes me complicit with my own powerlessness, how this will inevitably impact our work together. And who knows who I represent to each of them?

In the meantime, we will name ourselves family and celebrate it. The poster was at first imagined by Bia as an exact replica of those displayed on major streets in the city—Sunset, Hollywood, Olympic Boulevards. Bia wanted to print thousands and enlist a gang of lesbians to go out after dark, dressed in dark clothing and armed with industrial staples and thumbtacks. It spoke to that desire for lesbian visibility, the hunger to claim our territory in the world.

But in 1979, this visibility is still not safe; we imagine a legion of creepy men flocking to the Woman's Building, invading its safety to ogle or wreak vengeance on the lesbians. So Bia creates a single prototype, and we drive to Echo Park and staple this poster to the splintered wood of a telephone pole. We photograph it, taking pains to reveal its bold display on the street, just as careful to take it down before we go.

From this photo, Bia creates another poster, to be sent discreetly through the mail to a select list. Still, the poster invites the viewer to imagine a world in which the "Family of Women Dance" would be advertised on any busy street in the city of Los Angeles, a world in which we do not yet dwell.

Spring 1979

The color Polaroid doesn't do justice to the magic of that afternoon. Half a dozen women in shorts and tank tops lounging in a sunny backyard, surrounded by dozens of strips of vibrant pink cloth spread out on the grass, draped over shrubbery, hanging from clotheslines and tree branches. The photo obscures the purpose of our activity; neither does it reveal the delirium we feel—pleasantly stoned, the afternoon light on our skin, the explosion of shocking pink against the meticulous green of the lawn, the flush of communal spirit as we come together in our task.

We've gathered to dye 180 yards of white gauze to be used for the set of *An Oral Herstory of Lesbianism*, a performance piece collaboratively created by thirteen lesbians at my inception and under my direction. The pink gauze set has been conceived of by Bia and cast member Cheri Gaulke; they intend to completely enclose the performance space within this sheer drapery. The audience will feel like they are encased inside a big vagina. Viewed from the outside, the lighted interior will glow like a rosy lantern.

Neither Bia nor I have our own washing machines, and we've already been kicked out of more than one laundromat for trying to ply our Rit Dye in their Kenmores. When we'd attempted a wash after midnight at one twenty-four-hour establishment, figuring that the supervision would be lax to nonexistent, we'd encountered an old man in filth-encrusted jeans who'd unzipped them and flashed his penis at us before the first rinse cycle. We squealed in disgust and grabbed our dripping, half-dyed lengths of gauze, leaving the machines full of reddish suds. With only four weeks to go before the production opened, we are beginning to despair of ever getting all that fabric pink.

It is my friend Joanne Kerr who comes to the rescue, offering her large-capacity Maytag for our use; Joanne has until recently been married, and still owns many of the accoutrements of an Orange County housewife. She'd come to the Woman's Building as a Ph.D. candidate in anthropology; her dissertation has to do with gift-giving rituals across cultures and she wanted to study the practice of making art to be given as gift that was commonplace within the feminist art community. Since her arrival, she's "gone native," experimenting with relationships with women, immersing herself in the life of the community she'd set out to study.

That very life is throbbing in the terraced backyard of her house in Franklin Hills this April afternoon, as women pull armloads of gauze from the washing machine and spread the impossibly pink yardage out to dry. Those in attendance today—Clsuf, Geraldine, and Paula, among others— are not all cast members in the production. The women who drape pink gauze across green grass are part of the community of artists at the Woman's Building who are always eager to support the efforts of another woman artist, knowing that they might well call on you to help with their next project.

Sister Sledge's "We Are Family" blasts from the stereo speakers into the spring air. We pass joints in a desultory fashion; sunbathe between loads of wash; feast on pita sandwiches stuffed with tuna or cheese, sprouts, toma-toes, and roasted red peppers that Joanne graciously serves. Our labor seems ancient and tribal—the women of the village coming together on wash day, helping one another to hang and to fold, exchanging gossip and advice. At the same time the bright colors, sunshine, and music create a festival atmos-phere. And there is too the element of pure crackpot—Rit Dyeing 180 yards of fabric in a single washing machine—certainly another entry in that long and varied list of "What I Did for Art."

It is a moment that embodies for me my aspirations for lesbian art in those days: sensual, celebratory, communal, crackpot. A conscious refutation of the depressed, oppressed, downwardly mobile, or politically correct strains of les-bian life that seemed to dominate outside the realm of art. We are engaged in creating a myth of the lesbian as artist, and for that afternoon, giddy with the enormity and eccentricity and joy of our task, we are alive inside that myth.

Spring 1979

The poster for *An Oral Herstory of Lesbianism* is a long strip, a vertical col-umn composed of successive rows of women's faces, seven frames across. Each row a different color of the spectrum, each depicting one of the cast members of the performance.

Seven frames, and in each, the woman forms a distinct letter with her mouth. "L," the lips part, the tongue lodges behind the front teeth. "E," the open mouth stretches wide at the corners. "S," the teeth come together, while the lips still part. "B," the lips purse, almost pucker, before the "ee" sound blasts them apart. "I," the throat opens, the mouth stretches verti-cally. "A," a rounding of the mouth, teeth parted. "N," the tongue makes contact with the hard palate.

Hours spent in a photo booth in front of Woolworth's in Hollywood, plunking quarters into the machine, shooting strip after strip, trying to get the perfect visual representation of each letter. "L-E-S-B-I-A-N." Thirteen women articulating their identity.

Silkscreen and offset poster for An Oral Herstory of Lesbianism, *designed by Bia Lowe and printed by Cynthia Marsh, 1979.*

The concept and design are Bia's; the offset printing is done by Cynthia Marsh—who is not a lesbian, although many a woman wishes she were—on the old printing press in the Women's Graphic Center at the Woman's Building.

Oral—as we have affectionately and lasciviously dubbed the performance, has been created through a three-month process of workshops that I conducted. These sessions used theater games, writing exercises, and consciousness-raising to explore our experience as lesbians.

There are the inevitable coming-out stories, but one of our members, Brook Hallock, has recounted her experience of coming out to—and being rejected by—her teenaged daughters rather than her parents. We explore community life in the bars, on the sports field, and—in a piece Arlene Raven has written about the myriad attractions between women that often go unspoken—at a card table. We examine the challenges of relationship—finding, initiating, and maintaining an intimate connection. Chris Wong examines her identity as a Chinese lesbian, torn between the traditions of her culture and the lure of an alternative lifestyle, using the form of the Chinese Ribbon Dance. From this wealth of stories we weave the performance with the hope of creating a new tapestry that reveals and expands the meaning of "lesbian." It is clear to me that we do not represent all lesbians—we are all from approximately the same generation, all white women except for Chris and Brooke, who is Native American. It is, after all, *"An* Oral Herstory . . ." not *"The* Oral Herstory."

Still, in seven frames, thirteen women face the camera, ready to spell out our identity, ready to offer the stories of our lives.

Spring 1979

The scarf is blue and white, a long strand of chiffon. It comes from Paris, a place this working-class twenty-four-year-old can scarcely imagine. Arlene has given it to me, a gesture with resonance I have probably chosen to overlook, or am not equipped to receive, a token of our connection. I keep it on my altar.

It is scarcely possible that the two phone calls could have come in the same day, but they have conflated in my memory, two phone calls that shifted my foundations. Perhaps the whole month leading up to the opening of *Oral* has compressed in my mind into one long nightmarish day.

The first call is from my mother, telling me that she's decided to marry for the third time, barely a year since her divorce from my stepfather. In that year I have tried, from 2,500 miles away, to support her to be on her own, inundating her with my feminist cant, finding her a therapist, encouraging her to move when my stepfather started stalking her. I feel rejected by her decision to wed again, my puny efforts no substitute for having a man on whom to lean. It's small of me, but I am disappointed by her choice; I withhold my approval.

The second call is from Cheryl. It comes in the early afternoon, catches me off guard. She's excited, her words spit like the rat-a-tat of a machine gun, and it takes me a while to sort their meaning. "Lesbian porn . . . *Playboy* funding . . . Lesbian Art Project. . . ." It's a few moments before it comes clear.

When Cheryl and I were lovers we used to joke about a scam to make a lot of money marketing fake lesbian porn videos. We'd advertise our titles in the classified sections of *Hustler* or *Penthouse* and watch the cash flow in. "Lesbians Eat it Raw," for example, would depict short-haired women eating sushi; "Black and White Pussies Lap it Up" would in fact portray our cats drinking milk. It was a perfect scheme, we thought, for "ripping off the patriarchy," exploiting men's fantasies of lesbians but actually delivering normalized portraits of lesbian life. We congratulated ourselves on the political correctness of this scheme, though we did worry that the plan might backfire if our customers — frustrated at being so misled — decided to take out their ire on some unsuspecting lesbian.

Now it appears that Cheryl wants to pursue this project in earnest. She's had the brainstorm that she might get funding from the Playboy Foundation to do it. In the 1970s, the Playboy Foundation, under the direction of Christy Heffner, was eager to fund certain feminist activities, and this created bitter controversy in more than a few underfunded women's organizations. The Woman's Building Board has already voted decisively against going after *Playboy* money, and that's why Cheryl means to submit her proposal through the Lesbian Art Project. And to do so, she intends to become a formal partner with Arlene and myself in LAP, something I imagine she has wanted for a long time.

My limbs go cold with dread. There isn't an aspect of her idea I feel inclined to support, yet I fear the consequences of opposing her. I try stalling for time. "I don't know, Cheryl, there's a lot to think about . . ."

She interrupts me. "There's no time to think," she snaps, her tone insistent. "I need to know right now — are you going to support me or not?"

Here's the real issue, I think then, tasting the acid of fear on my tongue. "I need to talk to Arlene," I say, as calmly as I can. Trying to push back a plummeting sensation of doom, I cling to a corner of the bookcase; my knees are in danger of collapsing.

Through the receiver I hear a muffled exchange of words between them. I stare dully out my window at the line of palm trees framed against the horizon. Eventually Arlene comes to the phone, but her voice, so strained and distant, is almost unrecognizable to me.

"Arlene," I nearly plead, "I'm concerned about this. I mean, *Playboy?* And do we really want to change the whole structure of LAP?" *Rescue me, stand up for me,* a little girl inside me begs, but Arlene will never go against her lover to back me up.

She speaks to me as if we are strangers, as if she has no comprehension of my concerns. I have heard this tone in my mother's voice, years before, and again today when she announced her marriage plans. "I have no problems with what Cheryl is asking," Arlene insists, "but if you do you'll just have to say so."

Despite the blaze of sunshine out the window, the chill in my body intensifies. Like a bad dream from which I can't shake myself, I see there is no escape. It is a moment toward which I've been moving ever since I first met Cheryl, inexorable as in a dream, and now it has arrived. Too much is at stake. Both Cheryl and Arlene are in the cast of *Oral,* and it is so close to opening that to lose them will be catastrophic. Maybe Cheryl is counting on this as well.

Cheryl gets back on the phone.

"I can't decide right this minute," I tell her, "We need to have a meeting . . ."

Again, she cuts me off. "No," she insists, "I have to know right now."

I exhale deeply. "If I have to tell you right this minute, if there can't even be any process about this, then my answer is no."

Cheryl's anger is something I have always feared; unlike many women who learned to suppress their rage and power, turn it against themselves, or deflect it into passive aggression, Cheryl allows it full expression. Now it breaks over me in a wave of furious verbiage. She has supported my efforts all of these years; how dare I withhold my support from her? She bangs the receiver into the cradle of the phone, and I am left to anticipate the aftermath.

Neither Cheryl nor Arlene quits the cast of *Oral.* Cheryl begins to woo the other members of the cast, paying them compliments, being extravagant with her attention, inviting them to parties after rehearsal, parties from which I am conspicuously excluded. She finds private funding for her video project and hires several cast members to work on it. The gossip that filters back leads me to suspect that she uses these occasions to voice doubts about the production and my competency to carry it to completion.

No overt mutiny occurs; still, the cast—many of them heretofore friends and colleagues—grows unmistakably cooler toward me, less supportive of my artistic vision, more challenging of my leadership. The mutual support that characterized the workshop process has evaporated. I come to dread rehearsals, and more than once give serious thought to abandoning my own project. I take to spending the hours prior to rehearsal shaking with anxiety, pressed against my mattress to quiet my pounding heart, spinning fantasies of moving to another city and changing my name.

Then one afternoon, sitting on my bed in my apartment staring out at Echo Park Lake, an understanding stirs in me. I will never prevail, I know suddenly, by opposing Cheryl directly, scrapping to win back power in the eyes of my cast. I can only empower myself, I see with utter clarity, can only face my adversaries by becoming large enough to encompass them. The air in my apartment grows heavy, and I see myself expanding, not my body but the essence inside, swelling and widening, broadening its horizons. The animosity with which some members of the cast regard me will not threaten me if I am secure in my own authority. I can contain this dissonance, I decide; it need not define me or the art project.

In this moment something shifts in me that will never shift back. I learn a secret about power. I will be much older before I learn to apply it to my personal interactions, but it forever changes the way I approach my work with others. It will be still more years before I come to regard Cheryl with gratitude for being the agent of this lesson. A lesson about leadership, and also about the isolation inherent in this position.

I begin to reassert myself in rehearsal, taking the cast members' ideas and insisting that they push them further. I no longer look to the actors for validation, but become even more intently focused on the quality of the work. With just days to spare, the show takes shape and gels. It's good, and everyone knows it. The thirteen performances of *An Oral Herstory of Lesbianism* come off without incident, and each night audiences of women thrill to the tension and transcendence generated within the pink gauze performance space.

Some days after that disastrous phone call from Cheryl, I receive another.

"Because you have been so horribly unsupportive of me," she declares, "I want you to give back everything I ever gave you."

I don't argue or protest or plead my case. I don't resist or refuse. I do exactly as Cheryl asks. I am scrupulous in my sweep through my apartment. The big items are a bentwood rocker she'd bought me because I had no furniture, and the original drawing of my cat Ruby she'd made to illustrate an image from one of my poems. There is a little jewelry, the odd T-shirt, some record albums, notes she'd written to me, items from my altar. Exhaustive in the extreme, I even excavate an old toothbrush, bristles splayed and curled, that she'd once loaned me, and I add it to the pile.

Somehow, whether through an overzealous sense of thoroughness or because of unexamined resentments, the scarf Arlene had given me is also included in the heap of items to be returned. The blue-and-white chiffon scarf that Arlene had brought me from Paris.

A friend helps me haul everything to Cheryl and Arlene's house, the last time I ever visit that property. We pull into the driveway and quietly unload the items onto the porch, then we drive away. Perhaps some spell is finally broken.

My interaction with Arlene has been strained ever since I said no to Cheryl, and now she is even colder. I'm not sure why she's angry with me; perhaps it's the tension of mediating the estrangement between Cheryl and myself. We stop having meetings of the Lesbian Art Project without ever formally deciding to do so. We had planned to spend our third and final year of LAP working on a book about the project, but it seems mutually understood that this will no longer be possible.

We do have one last meeting, about six weeks after the completion of *Oral,* at a Mexican restaurant not far from Arlene's house. It's a dark dive, a cool refuge from July blasting on the sidewalk outside. I scoop mouthful after mouthful of blistering salsa onto corn chips as Arlene and I inter the Lesbian Art Project.

Just as we are getting up to leave the restaurant she asks me, "Why did you give back the scarf?" and I can see that she is wounded. I can scarcely remember doing so; certainly it wasn't my intention to reject her. "Your argument was with Cheryl," she insists, "not with me."

How can I explain the ways I'd felt betrayed by her, that I'd seen the two of them function as a unit, how I felt she'd set me up and let me down? How the family of women had too perilously replicated my own family?

I am sorry to have hurt her, and dumbfounded that I actually could. I have felt unloved, but now she tells me I have been unloving.

"I'm sorry," I say, lamely, "it was a mistake." And this is partially true.

The rest remains unspoken, a story for the talking bead.

Offset poster for the Great American Lesbian Art Show (GALAS), *designed by Bia Lowe, 1980.*

Spring 1980

XX chromosomes determine femaleness. The symbol XXX imagines the parthenogenic woman, she who creates from her own source—the lesbian artist.

—quote from the poster for the "Great American Lesbian Art Show"

We are painting the walls red. Not an elegant burgundy or an understated rust. Matador red, waving our sexual cape at the furious bull of homophobia.

We are painting the walls of the Woman's Building gallery for the "Great American Lesbian Art Show" (GALAS). An unapologetic scarlet.

We grip the long extension poles, spreading color from floor to eighteen-foot ceiling, straining the muscles of our shoulders and backs. Our skin is splattered with flecks of red, like bright blood or an erotic flush. The walls soak up our crimson wash; they demand coat after coat. We paint for days. At night when I close my eyes, my vision is suffused with green, red's vibratory opposite.

GALAS is not simply this exhibit, but a yearlong project to bring national recognition to lesbian art and artists. It is the brainchild of the artist Tyaga, an open-faced blonde with a crew cut. She has assembled a collective of women[16] to plan a national exhibition of lesbian art. Inspired, without question, by the Lesbian Art Project, GALAS has sprung up in the wake of LAP's demise. I am still in shock from its dissolution; it feels on the one hand natural to be working on this lesbian art endeavor and yet it also feels profoundly odd.

These red walls will be graced by the work of ten artists[17] who've been visible as lesbians in their careers. We've chosen erotic line drawings by Kate Millett; wry, moody neons by Lili Lakich. An enormous wrapped sculpture—suggestive of a hungry mouth or a greedy vulva—by Harmony Hammond; the disarmingly domestic dough sculptures of Nancy Fried; and somber, brooding oils by Gloria Longval.

We've chafed under the limitations of budget and geography, and the absence of scholarship and critical discussion about the work of contemporary lesbian artists. We can't claim to represent lesbian artists across the United States (let alone the Americas); all of the artists in the GALAS invitational reside in New York or L.A.

So in addition to the Woman's Building show, we've also sent out a call—via the feminist press—urging lesbians to organize exhibits in their own communities and to send us documentation of these works. Over two hundred art shows and events are planned across the country,[18] including nearly twenty satellite events in Los Angeles. Slides of work from these shows will be on continuous view as part of the GALAS exhibition at the Woman's Building.

---

[16] In addition to Tyaga, the GALAS collective members were Jody Hoeninger, Bia Lowe, Louise Moore, Ba Stopha, and Terry Wolverton.

[17] Lula Mae Blocton, Tee Corinne, Betsy Damon, Louise Fishman, Nancy Fried, Harmony Hammond, Debbie Jones, Lili Lakich, Gloria Longval, Kate Millett.

[18] In addition to expected locations such as New York, San Francisco, Boston, and Chicago, there were also shows in Bozeman, Montana; Winter Park, Florida; Lawrence, Kansas; Alexandria, Virginia; and Anchorage, Alaska.

The working process of the GALAS collective bears no similarity to that of the Lesbian Art Project. We haven't probed our personal histories or dissected our feelings; we haven't formulated theory. The group is task-focused and the tasks have been multiple: research, curating, fund-raising, installation, and publicity. The GALAS Collective has made no attempt to bond as a family, which, after the turbulent years of LAP, I've found to be a relief. Still, it is odd to work on a lesbian project without Arlene. She is curating her own exhibit — Woman•Woman•Works — which will be installed in the first floor gallery of the Woman's Building concurrently with GALAS. There is no interaction between us about these shows.

The almost yearlong process of organizing GALAS was a phenomenon in itself, and included the organizing of several other events along the way. Dozens of local artists and writers flocked to "Amazon Ambrosia," a day-long lesbian art worksharing with featured presentations by artist Harmony Hammond and Liza Cowan, former publisher of *Dyke* magazine. An upscale crowd of politically active lesbians and gay men were drawn to the benefit reading by Kate Millett and Paul Monette (in a display of co-gender cooperation uncharacteristic of the time), hosted by our organizational cosponsor, the Gay and Lesbian Community Services Center. The crackpot element was in full force at *An Intimate Dinner for 150 Celebrating Eleanor Roosevelt and All Great Lesbians,* a performance art dinner I created, catered by Clsuf and Twolip Art, with appearances by The Waitresses and singer Silvia Kohan.

It is the spring of 1980 and we are flushed with bravado. The red walls signal the unabashed spirit of GALAS, our determination to claim territory, be visible, revel in unsubtle beauty. They signal the breadth of our ambition, our insistence upon being public — as we are rewarded with a feature article and review in the *Los Angeles Times* and a review in *Artweek,* the first time lesbian art has received this level of mainstream recognition. The red walls speak of our intent to mythologize, our adoption of three X chromosomes — whimsical, dancing DNA — as our logo, a bold assertion that lesbians are, as writer and philosopher Monique Wittig posited, "a third sex."

We don't know that the world is about to change. It is May; we can't foresee the presidential election in November that will turn our revolution upside down. The disappearance of arts funding and the emergence of economic hard times that will send the Woman's Building scrambling for the cover of mainstream respectability, making us think twice before using the word "feminist," let alone "lesbian," in grant proposals, brochures, or exhibitions.

In the spring of 1980, we think we've moved from the reinvention of ourselves as lesbians to taking over the planet with our mutant biology, our crackpot sensibility. We can almost taste the world we've conjured through our art: life-affirming, celebratory, erotic. So we paint the walls red, as if against the long chill we don't yet know is coming.

Postscript: Fall 1990

The banner—ten feet by eight feet—spills down the side of the three-story building on Industrial Street in the heart of the downtown arts district. Eyes gaze between open palms, and the text reads, "I feel what I want/I want what I feel." Designed by artist Susan Silton, the banner announces the exhibition, "All But the Obvious," the first lesbian group show to be mounted in Los Angeles since GALAS, ten years earlier.

This exhibit takes place not at the Woman's Building but at LACE (Los Angeles Contemporary Exhibitions); by this time the Woman's Building is no longer considered the center of contemporary feminist discourse. In fact, this next generation is not looking for a feminist center. The theoretical bases have shifted from the activism of a women's movement for social change to academy-based consideration of postmodern European philosophers— Foucault, Mann, Derrida, and women such as Julia Kristeva and Luce Irigary. Seventies feminism has been dissected, criticized, and summarily dismissed.

The work in "All But the Obvious" is made by a new generation[19] of

---

[19] When I speak of a "generation" here I am not strictly speaking of the artists' chronological age, but of the point in time at which they came to artmaking and the social, political, and philosophical structures with which they are aligned.

artists, and points up two distinct trends in lesbian art of the late eighties and early nineties: theoretically based works such as *Disturbances* by Millie Wilson, which embeds multiple layers of theoretical references, and post-punk "Bad Girl" art, such as S/M-laced photographs—*Be My Bitch* is one title—by Della Grace.

The curator of "All But the Obvious," Pam Gregg, has no knowledge of the Lesbian Art Project or the Great American Lesbian Art Show, and expresses only mild interest when I approach her to talk about it.

A few months later I am commissioned by the *Advocate* to write a feature about this new generation of lesbian artists. This gives me an excuse to call a dozen young women in Los Angeles, New York, San Francisco, and Chicago; during my interviews I ask them what they know of lesbian art in the seventies. I am stunned that almost none of them has any idea of their predecessors. One mentions Barbara Hammer, the lesbian film-maker who's been working since the early seventies; at least two cite the avowedly heterosexual Judy Chicago. Perhaps Judy's name comes to mind because she used vaginal imagery?

I feel profound discouragement at my findings—it seems all of our work has been so entirely erased. I have no doubt that these young artists can only make the work they are creating because of the pioneering efforts of LAP and GALAS a decade earlier; in this way we were not ineffective, in this way I see our legacy. But the artists and theories of LAP and GALAS are unknown to these women, rendered invisible or ridiculous. I am once more thrown back on my question—in so utterly rejecting the structures of the dominant culture, did we marginalize ourselves irredeemably? Or was it only in turning our backs on those dominant structures that we were able to spawn a next generation, oblivious to us as they might be?

"I feel what I want/I want what I feel," Silton's banner proclaims. It's a resonant statement, insistent on both sensation and emotion, the body and the heart. In this postmodern, theory-driven time, it's almost subversive. Yet there is a collective vision, a social intention, that is absent from the work in this show that speaks of personal gratification or weaves intricate webs of intellectualism.

The walls of the gallery remain stark white.

Wolverton (right) brings light to the planet Femina in FEMINA: An IntraSpace Voyage, *as codirector Ann Shannon observes, 1978. (Photo by Bia Lowe)*

Performativity
1978–1986

. . . the true theater has its shadows too . . .
—Antonin Artaud,
The Theater and Its Double

EVEN AS A CHILD, I PERFORMED. I'D STAND IN THE HALLWAY OF MY GRAND-parents' flat, in front of the full-length mirror. I'd sing and dance to my favorite phonograph record—"Talkin' to the Angels in the Sky"—and stare into my own eyes. In a family that could not mirror me, I hungered for some reflection of myself as vibrant, creative, but there was more: that girl dancing in the glass kept me company, made me feel less lonely.

Perhaps my pull toward the performing arts had in part to do with my longing to relieve isolation. The work I created in high school and college and the feminist theater experiments in which I engaged were, at least in part, attempts to find solace and kinship in creative collaboration.

When I first arrived at the Woman's Building, I didn't understand the difference between theater and performance art. I assumed that "perfor-mance art" was the same as the experimental theater work I'd been doing in Toronto and Grand Rapids; maybe this was just a California term for it, the way "pop" was known as "soda" here and "expressways" were called "freeways." Over time, I learned that performance art sprang from an entirely different tradition — not from theater at all but from the visual arts.

I learned that in the early decades of the twentieth century, artists began to question the notion of art as object, to become more interested in conceptualization than in an end product. Futurists, Dadaists, and Surrealists still made art objects, but appreciation of these was enhanced by knowledge of the theories and processes that gave rise to them. In the 1950s, the "action painters" emerged; their focus was on the *process* of applying paint to canvas — throwing or spilling paint, or covering their bodies with pigment and rolling across the canvas. It was in the *gesture* of painting, they believed, that art resided, more than in the product that resulted.

By the 1960s, the Fluxus artists had coined the term "conceptual art," declaring that art resides in its ideation. Some artists simply typed up their ideas on three-by-five cards. Yoko Ono published a book, *Grapefruit,* containing page after page of ideas for possible performance actions. It was enough for the audience to imagine the concept; actually manifesting it was beside the point.

Some posited that — just as a painter or photographer might frame a landscape or a scene — an artist could put a frame around some aspect of experience, whether an instant or a prolonged span of time, and declare that the work of art. Although some artists framed everyday experiences (in a performance created for Womanhouse, artist Karen LeCoq sat before a mirror, repetitively applying and removing makeup), others set about to concoct an experience that might not have otherwise happened, and thus impact directly the lives of their audience. Artist Joy Poe staged her own rape during an opening at Artemesia Gallery in Chicago, creating a moral dilemma for her viewers: should they intervene against this crime and risk disrupting "art," or should they remain passive spectators and in doing so, become complicit in Poe's violation? Being faced with this quandary angered many in the audience who felt entitled to a clearer delineation between art and life.

Performance actions might be performed privately, as a kind of personal ritual, and later revealed to an audience through documentation — as when Linda Montano committed herself to listening, via headphones, to a single musical note, tuned to one of the seven chakras or energy centers in the body, ceaselessly for one year. Others might be witnessed only accidentally by passersby, as when Adrian Piper dressed as a man to walk around the streets of New York.

Such events might take place before an invited audience that was frequently incorporated into the piece, being asked to participate either through directed action or randomly. Suzanne Lacy, for example, dressed as a vampire and spent the night in a coffin while the audience was instructed to file past and gaze, as mourners, into the open casket. Here the audience transcended their role as spectators to become performers in the tableau.

Feminist artists gravitated to performance for several reasons. Both performance and video were emerging art forms in the early seventies, without established traditions or hierarchy. It was hard for a woman painter to make a name for herself in a centuries-old tradition where men predominated, but in performance a woman could get in on the ground floor. Feminists were further drawn to performance's focus on process over product and to the form's use of the body as art medium. And one could use it as a means to build community, whether through collaboration with other artists or by involving the audience in direct dialogue about the issues addressed within the work, C-R style.

Feminist practitioners contributed four significant elements to the medium of performance: first, an exploration of alternative personae, which was in keeping with the feminist intention to redefine roles for women. Second was the use of confessional text, which grew out of both consciousness-raising sessions and then-pioneering practices in feminist literature in which writers revealed intimate details of their lives and allowed the reader to eavesdrop on their internal monologues without the veil of fiction.

Interestingly, those two directions both tended to push performance art in a more theatrical direction, as did number three: the incorporation of ritual and feminist spirituality, returning to theater's earliest roots as religious ceremony.

The final contribution made by feminists was the promulgation of performance art as media event, the creation of spectacle designed to attract the eye of the media, and thus gain a mass audience for the feminist statement being made. In 1978, Leslie Labowitz and Suzanne Lacy teamed up with Bia Lowe and other artists to create *In Mourning and in Rage,* a large-scale public protest performance. The purpose was to challenge the media's sensationalizing of a rash of murders of women perpetrated by the so-called Hillside Strangler; the tone of the press coverage was heightening the climate of fear and reinforcing the victimization of women. Exceptionally tall women, made taller by towering headpieces, were transported by hearse to city hall. Dressed in black, they debarked and formed a circle in front of the steps beneath a banner reading, "In memory of our sisters, women fight back." The artists designed the performance action and imagery specifically to captivate the interest of television news and, in successfully achieving this network coverage, not only used the media to critique itself, but extended the impact of the piece far beyond the usual feminist and/or art audiences.

Even already established elements within the performance medium were altered by feminist practice. Male artist Chris Burden, for example, used the body as art medium by arranging to have himself shot in the arm with a pistol, then documented the experience as a performance. FSW participant Jerri Allyn, by contrast, placed a rented hospital bed in her studio and spent a week there exorcising her fear of cancer, the disease that had taken her mother's life. Viewers could attend "visiting hours" and hear Allyn read from her journals, or listen to a parade of researchers and alternative healers discuss the latest approaches to cancer treatment.

The Woman's Building was a central hub of feminist performance activity during the 1970s and early '80s. Seminal artists performed or taught there — Eleanor Antin, Suzanne Lacy, Rachel Rosenthal, Martha Rosler,

Carolee Schneeman, and Barbara Smith are just a few of a long list—and encouraged a second generation of feminist performance artists, among them Jerri Allyn, Cheri Gaulke, Vanalyne Green, Linda Nishio, and myself, who in turn broke ground for those who came after us.

~

WRITING IS A SOLITARY PURSUIT; performance is about the capacity to engage others and create community. This aspect of performance captivated me, held sway over the writing I also longed to do. My background in theater had already well acquainted me with the notion of collaboration. A staged production is of course the product of many visions: that of the playwright, the director, the designers of sets, costumes, graphics, and lighting, and one hopes, the performers. In the experimental theater of the 1960s (such as the work of the Living Theater in New York) and most of the feminist theater groups active in the 1970s, collaboration also involved the collective development of content and the dismantling of stratified roles. A performer might write her own monologue, offer suggestions for its staging, and troll thrift stores in search of her costume.

For those who'd trained in the visual arts, however, collaboration was a more radical idea, a challenge to the myth of the lone genius who creates in solitude. Within the feminist art movement, collaborative process was highly regarded as a means to create support, share power, and expand the vision of a given work.

Several ongoing collaborative performance groups emerged from the Feminist Studio Workshop, including Mother Art,[20] whose members bore the dual identities of artist and mother and whose works addressed the struggle inherent in this duality; the Feminist Art Workers,[21] who used

---

[20] Formed in 1976 by Jan Cook, Gloria Hadjuk, Christie Kruse, Suzanne Siegel, and Laura Silagi.

[21] Comprised of Nancy Angelo, Candace Compton, Cheri Gaulke, Vanalyne Green, and Laurel Klick.

feminist educational theory and process as the basis for audience-participatory performances; The Waitresses,[22] whose works addressed issues facing working women such as unequal pay, sexual harassment, and woman-as-servant; and Sisters of Survival,[23] who dressed in nun's habits in all colors of the rainbow to represent an image of "global sisterhood."

I was never a member of these ongoing groups, but I used the resources of the Woman's Building to create a series of performances that employed different models of collaboration. Working on these projects did provide me great succor, and I found myself able to accomplish a level of work that far exceeded my individual vision and capacities. But power is not easily shared, especially by those unaccustomed to having it, uncomfortable with acknowledging it, or unequipped with a language to speak of it. Collaboration had its shadow side. Yet I persisted, certain I would find the right structure that would provide the community for which I so desperately longed.

FEMINA: An IntraSpace Voyage[24]

A group of women decides that life on Earth has grown intolerable, and sets out to create a new society on a distant, undiscovered planet. In 1978, in the throes of my involvement with the Lesbian Art Project, I proposed to explore this vision of a feminist future in a collaborative performance. In Toronto and Grand Rapids, I'd previously developed experimental the-

---

[22] Founding members were Jerri Allyn, Leslie Belt, Anne Gauldin, Patti Nicklaus, Jamie Wildman, and Denise Yarfitz.

[23] Jerri Allyn, Nancy Angelo, Cheri Gaulke, Anne Gauldin, and Sue Maberry.

[24] FEMINA: An IntraSpace Voyage was created and performed in 1978 at the Woman's Building in Los Angeles. Initiated and produced by Terry Wolverton, the work was collaboratively created by Norma Fragosa, Chutney Lu Gunderson, Pam MacDonald, Jade Satterthwaite, Ann Shannon, Dyana Silberstein, and Terry Wolverton, and directed by Ann Shannon and Terry Wolverton. It also included set design by Carol Jefferies, graphic design by Bia Lowe, original music by Sandra Wilson, film by Holiday Temple Jackson, and masks by Barbara Stopha. The work was based on an unpublished short story, "A Clear but Distant Memory" by Wolverton.

ater pieces within the structure of a workshop, so I decided to use this process again and designed twelve sessions through which *FEMINA* would be created.

With the exception of Ann Shannon, with whom I'd worked previously, the seven women who signed up to participate were not experienced performers. I viewed this as a plus; it both served my notions of the democratization of art (the belief that "everyone has the capacity to be creative") and promised to facilitate a particular notion I had for *FEMINA*. In theater, we always ask the audience to "suspend disbelief," but in the process of creating *FEMINA*, I wanted the *performers* to suspend disbelief. I asked these women to act as if, come June, we were really going to leave the planet.

In workshops, I used theater games, writing exercises, guided meditation, and consciousness-raising sessions to explore three questions: Why do you want to leave Earth? What keeps you tied to Earth and this way of life? And what do you imagine a new women-centered planet will be like? To the first question, women responded with apocalyptic visions—bombs, earthquakes, mass destruction. But there were also smaller, personal reasons. Dyana constructed a monologue about having spent her life holding in her stomach. Pam recalled the birds in the trees from her childhood, but realized that the birds were now being killed with pesticides and acid rain. Norma talked about her Mexican heritage, how her people thought she should stay and fight for *la revolución* but that she hungered for a life beyond struggle.

There were certain pitfalls in the working process I'd chosen. One woman found the six-month commitment—three months of workshops, three months of production—too demanding and left the cast midway, though her photo was already on the publicity poster. Another cast member developed philosophical differences: Jade decided she could not leave Earth with us; the vision was too separatist. She had a son and she needed to stay and raise him. We solved this problem by reshaping her character as the storyteller, the one who witnessed the women's departure and remained behind to tell about it. Still a third came to me one day and con-fessed, "I have to drop out. I've enrolled in school in the fall and I won't be able to go to Femina."

I stared at her for a long moment, then said, "I know I've asked every-one to imagine we're really going to go, but we *are* just doing a perfor-mance. You'll be free to do whatever you want in the fall."

She nodded slowly as she took this in. "Okay," she said at last, visibly relieved.

I was gratified that the participants had so taken to heart the "suspen-sion of disbelief," but a little scared by it too. It was the late seventies, and so many of us who were committed to feminist cultural revolution were already walking a blurred line between reality and imagination. We had to distrust the world we'd been raised to believe in and invest our faith in things that didn't exist, things we couldn't see, a world still to be created. *FEMINA* was of course a metaphor for feminism; we were all taking a big leap of faith away from what we'd been taught, from all that was familiar and approved of. How thin was the line between faith and madness?

In addition to the cast, I was also working with a number of artists in other disciplines, who saw the production as a worthy vehicle for their artistic visions. This opportunity for collaboration across disciplines was a direct benefit of working at the Woman's Building. FSW student Carol Jefferies was photographing the demolition of a building in Pasadena and thought these images would make an interesting backdrop for our piece. Her friend, Sandra Wilson, came to me and asked if she could write music. Holiday Jackson wanted to make a short film to incorporate into the piece. Bia Lowe had proposed a poster design that revealed the piece as cosmic and magical. These artists not only contributed their labor and creativity, but also paid for the materials and processes necessary to manifest their work. These collaborations were the most effortless part of the production: with each artist given free reign to make her own creative statement, my task was to weave them into the whole.

What was not effortless was my working relationship with the cast. We were forced to confront differing levels of investment, discrepant visions and sensibilities (both aesthetic and political), and incompatible work habits. Some members accepted their roles and wanted no larger responsibility, but others complained that I was stifling them, refusing to share power. Although I welcomed the creative ideas of each member, I was not open to sharing leadership of the project: I had a specific vision in which I was invested.

At twenty-three, I had neither the skill nor the inclination to endlessly engage in interpersonal dynamics. I am by nature a task-oriented person, and it took some years for me to gain the patience to appreciate a process by which everyone states their feelings and endeavors to achieve consensus. In 1978, I preferred everyone deal with her feelings on her own time; how could I accommodate the emotions of others if I was unwilling to address my own?

I was, however, interested in the experiential process of the audience, which was encouraged to believe that the events they would be witnessing were real, that they had come to bid good-bye to this group of women who were leaving to explore the realms of space. The audience moved first through the Femina Museum, commemorating each woman who was leaving. A biographical statement about each woman explained who each had been on Earth. Shelves displayed personal objects emblematic of each woman's personality; mine included a dope pipe and the pair of snake bracelets that had belonged to my step-grandmother.

The audience was then escorted into the performance space, where each of the performers had created a "nest" onstage in which to prepare for the journey. Each woman was being attended by a lover or close friend whose job was to help us get ready — to brush hair, massage shoulders, reassure. Audience members were invited to bid us good-bye, offer their good wishes, or say whatever they might wish to before never seeing the travelers again. They were also invited to leave some personal object on an altar, which would be transported to Femina, and thus represent them in the new world.

As the performance began, we gathered in a circle to focus our energy. Sandra's score began to play; she had set to music the title poem from my book *Blue Moon*. Jade, the narrator, began to tell the tale of how the women had decided to go. Each performer talked about what had happened to make her want to leave the Earth. Carol's slides of the razed building were projected over our bodies, underscoring the sense of things falling apart.

Other scenes addressed the women's reluctance to go; Pam had devised a wonderful bit about her head being stuck to the Earth; her body flailed in its effort to depart while her cranium stuck firmly to the stage floor. Still, the destruction escalated; Holiday's film about escaping devastation was screened against the scrim. Barely eluding destruction, we found one another, gathered our energy, raised power, and blasted off. It had been decided early on that the women wouldn't be traveling in a spaceship—women don't have access to that kind of hardware and, besides, we didn't need it. We would journey by generating our psychic energy, the fusing of each woman's individual power into a collective force, a method we called "intraspace voyaging."

The space journey was depicted as three women dancing on the stage, while three others moved through the audience in darkness, whispering women's secrets, bits of folk wisdom, lore, and buried history.

Arriving on Femina, each woman found herself transformed by the journey, taking on a new name and new qualities. Ann became AnnChantment, and discovered the breath of the planet. Chutney Lu emerged as Lixa, the source of laughter. I became D'light, and brought illumination to Femina. The performance concluded with the birth of a child, leaving the audience with the sense of something new being born, but not yet fully formed. Just as feminism was at the time.

My goals for *FEMINA* were not only artistic but activist, and from the beginning, I'd been determined to use the piece to inject a feminist vision of the future into the cultural mainstream. Shamelessly capitalizing on the *Star Wars* hype, we used the media to get the message out. Bia's posters included the tag line "The future is **closer** than you think," referencing the title of *Close Encounters of the Third Kind*. *FEMINA* received a lot of attention in the press, including a story in the *L.A. Times* and another in a downtown business paper called the *Enterprise*; even the *Hollywood Reporter* devoted a column. It was highly unusual for a work of feminist art to gain this level of media attention at that time.

As an art project, *FEMINA* was extremely successful, but the process had been arduous. I'd run up against the limitations of working with non-performers, especially the tenuous nature of their commitment, as well as my own personal limitations that kept the project from providing the community I sought. At the conclusion, I returned with the rest of the cast to our disparate lives on Earth; some of them I never saw again.

An Oral Herstory of Lesbianism [25]

The next year, I set out to improve on the collaborative model by which I'd created *FEMINA*. Still working in the context of LAP, I proposed to create a piece that would chronicle the lives of lesbians, and advertised for women who would collaborate on the performance.

This time I had a track record, and I drew a cast of artists who were my peers, some already experienced performers, others with a level of accomplishment in other artistic fields. There were also more complicated emotional dynamics among the group, women who were friends and colleagues with one another, lovers and ex-lovers and lovers-to-be. Both Arlene and

---

[25] *An Oral Herstory of Lesbianism* was created and performed in 1979 at the Woman's Building in Los Angeles. Initiated and produced by Terry Wolverton the work was written, performed, and directed collaboratively by Jerri Allyn, Nancy Angelo, Leslie Belt, Cheri Gaulke, Chutney Gunderson, Brook Hallock, Sue Maberry, Louise Moore, Arlene Raven, Catherine Stifter, Cheryl Swannack, Terry Wolverton, and Christine Wong. The piece also included art direction and graphics by Bia Lowe.

Cheryl joined the cast. I chose to overlook the explosive potential of these dynamics and concentrate on the performance I wanted to create.

In a series of ten workshops designed to generate the content of the piece, each woman was asked to examine aspects of her own experience, then to manifest her stories on a physical level through gesture, movement, and action. In this production I tried to take more care to focus on relationships among the cast members, the process of our work together, and to create a sense of bonding within the group. One week we focused on the body; I assigned each woman to play a part of the body — head, arms, legs, breasts, vagina and so forth. Everyone had to figure out how to portray their individual parts and then the group had to work together to depict the whole body.

Through the course of the workshops, we explored issues of internalized oppression, lesbian relationships, homophobia, and our relationships to family. Revealing our stories required trust of one another, and although all cast members liked each other, over time we built a mutual respect for the risks everyone was taking.

For one of the later sessions we met at Cheryl and Arlene's house instead of at the Building; this session was to focus on sexuality and I had requested that everyone be naked. We were all nervous, but each woman dutifully answered the questions I posed about her sexual experience. Still, it was one of the most constrained of the workshop sessions, everyone bare-assed and tight-lipped; no great stories or images came out of it. We didn't really want to be seeing each other in this way — with our complicated histories and involuted bonds, women working together with spoken and unspoken attractions. Rather than open us up to explore deeper reaches, our nudity may have actually served as a barrier to further intimacy.

Upon completion of the workshop sessions, we moved into the next phase of the production: sifting through stories and images we'd generated, developing them into actual scenes, stringing those scenes together into a cohesive narrative. It's always a messy process — everyone gives feedback to everyone else, often the original ideas transform entirely, sometimes two stories are merged to make a different story, sometimes it works better for someone not to perform her own story. The participants found this phase frustrating, chaotic, and undefined, and, although it seemed normal to me, the cast members couldn't quite see how a product would ever be achieved. A lot of doubt was projected onto me—was I doing my job, was I competent to do my job? This was exacerbated by the conflict with Cheryl that erupted over the grant from the Playboy Foundation just weeks before *Oral* was to open. Although I felt they were attacking my leadership, I came to understand that they were actually looking for *more* leadership from me, reassurance that I was not going to let them make fools of themselves onstage. And I needed to grow within myself to be able to contain their fears without becoming overwhelmed by them.

The behind-the-scenes struggles were not apparent in the performance, which ran for twelve nights to full houses. As with *FEMINA*, the piece began with a pre-show as the audience entered the Woman's Building. Three cast members had created a tableau on the second floor. Wearing workout clothes and doing physical warm-ups, they represented those lesbians who are sports-minded, who like to feel the strength and power of their physical bodies.

The audience continued up to the third floor and encountered the performance space, which was encased in deep pink gauze, like a very large tent. This interior space was set up like a lesbian bar, complete with disco music; the audience was invited to dance onstage with the cast. Suddenly the women from downstairs came racing into the bar, a triumphant soccer team after the big game, and at this moment the performance began. The athletic boasting of the team members caused one woman to complain about feeling marginalized as a femme within lesbian culture, and this triggered a butch-femme conga line, with each woman aping extremes of this spectrum. Before leaving the bar there was a solo scene in which a woman talked about the inherent loneliness of going to a bar to find love.

That scene was followed by a series of coming-out stories: coming out to parents, to oneself, to one's children. This culminated in a kind of birth canal in which each woman moved through according to her own coming-out process: Arlene was dragged kicking and screaming; Nancy minced through with her legs crossed; Leslie tripped and fell, only to be coddled back to her feet by a circle of women. In no time, this nurturing circle began to hurl accusations in our exploration of "political correctness."

Oral included scenes about how lesbians relate in community: rituals of attraction and coming on, the difficulties of bonding and trust. We also explored other issues that affect lesbian identity: a rigorous piece by Leslie Belt in which she jumped rope while chanting about being molested by her grandfather, and a scene by Chris Wong in which she used the form of a traditional Chinese ribbon dance to talk about being Asian and queer.

Oral addressed sexuality but did so neither explicitly nor with the intention to arouse. One scene concerned itself with flirtation and seduction, a dance of moving forward and pulling back. Another piece tackled the topic of "lesbian bed death" (that is, long-term relationships in which the sex has ended), staged with two women on opposite sides of the stage yelling at the top of their lungs. There was also a fantasy sequence with women in animal costumes dancing wildly, a tongue-in-cheek send-up of orgiastic frenzy, but all these scenes were really "about" sexuality. There was no scene that actually attempted to seduce the audience or in which a performer was asked to be sexual onstage, strategies that became more commonplace in feminist performance of the 1980s.

Predictably for 1979, *An Oral Herstory of Lesbianism* was ignored by the mainstream media, but received glowing reviews in the feminist press. Still, I came out of the process exhausted and disillusioned. The Lesbian Art Project was in shambles, and I felt estranged from many of the women in the cast. Judy Chicago had written in *Through the Flower* about the alienation experienced by women in leadership roles who become targets of projection, envy, sabotage, and women's unresolved problems with authority. Now I'd had a taste of this, and it soured me on future large-scale collaborations.

~

AFTER *ORAL*, I either worked alone or in collaboration with just one other woman. My next piece, in fall 1979, *In Silence Secrets Turn to Lies / Secrets Shared Become Sacred Truth*[26] was a solo work that explored my history of sexual abuse. That was followed in January 1980 by *Ya' Got Class, Real Class,* a collaboration with FSW member Vicky Stolsen, which used the format of a TV game show to explore complications of class differences among women.

That process was more satisfying; we approached the work on equal terms and shared responsibility for the outcome. Neither of us was the designated leader; we were instead partners. *Ya' Got Class* was performed outside the Woman's Building in a series sponsored by *High Performance* magazine and Los Angeles Contemporary Exhibitions (LACE). Still haunted by the rejection I'd experienced in the theater program at the University of Detroit, I was relieved to be invited to perform in this series, to be seen as part of the large performance art scene.

In spring 1980, I produced an event that was both fund-raiser and participatory performance. As part of my duties on the organizing collective of the "Great American Lesbian Art Show," I created *An Intimate Dinner for 150 Celebrating Eleanor Roosevelt and All Great Lesbians.*[27] I used a model of collaboration that had worked well in the past: assigning artists different areas of responsibility and giving them autonomy to fulfill their task. Bia

---

[26] This performance is described in detail in the "Recovery" chapter.

[27] Why Eleanor Roosevelt? That spring a book of journalist Lorena Hickock's letters to Mrs. Roosevelt had been published, containing such telltale lines as "I ache to hold you close." Ever on the lookout for members of our tribe, the letters were enough for many lesbians to claim the former first lady as one of us.

Lowe worked with Anne Mavor to create an invitation that looked like a table setting. Nancy Fried raided the gardens in her neighborhood for days to string flower-braided vines and streamers across the vast warehouse ceiling. Clsuf took charge of the kitchen and designed an exotic menu that reflected her interests in natural foods, including red clover soup and seaweed crackers. Sandra Wilson provided the evening's musical entertainment, which included a set by songstress Silvia Kohan. And The Waitresses created a tribute to Eleanor Roosevelt, applauding her service to humanity by designating her "The Waitress to the World."

By summer of 1980 I was severely burned out; in addition to my performance work I had been volunteering on two immense projects: the Incest Awareness Project and GALAS. I produced no more performances between fall 1980 and fall 1983. Instead I performed in several pieces that were organized by other artists — Cheri Gaulke and Nancy Angelo's *The Passion; Heaven or Hell* by the Feminist Art Workers; a political street performance called *Combat Billboredom* by Midnight Graphics; the more theatrical *The True Story of Karen Silkwood* by Cyndi Kahn; and an experimental music piece, *Audible to Oneself,* written and scored by Anna Rubin. Working in other artists' performances allowed me to remain active and visible, but relieved me of the headaches of production. It wasn't as if I had planned the withdrawal, but I was consumed with other projects: In fall 1980 I launched an Anti-Racism Consciousness Raising Group for White Women; in 1981, I took a job as administrative assistant to the new executive director of the Woman's Building.

During this span of time my writing consisted mostly of journalism for art publications — reviews and editorials, an occasional feature — something I'd begun to do in 1977. This gave me the illusion of writing without requiring me to be introspective. I had also joined a writing group that met in the home of Eloise Klein Healy, a poet who'd been inspired to take herself seriously when she'd attended the Women's Words conference at the Building in 1974. During my membership in that workshop I produced a few desultory poems, but my time and creative energy were always being siphoned by the external demands of community, and I gladly gave in to them.

In fall 1983 I was invited to be part of an evening of feminist performances that was part of an exhibition at the Long Beach Museum of Art. The "At Home" exhibit had been conceived and curated by Arlene Raven to honor the tenth anniversary of the Woman's Building and to evoke the tradition of Womanhouse. The performances were to be site-based works, as Womanhouse had been; each artist was asked to choose a space inside the museum or on the grounds. I found myself drawn to the little back porch area of an outbuilding that housed the museum's gift shop, which I curtained off for privacy.

The project marked my return to producing my own work. Not only would this be a solo piece, I also made the decision to define a different relationship to my audience: I met with them one on one.

Medium: Memory/Muse

As the "At Home" exhibit addressed the preceding decade of feminist art, my performance focused on the music of the previous ten years and the way popular music is a powerful trigger for memory. I adopted the persona of The Medium, a fortuneteller in a pink sequined turban. As each person was admitted, one at a time, to my chamber, he or she was invited to sit at a little table across from me. Arrayed on the black tablecloth were a cassette player and a deck of cards. I placed a pair of headphones on the person and let them listen to a piece of music; at the same time I handed them a fortunetelling card on which was printed the story of my memory of that song. As we listened to the tune, they read my story on the card. Then I handed them a blank card and asked them to write a story too: either from their own memory of that song, or a story from that time period, or a recollection that was triggered by something in the episode on the card. Each person received a different song and a different story. The songs were my personal favorites from the decade—

Stevie Wonder, Ohio Players, Aretha, with a smattering of Joni Mitchell and Stevie Nicks.

Outside the chamber was a wall on which my stories were displayed and beneath them, the stories written by the audience — two parallel narratives. It was the first time I had engaged in this kind of direct collaboration with my audience. I loved the intimacy of the piece, how it was not just about performing but about authentically being with each person for a small amount of time.

In spring 1984 I was invited to take part in a performance series sponsored by UCLA. I wanted to present the information and insights I'd gained from doing antiracism work for the past three years, and I created a performance called *Me and My Shadow*.[28] The piece examined the ways in which we learn racism as children and how it distorts our view of ourselves and others. After the UCLA event, I performed this work at the Woman's Building, then toured it to Sushi Gallery in San Diego and to ABC No Rio in New York. A friend, Tina Treadwell, produced and directed a video of the piece, which won a Merit Award in the JVC Tokyo Video Festival that same year. I experienced a flurry of optimism — perhaps I was finally on the verge of establishing a national reputation as a performance artist, and throwing off the specter of failure that still lurked at my side.

In fall 1984 I was invited to be part of an exhibition that would examine the contemporary practice of making altars across cultures and within a feminist tradition. I'd been requested to create an installation, so I proposed to mount a performance out of which my altar would grow. I invited artist Kim Dingle to collaborate with me on the visual elements of the piece.

Familiar explored our relationship to our pets, the way we achieve an intimate bond with animals that we sometimes cannot forge with other humans. I envisioned the performance as ritual in which the audience would participate. In the publicity I instructed people to bring with them objects

---

[28] This performance is described in detail in the "Recovery" chapter.

or photos or other representations of a beloved pet, past or present. When the audience arrived, each person was handed a stick of modeling clay—we'd purchased clay in a rainbow of colors—and asked to hold it during the performance, to infuse it with the feelings that came up for them as they watched the action. During the performance I told stories about my cat Ruby, who had died the previous year. I also invited five other women[29] to perform vignettes about the significant animals in their lives. Their involvement was a way for me to collaborate without having to engage in any bruising group process; each was responsible for her own part.

In the middle of the piece there was an intermission, and the audience was led from the performance space into another room where tables had been set up with art supplies—paint, crayons, paper, glitter, magazines. We invited each audience member to make a totem to his or her beloved familiar. Those who attended were, for the most part, passionate about animals; they seemed to appreciate the opportunity to express their deeply held feelings for their pets. The performance ended with everyone presenting the totems to me, and with these objects, the altar was created.

The successes of *Medium: Memory/Muse, Me and My Shadow* and *Familiar* created a new momentum for me. I felt certain that my career was about to take off, that I would at last redeem myself from my own self-doubts. I began submitting grant applications to the National Endowment for the Arts. My confidence stoked, I was ready to take on another large-scale project.

Excavations[30]

In 1985, I received a California Arts Council grant to conduct oral history interviews with lesbians and use these as the basis for a performance.

---

[29] Performance artist Rachel Rosenthal, writers Jacqueline de Angelis and Bia Lowe, sculptor Jere Van Syoc, and performance artist Nancy Angelo participated.

[30] *Excavations* was created and produced in 1985 at the Barnsdall Park Gallery Theater by Terry Wolverton in collaboration with fifty-three lesbians from southern California. It was performed by Joan Coleman, Linda Klein, Alyssum Long, Marilynn Cruz Rodriguez, and Tina Treadwell. Original music and sound engineering by Sandra Wilson.

Working under the sponsorship of the Gay and Lesbian Community Services Center, I conducted audiotaped interviews with fifty-three lesbians. To reflect the diversity of the community; I interviewed young women and old, lesbians who'd been married to men and those who'd been lifelong lesbians. I spoke to women from a range of cultural and national backgrounds, women with children, one who'd been a nun, one who'd gone back to men, one who'd been in the military. They told me their stories and I recorded them.

Then I worked with composer and sound editor Sandra Wilson to edit these stories and splice them together into a cogent narrative. She composed original music and set about laying down the tracks.

I offered workshops in writing and performance to develop the action that would take place onstage while the audience listened to the audio. Playing off the theme of "excavations," I enlisted a student to find as many images as she could that had to do with layers—geological, biological, and so on. Slides of these images were projected over three tableaux onstage, each representing a different state of lesbian visibility in our culture: One woman paced on all fours inside a Lucite box about the size of a phone booth turned on its side; she could be clearly seen but was imprisoned in that visibility. A second woman was positioned behind a screen made of spandex; as she moved behind the fabric we could see her outline, but never a direct view of her. A third woman was buried entirely in a pile of sand, her body fully obscured. Over the course of the piece she emerges, slowly, imperceptibly, and at the end she rises, becomes visible. These actions occurred while we listened to the voices of lesbians telling their stories.

Primarily an audio work, *Excavations* was dependent on technology. This not only made it costly but also meant I was working outside my area of expertise. I was totally reliant on other people without the resources to adequately compensate them. The grant I'd received was modest, and the piece I'd created required a larger budget than I could muster. I'd rented

Sheila de Bretteville and Suzanne Lacy move sheetrock in the restoration of the new Woman's Building site on North Spring Street, 1975. (Courtesy of the Woman's Building Slide Archive)

Students and teachers of the Feminist Studio Workshop renovate the North Spring Street building in preparation for the Woman's Building's move downtown in 1975. (Photo by Maria Karras)

The Summer Art Program was another aspect of the arts education offered at the Woman's Building, taught by Feminist Studio Workshop participants who had been trained in feminist educational methods. (Photo by Mary McNally)

Deena Metzger with Meridel LeSeuer at the Woman Writer's Series at the Woman's Building, 1976. (Photo by Sheila Ruth, courtesy of the Woman's Building Slide Archive)

Katya Beisantz and Syl Booth explore fantasy personas in Suzanne Lacy's performance class at the Feminist Studio Workshop, 1976. (Courtesy of the Woman's Building Slide Archive)

Blueprint poster for the Women in Design conference, designed by Sheila de Bretteville, 1975. (Courtesy of the Woman's Building Slide Archive)

In Mourning and In Rage, *by Suzanne Lacy, Leslie Labowitz, and Bia Lowe, a performance on the steps of Los Angeles City Hall to protest media coverage of the Hillside Strangler case, 1977. (Courtesy of the Woman's Building Slide Archive)*

Woman's Building founders — (l. to r.) Judy Chicago, Sheila de Bretteville, Arlene Raven — at the WB's 5th anniversary celebration, 1978. (Photo by Maria Karras)

This Is My Body, *performance by Cheri Gaulke, 1982. (Courtesy of the Woman's Building Slide Archive)*

When Nancy was a child, her grandmother told her the story of the difference between Heaven and Hell. In Hell, a long banquet table is piled high with sumptuous food and all the people are desperately trying to feed themselves with four-foot-long forks. Heaven is exactly the same scene – the long banquet table and the sumptuous meal. The difference is that in Heaven, people are using the four-foot-long forks to feed each other.

(l. to r.) Feminist Art Workers Nancy Angelo, Laruel Klick, and Cheri Gaulke perform Heaven or Hell, 1981. (Photo by Sue Maberry, courtesy of the Woman's Building Slide Archive)

Offset poster for FEMINA: An Intraspace Voyage, *designed by Bia Lowe, 1978.*

The Waitresses perform a tribute to Eleanor Roosevelt at An Intimate Dinner for 150, *1980. (Photo by Jo Goodwin, courtesy of the Woman's Building Slide Archive)*

"Once she thought incest was something she had to carry around all by herself," logo for the Incest Awareness Project designed by Bia Lowe, 1979.

Shovel Defense, *a media performance in front of Los Angeles City Hall by Marguerite Elliot and Sisters of Survival (Nancy Angelo, Anne Gauldin, Cheri Gaulke, and Sue Maberry), 1982. Photo by Sheila Ruth (Courtesy of the Woman's Building Slide Archive)*

Offset poster by Patssi Valdez was one of several commissioned by the Woman's Building as part of "Cross Pollination," 1985. (Courtesy of the Woman's Building Slide Archive)

Ceramic "cake" by Beatrice Wood created for "Having Our Cake," the 15th Anniversary show, 1988. (Courtesy of the Woman's Building Slide Archive)

Wolverton, dressed as a birthday cake, poses with Sue Maberry at the Vesta Awards, 1988. (Photo courtesy of Terry Wolverton)

"Love slave to the Woman's Building," Wolverton keeps company with Trudy Reilly (left) and Mary Lou Muir (right) while tied to a pole at her goodbye performance party, 1988. (Photo courtesy of Terry Wolverton)

the Gallery Theater at Barnsdall Park, but I could only afford the fee for the two days of performance; this meant our tech rehearsal had to be on the same day as our first show. My lighting designer was still hanging fresnels when the audience arrived for the performance, and I actually ended up running the lights — something in which I had no training. I didn't even see the performance; a colleague sat in the house taking notes for me.

Even from backstage I could tell it wasn't going well — I sensed lackluster energy in the audience. Aside from the fact that we were unrehearsed, the sound track was completely muddy, the music too loud, the stories inaudible. Sandra had only completed it the day before; I'd never had the chance to listen to it.

By the time I took a tepid curtain call, I was completely depressed. Although I'd always feared it, I never really expected to fail. This evening had flopped on a grand scale. *They'd been right,* I heard a voice in my head, *those horrible men at the University of Detroit. I was no good.*

I came home despondent, certain my career was over, my reputation washed up. My plan was to crawl into bed and never get out, but just as I was burrowing my hot cheeks into a nest of pillows, a friend called and said, "Okay, you have twenty hours before the next show. Fix it!"

I could feel determination stir in me once more, my heart and breath accelerating. Self-pity burned off with the prospect of redemption. I called Katja Beisanz, my choreographer, and she agreed to rehearse the performers again the next afternoon, to make their movement more refined and committed. I called my lighting person and badgered him to run cues before the next show. Then I called Sandra and said, "Guess what? We're not going to sleep tonight." At my insistence we went back into the studio — this was the place where she worked and we had to use it in off-hours — and remixed the entire tape. I came home at about six in the morning, slept a couple of hours, and met my cast at the theater at noon. These women were wonderful; they'd done the best they could the night before without ever having had a run-through. The second night's performance was tight and compelling; it fulfilled my vision for the work. The headline for the review in *Artweek* was "Buried Treasure."

~

IN THE AFTERMATH of *Excavations,* I needed to rethink my relationship to performance art. I could see that the work was suffering because it was underfunded, even as I was digging my way into a hell of credit card debt from which I didn't know how to emerge. And this was with everyone doing me favors—artists working for free, professionals giving me seriously discounted rates, Sandra going in to work at off-hours so we didn't have to pay for editing time.

By the mid-eighties, some performance was being funded—artists like Laurie Anderson in New York and George Coates in San Francisco were spending tens of thousands on their pieces, which relied on the latest in audiovisual technology. One of the inaugural events of the new Museum of Contemporary Art in Los Angeles was a series of performance art, thus officially announcing the "arrival" of the art form in the city where it had in fact been going on for years. Performance art was no longer just a bunch of people doing it out of their garages or lofts. Production values were escalating. Audiences were getting more sophisticated; expectations were being raised. Audiences were hungering for spectacle, not heartfelt content. It was growing more and more difficult to compete on a limited budget.

I'd grown frustrated with my inability to attract more substantial support for my work. My performances were always well attended and usually well reviewed by those publications that published critical response to performance art—the *Los Angeles Times* would not begin to do so for another few years—but I could never seem to convince the National Endowment for the Arts that my work held "national significance." I grew discouraged at seeing my grant applications denied. Was it my lesbianism? My lack of an advanced degree? Despite the positive responses I'd received, doubt nagged at me: Was my work just not strong enough?

Additionally, although I'd had deeply rewarding artistic exchanges with a few key individuals, my efforts to forge community through collaborative performance had proved largely unsatisfying. Indeed, the responsibilities of producing and directing, of leadership, often left me feeling isolated from the group. Maybe I'd failed to choose the right people; maybe I'd clung too tenaciously to creative control. I'd certainly felt more solidarity in project groups in which the focus wasn't a product I considered "mine."

Despite these misgivings, I did create one more performance at the Woman's Building in 1986, collaborating with Catherine Stifter on *dis•abuse*.[31] Our work together was a satisfying experience; it fulfilled our artistic intentions and reinvigorated our friendship. Our piece was praised and admired, well reviewed in both *Artweek* and *High Performance*. Still, when *dis•abuse* was done, I made the decision to give up performance art.

What is the meaning of success? Of failure? We didn't discuss this enough in the FSW or at the Woman's Building. The founders—Judy Chicago, Arlene Raven, Sheila de Bretteville—had already achieved considerable mainstream recognition before investing their time in the feminist art movement, and for each of them, this success continued to grow. But for what were we—the generation of students that followed—supposed to strive? We were driven by feminist ideals, certainly, the desire that our art would help to bring about the cultural change we sought. But how could we avoid being lured by notions of fame, recognition, or at least, sustainability?

I'm reminded of the question Arlene and I used to ponder: how to measure the effectiveness of the Lesbian Art Project. Was it by an external ruler—number of people who attended, the quantity of press coverage, the amount of funding received? Or was there another yardstick, deeper though less apparent, something to do with the energy generated in an unseen realm, its subtle influence on consciousness?

Between 1973 and 1986 I had created sixteen performance or experi-

---

[31] This performance is described in detail in the "Recovery" chapter.

mental theater works that were presented in Toronto, Grand Rapids, Los Angeles, San Diego, and New York. These pieces all had something to say; they were presented, albeit on a modest scale, with concern for artistry and craft. Each of these drew full and receptive audiences; most were reviewed favorably. By what gauge did I imagine myself unsuccessful?

The answer: by two equally unrealistic standards. I'd grown up expecting the Cinderella experience, that at a certain point I would be recognized as brilliant, exceptional, and then elevated into the pantheon of "Art Stars." The Mount Olympus of Culture. We're sold this myth as children; it's reinforced in the cult of celebrity. This illusion erases all notion of *process;* it obscures the true path of deepening one's skill and message over time. The notion of "Art Star" was at its peak in the 1980s; painter Julian Schnabel and writer Tama Janowitz beamed at us from the glossy ads in magazines, selling vodka and lifestyle. How could a lesbian from a working-class family whose work had a heavily progressive and confrontive agenda ever expect to sell liquor to the readers of *Vanity Fair?* And what exactly would I have gained had I been able to do so?

The other false measuring stick was that success in one's art career would change the quality of one's life, transform it, make one fulfilled and content. *If only I were successful, I would be happy.* Years later, after the publication of my second book, I spoke with a colleague about this delusion. "If you're a lonely, insecure person and you get published," my friend rued, "then you're a lonely, insecure person with a published book."

I see it all so differently now, from the perspective of time, maturity, and healing. I promise my students that art is all about risk, and most risk results in failure. "If you succeed too much of the time," I warn them, "chances are you're not attempting enough." I advise them to concentrate on honing the work as fully as they can to their own satisfaction. "Fall in love with the process. That's the part you can control," I tell them, "What the marketplace does with it is out of your hands. Yes, make a place for yourselves there, but don't invest yourselves in its values."

And I know now too that sometimes a path is blocked because we're meant to take another road. That was true for me. The decision to give up performance was not easy; in many ways, it felt like amputation. Disillusionment did, of course, play a part; I could not recognize my own success in the external reflections that were coming back to me.

But it was not, ultimately, discouragement that motivated my decision. What happened was that I'd begun to feel the pull of my writing, tugging at my sleeve like an impatient toddler who'd been neglected for too long. In contemplating this, I saw the ways I had sacrificed my writing to my performance career.

For years I'd announced myself as "a writer and a performance artist," yet my literary output consisted of the slim, self-published *Blue Moon,* a few scattered poems in journals, a fistful of performance texts, and a rather more substantial body of published journalism toward which I felt little emotional investment. I was thirty-two years old and had not yet begun to fulfill my mission as a writer. Instead I'd occupied myself with workshops and rehearsals, marketing and publicity campaigns. The extroversion I so craved in performance had crowded out the introversion required to produce writing of depth.

I was not a woman given to keeping company with myself. The loneliness of my childhood had made solitude seem like solitary confinement. I'd set up my life to elude introspection, avoid the demons that surfaced whenever I let things quiet down enough to hear their shrieks. I'd spent years cultivating applause to drown them out. Now I was beginning to understand that if I really wanted to write, I was going to need to face those demons, to still the distracting ovation and listen to what they had to say.

A little girl once gazed into the mirror and sang "Talking to the Angels in the Sky." The girl in the mirror smiled and sang back, and neither of them had to feel alone. Now it was time to return to the mirror, to claim my reflection in all its flawed, terrible, vulnerable beauty, and begin to sing again, this time in a single, unified voice.

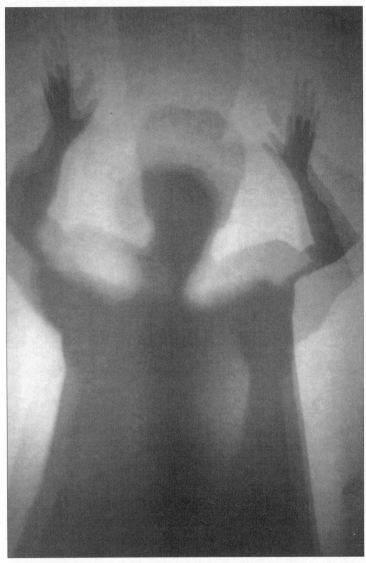

Wolverton confronts her shadow in Me and My Shadow, *1984. (Photo by Bia Lowe)*

Recovery in Four Movements
1979–1989

Fear is a natural reaction to moving closer to the truth.
—Pema Chodrön,
When Things Fall Apart

IT IS COMMONPLACE NOW FOR ARTISTIC WORK TO BE ROOTED IN AUTOBIOG-raphy. The 1990s were the decade of the literary memoir; theater abounds with one-person shows in which the writer/performer chronicles his or her life; director Cameron Crowe makes a celebrated film about his years as a teenage journalist; choreographer Bill T. Jones creates dance about living with HIV and AIDS. Television is awash with talk shows on which people come forward to reveal their most intimate secrets. It's hard to remember that in the 1960s and '70s, such self-disclosure in art was nearly taboo. "Confessional" writing was scorned by the literary establishment; within the visual arts, only formal exploration received critical validation.

Feminist art changed the paradigm, insisted that women use their lives as the material for their art. It was initially a political assertion: that women's lives have value, that creating art should be an internal experience, not merely a matter of technique, surfaces, and style. Perhaps unanticipated was the effect that such a strategy of artmaking would have on the lives of the artists.

Some scientists believe that to study something is to change it; the very presence of the observer alters the event or entity that is being scrutinized. Similarly, when a feminist artist makes art based on her life, that life is inevitably changed. And often such a work demands personal change or growth on the part of the artist before it can come into being.

Arlene Raven defined feminist art as art that "raises consciousness, invites dialogue, and transforms culture." To her definition, I would respectfully add that feminist art also transforms its maker.

I came to the Woman's Building at the age of twenty-two with an equal measure of creative drive and emotional damage. I had high hopes for the former and only the dimmest awareness of the latter. I had used political anger to displace responsibility for my distress on everything outside of me—men, the military-industrial complex, the Establishment, the patriarchy. I had not begun to see where my own responsibility might lie. Nor how, unaddressed, my damage would subvert my creative potential.

Through the process of making art, I found both the necessity and the means to recover myself. For a number of years, I didn't know that I was doing that. Yet an artwork would yield an issue, and I would undertake to explore that issue, and sometimes that would lead to another issue or to another work of art. As recovery took root, my art grew stronger. Creating and healing, healing and creating, each process feeding the other. The interdependence of artmaking and self-development was perhaps the most potent of all the values I learned at the Woman's Building. Today, my students blanch when I tell them, "You can't be a better writer than you are a person," that the issues lying unprobed in the psyche inevitably reveal themselves as flaws in the artwork, but I know it is so.

The Incest Awareness Project: 1979–1981

I was never in denial about my experiences of being molested by my stepfather as a child. The memories were never repressed. I had at various times attempted to discuss them with others. When I was six, I told an older girl, a teenager named Barbara who lived across the street, that my stepfather got me to touch his penis. She gasped and responded, "Your family is bad and dirty." I didn't think that was true, but I didn't mention it again until I was a teenager, when I confided in my first boyfriend, Ray. His compassionate response was to suggest that this must be why I was "frigid" and to encourage me to seek out books about female sexual dysfunction to "help" with my "problem."

At eighteen, I made an attempt to tell my mother. We were lunching at a restaurant outside of Detroit. I began to circle around the subject, hemming and hawing, not revealing much but testing the waters. The look in her eyes grew so dangerous that I backpedaled, retracted even the little I'd spoken, made up some lame excuse that she was only too willing to believe. My mother was still married to my stepfather at the time, and although there was ample reason for their marriage to end, I didn't want to be that reason.

My next attempt was with a former high school teacher, who had, after graduation, lured me to his apartment, no doubt with seduction on his mind. I felt so adult at eighteen, in my short dress, having a drink with an adult man in his apartment on West Grand Boulevard. For some reason I ended up disclosing this part of my history. His response, "Big deal, all fathers do that," left me stunned and furious; I was up and out of there in about two minutes. Even at that time I had sufficient feminist analysis to recognize him for what he was. But I had no way of understanding the emotional reverberations set off by these incidents; like stones dropped into deep water, they made no ripple on the surface.

Of course I told my woman lovers, who generally responded with angry solicitude. "Goddamn patriarchy," I remember one muttering, "It makes me want to just kill the next man I see." Like rape, we recognized incest as a social crime, a political crime, but we were not sophisticated in our understanding of its personal aftermath.

In the summer of 1979, artist Leslie Labowitz announced her intention to launch a Social Art project[32] at the Woman's Building that would deal with incest. For the purposes of this project, incest was defined as "sexual assault within the family—including all forms of sexual contact, not only intercourse—in which an imbalance of power, knowledge, or both exists between the perpetrator and the victim. This can occur not only between blood relatives, but in any relationship in which the perpetrator holds an authority position in the household, such as a stepfather or mother's boyfriend."

Labowitz was responding, in part, to advance publicity for the Bertolucci film, *Luna,* which promised to depict an erotic relationship between a mother and her teenage son. The Incest Awareness Project would attempt to deflate this kind of myth and present the reality of incest.

My girlfriend encouraged me to become involved with the Incest Awareness Project. One of our first project activities was to attend a talk given by psychologist Dr. Susan Forward, who had just published *Betrayal of Innocence,* a book about incest.

Perhaps a dozen of us from the Woman's Building were scattered throughout a packed auditorium in Santa Monica on a July evening. Dr. Forward wore a cream colored suit with a trim skirt, and her auburn hair was salon styled; she was unquestionably "straight," not only in terms of her sexual orientation, but as that term had been used in the sixties, to designate a member of the Establishment. I disliked her on sight.

As she spoke, though, my slow burn began to escalate. She kept talking about the "incest victim," "the damage," "the pathology." I didn't want to hear it. To me, incest was a political crime, something men did to little

---

[32] Social Art is a movement in which artists align with or become activists themselves to directly bring about social change. In 1977, artists Suzanne Lacy and Leslie Labowitz founded Ariadne: A Social Art Network at the Woman's Building. Through this program, they sought to combine performance, mass media, and community activism to address issues of violence against women. Among other actions, the group had mounted *Three Weeks in May* (1977), a citywide project designed to raise awareness about rape, and the previously described *In Mourning and in Rage* (1978).

girls,[33] and less frequently, to little boys. Susan Forward made no claim to be a feminist, and seemed to be more willing to study the problem than committed to ending to this form of assault.

"If she says 'incest victim' one more time," I hissed to my girlfriend, who was sitting next to me, "I'm going to stand up and start screaming."

The psychologist seemed bent on objectifying the woman who'd experienced this crime, suggesting that she was the one with the problem. Even her terminology served to define the individual by what had been done to her. To my ears, Forward's was a psychology of obfuscation, a refusal to address precisely who was doing what to whom.

"I have to leave," I muttered, then stood and strode out of the hall. I waited in the foyer, shaking with rage. My girlfriend followed me out, concern for me furrowing her forehead. She, too, had found the presentation objectionable, but was having a less visceral reaction. All of the volatile and unexamined feelings I harbored about my own incest experience were in that moment directed toward Forward and her ideas. It was so much easier to feel political anger than the welter of emotions beneath.

As the rest of the group joined us at the end of the lecture, our conversation was fervid. This message — wrapped as it was in the dressing of the social sciences — was surely as false and harmful as Bertolucci's soft-core fantasies. How should we refer to the individual on whom such abuse has been enacted? How should we think of ourselves? I can no longer remember whether it was Paula or Nancy, Leslie or Annette who suggested the term "survivor." Incest survivor. And so we became.

The Incest Awareness Project spanned three years and encompassed many facets. Its first public manifestation was an art exhibit, "Bedtime Stories: Women Speak Out About Incest," which opened simultaneously with the launch of our media campaign on the issue. Additionally, the project would

---

[33] According to the statistics available in 1979, 97 percent of all perpetrators were adult men, and 87 percent of its victims were female children.

form alliances with social service agencies to provide links to community resources—hotlines, counseling, and legal and medical resources. Nancy Angelo would mount a video project that would become groundbreaking, both as an artwork and as a potent tool for community education.

In the summer of 1979, after the completion of *An Oral Herstory of Lesbianism,* I devoted myself to the Incest Awareness Project. I had simultaneously begun working on the "Great American Lesbian Art Show," and my days and nights became a frenzy of phone calls and meetings, trips to the typesetter, copy shop, and office supply store.

Bia Lowe had been enlisted to design a logo for the Incest Awareness Project, and she racked her brain for an image that would deliver a potent and easily understandable message. Her poignant solution was a photographic portrait of a little girl, perhaps ten or eleven, in overalls and tennis shoes. She is collapsing beneath the weight she carries on her shoulders: an oversize globe of the world. Superimposed on the surface of the globe is a photographic negative of a family portrait, the images ghostly against their dark background, but the roles unmistakable—dad, mom, two kids. Text reads: "Once upon a time, she thought incest was something she had to carry around all by herself."

That was our message: the unspeakable can be spoken, there are others available to hear it, and through speech healing can come. It is essential to remember that these were the days before Jenny Jones and Jerry Springer; in the 1970s, one's history of sexual abuse was a shameful secret, to be confided—if at all—only to one's most intimate companions and probably only once, never to be mentioned again. Speaking was revolutionary, we understood, a defiant act against the "conspiracy of silence"[34] that allows incest to continue without challenge.

Sparked by the vision of the project, I made a pilgrimage home to visit

---

[34] *The Conspiracy of Silence* is the title of a groundbreaking book about incest by Sandra Butler, one of the first texts to present a feminist analysis of incest.

my mother that summer. Knowing what I intended to disclose, my girl-friend accompanied me; we made the decision to rent a motel room rather than stay with my mother. One afternoon, my mother and I embarked on our ritual of spending time together. This began with lunch at Hudson's department store — Maurice salad for her, shrimp salad on toasted cheese bread for me — followed by shopping. Afterward, we returned to her townhouse.

We sat across from each other at the glass-topped dining room table, as we did when we played gin rummy, another of our rituals. Her frosted hair was sprayed into the shape her hairdresser had sculpted, and she had reap-plied her lipstick after lunch. She left a deep pink half-circle on the rim of her martini glass. She was just about to reach for the deck of cards when I stopped her.

"Mom, there's something I need to tell you." I was cold all over despite the humidity of a midwestern August.

She said nothing. Something in my voice must have caught her attention.

I took the deepest breath I could. "When I was little . . . Mac was . . . he molested me. Sexually." I gave out then, unable to produce another word from my swollen throat.

"Did he have . . . intercourse with you?" she asked sharply. I was struck by the formal word in this most intimate moment.

"No, but . . . it was more than once and . . . no."

"Why didn't you tell me then?" she demanded, her face growing red and dangerous.

"I tried once," I said. I wondered if she remembered that long-ago after-noon. This time I was not going to retreat. "I didn't want to be blamed for breaking up your marriage."

"Then why tell me now?" Her rage was growing. "Are you trying to punish me?" It was her tragedy, she the injured party.

I was so calm that day; I had prepared myself for this visit, made myself hard and hollow as steel inside. I needed nothing from her, was prepared to get nothing. Her anger glanced off me. My sole purpose was to be able to tell the truth.

At twenty-five, I thought I could simply decide this, set my mind to it and it would be so. But my needs—to have my mother hold and comfort me, say she was sorry, to grieve *with* me—could not simply be erased by will. Swept aside, those needs just burrowed deeper underground.

At the time, though, I felt victorious, unburdened. I had told the truth. Later that night in the motel room, my girlfriend would hold me while I shook, but did not cry. I returned to L.A. to work on my performance for the "Bedtime Stories" exhibit. This performance, *In Silence, Secrets Turn to Lies / Secrets Shared Become Sacred Truth,* owed its form and content entirely to this conversation with my mother.

I'd originally conceptualized the piece to be about keeping secrets, the way that silence around incest had made me a liar, separated from my authentic self. But in writing the text, I realized that I had tried to protest what was happening in my family, but had not been heard.

I created an environment for the performance by hanging a dark red canopy from the ceiling, with dozens of crepe paper streamers hanging from the fabric. On the periphery were several layers of blood-red streamers, and on each streamer was written one of the truths that I'd been forbidden to speak.

Don't say, "No!"
Don't say, "Please don't get drunk tonight."
Don't say, "Daddy, I don't want to touch your penis."

I began the piece standing outside this environment. I talked about how for girls, being good is equated with being quiet. I then entered the thicket of streamers, chanting the words written on them, the unspeakable. Inside, I recalled that I did speak out about these events as a child, but wasn't believed.

That's when I learned that a good girl said only what others
were willing to believe. Then I could scarcely tell anymore
what was true and what was acceptable.

Moving deeper into the environment, I came to a ring of black streamers, on which were written the lies I'd told myself:

I'm ugly, I'm not angry, no one will ever love me.

These are messages internalized because of abuse. One by one, I ripped
down these streamers, claiming the primacy of my own truth. Then I
poured a circle of salt—for purification—over the discarded lies.

At the very center of the environment was a chair and a music stand on
which rested a notebook. I sat then and read a letter to my mother,
recounting my recent conversation with her.

I have to remind myself that it is not I
who brings this pain into our lives.
I have to remind myself that ending this silence is a gift
that I give to my life . . .

As the performance concluded, I invited the audience to enter the space
and write their own stories in the notebook, which people did throughout
the course of the exhibition. Some people just wrote notes congratulating
me on my "courage," but others wrote about their own experiences with
incest, some in very intimate detail. Some wrote that they'd never told anyone before. One woman confided she hadn't remembered what happened to
her until she came to the exhibit.

Although I'd always had a strong concern with "being myself," I think
I'd always constructed that self out of scraps of what I saw around me—
social rebellion, cinematic drama, the pose of fashion. I had little familiarity with the concept of an authentic self, rooted in interiority; my work on
this performance had begun to suggest why that might be true.

The design of the "Bedtime Stories" exhibit contained a graphic depiction of this kind of schism, common to survivors of incest. In the gallery,
the walls were split horizontally—the bottom half painted yellow, the top
half painted black—to illustrate the split reality of children undergoing
incest: playing the role of a normal child during the day, but plunged at
night into the terrors of adult behavior. Along the border where the colors

met, artist Dyana Silberstein ran an endless row of color Xeroxed paper dolls bearing her own face in expressions of anger, fear, confusion, and grief. An installation by Lyricon Fire Jazzwomin depicted a military uniform, stuffed as if inhabited by a body, sitting in a chair surrounded by empty liquor bottles.

In addition to paintings and installations by eighteen artists, the exhibit also featured drawings from an art therapy workshop and a section called "Letters Home," in which women from the community had written to family members about their own experience of incest. Throughout the installation, the curators had placed child-size chairs and tables at which the audience was invited to sit and realize how small were the bodies undergoing this abuse.

The exhibit, coupled as it was with the media campaign, generated a great deal of public attention and had a profound effect on its audience. More people attended "Bedtime Stories" than had visited any previous exhibit at the Woman's Building. One television news producer who came to tape a segment on the exhibit broke down in the taping as the memory of her own molestation came flooding back. Hundreds of people called the hotline and were referred to social services, low-cost counseling, and support groups. Mayor Tom Bradley declared the month of October 1979 to be "Children's Defense Month," and commended the efforts of the project.

Across the country, feminists were taking up the issue of sexual child abuse by family members, and our work was part of this larger effort. Still, it is not an exaggeration to state that the Incest Awareness Project helped to raise consciousness about and redefine the issue of incest, and to reshape the public debate around it.

I also involved myself with Labowitz, Angelo, and Nancy Taylor—who worked in the Public Policy office of the Gay Community Services Center—on the Incest Awareness Project Media Campaign. This included not only strategizing the campaign and writing press releases and supplementary material, but also appearing on talk shows and in news interviews.

Some women in the project were reticent to make their experiences so public, but I readily offered myself to become the "poster child," the Incredible Walking Incest Survivor.

I didn't imagine there would be any repercussions to this. My mother and stepfather were divorced; I lived 2,500 miles from either of them; my stepfather and I were not in contact. I had made my mother aware of the truth and informed her about my involvement in the project. I felt no impulse to protect them from the consequences of their actions. I viewed my participation in purely political terms: in speaking about my experience, I would help other women come to terms with what had happened to them.

The format for the talk shows was that Leslie was the expert; she recited the statistics, provided the political framework. I was the case study. I sailed through those interviews with poise and ferocity, stared into the lens of the television camera and never flinched as I spoke about my stepfather's actions. Full of a sense of mission, I walled off the feelings of vulnerability and fear, replicating the very strategy I'd used as a child to withstand the incest. When the fallout came, I didn't even recognize it as such, so effectively had I separated from myself.

The completion of the "Bedtime Stories" exhibit did not signal the end of our work. Almost immediately I, along with sixteen other women, began meeting with Nancy Angelo about her video project, *Equal Time in Equal Space*. And the work of the collective organizing the "Great American Lesbian Art Show" was accelerating simultaneously. There was no opportunity to pause and contemplate the tumult of the previous six months, to absorb the impact of my public actions on my inner world. Even if there had been time, I wouldn't have wanted to engage in this reflection. "Keep moving," was my inner mantra, as if I could forever outrun my feelings. I was smoking dope all day long—from the joint before breakfast to the one just before bedtime—and this too kept my demons, and my self-awareness, at bay.

There was no time to ask why my sexual responsiveness to my lover had disappeared, how I froze whenever she moved to touch me. I loved this woman—why did my senses grow numb, skin brittle and deadened, with our intimacy?

In conceiving of *Equal Time in Equal Space,* artist Nancy Angelo envisioned a work that would reproduce the consciousness-raising process, both in its development and in its presentation. Six "performers"[35] would conduct a conversation about our incest history, each of us being taped by a separate camera. When presented to the public, there would be a circle with six separate video monitors, one of us on each, the tapes synchronized to re-create our conversation. The audience was seated in the circle too, on chairs set between the monitors, becoming part of the conversation.

Each performer was paired with a camerawoman,[36] and we were encouraged to bond with that partner. Angelo wanted us to feel that the camera was an ally, not a voyeur or interrogator. Ten preparatory sessions were scheduled to address topics related to incest. We each told our stories of what had happened to us; our experiences were with fathers, stepfathers, brothers, grandfathers. One woman had been molested by her mother. We looked at our experiences through the filter of religious background, race, ethnicity, and class. Each of us was asked to talk about our current relationship to power, authority, and anger. In one session, we discussed our bonds with our mothers, how incest had affected these. Nancy asked us to examine our ability to trust others and to receive their support; many of us found this to be impaired. We were asked to talk about our bodies and sexualities. This proved no easier than when I'd asked women to do the same in workshops for *Oral;* significantly, I did not discuss what was currently going on in my relationship. In another session we talked about addictions, family and personal; so many of us had come from alcoholic families.

---

[35] Anita Green, Lyricon McCaleb Jazzwomin, Bia Lowe, Paula Lumbard, Terry Wolverton, and Chris Wong.
[36] Jerri Allyn, Cheri Gaulke, Chutney Lu Gunderson, Geraldine Hanon, Catherine Stifter, and Jane Thurmond.

Through these C-R sessions, we developed the content of our on-camera conversation.

Once again, I saw myself as bold, risk-taking, not aware that my fragmentation was accumulating, parts of myself shut off in order to present the public face. I think that if I were to watch the woman on-camera, too thin and with long hair hennaed, she would strike me now as brittle, abstracted, not quite inside herself.

Equal Time in Equal Space premiered at the Woman's Building that fall. Bia Lowe designed and constructed a protective and comforting environment in which the audience could bear witness to our stories. There were seven screenings at this initial showing. I sat in the dark and watched the women with whom I'd worked relay their stories:

It was my father . . .
. . . my stepfather . . .
. . . my brother . . .
I was five . . .
I was eleven . . .
It happened only once . . .
It happened every night for years . . .
He'd come into my bedroom . . .
. . . out behind the garage . . .
. . . in the bathroom . . .

I sat in the dark and watched my own face on the monitor, eyes striking an expression of anguish or tough resolve, lips molded into a replica of wounded courage. After each performance there was a discussion, facilitated by a therapist. Members of the audience would confess their own stories. They would break down. They would ask us questions. They would thank us.

I answered their questions earnestly, always encouraging them to speak out too. Did anyone notice I was missing? I certainly had no idea. Did they see the brittleness in me? Or did they only see and admire the Incest Warrior, never suspecting how much of me was hollowed out?

135

Once the Incest Awareness Project was ended, I was more than relieved. I had had my fill of being a poster child for incest, and although I couldn't have said this to myself, I needed to retreat.

As happened so frequently in those fervent days of Second Wave feminism, political fervor outpaced our skills for dealing with its personal ramifications. The slogan "the personal is political" demanded that our lives inform our politics, but offered scant advice to deal with what our politics would do to our lives. I, perhaps even less than most, was scarcely inclined to attend to emotional needs or inner process. I was determined to spend myself on politics until I was used up. I had not learned to be careful with myself, to even imagine that I might need to.

Still, this work was the cornerstone of a transformation in my life and art. It was the beginning of a journey of healing, and it was the first time my performance work had dealt with such a profoundly personal topic. The theme of incest has recurred in my poetry and fiction, and always there are women who thank me for making this experience visible, discussible. It does, in fact, give them courage to face this issue in their own lives.

And although my work on the Incest Awareness Project would eventually lead to recovery, it is also true that in the process of healing, one often grows sicker before getting better.

Antiracism: 1980–1984

Had anyone asked, I would have sworn that I was not a racist. Even as a child, I'd been drawn to the gray, flickering TV footage of orderly civil rights marchers, dressed in their Sunday best, beset by water cannons, attacked by dogs; of white-shirted, dark-skinned young men handcuffed and dragged from the stools of lunch counters. The rhythms of Motown, soul music, and R&B were in my pulse, the radio my constant companion through years of insomnia. I'd been twelve when the riots erupted in Detroit, five days of burning and looting. Although my neighborhood had not been directly under siege, smoke clung to the July air, graying the sunsets to a deep taupe, and pieces of ash dropped from the sky like a thick and somber snow. I watched tanks lumber down Grand River Avenue, National Guardsmen with rifles perched on top. My allegiance was entirely with the rioters, the members of the black community who'd had enough. In my soul, I understood the urge to burn, the pain that erupts in conflagration.

Within this empathy, I began to feel kinship, believed that black people were, on some cosmic level, my family.[37] African Americans did not, necessarily, see it that way. By the 1970s, Black Nationalism had replaced the strategies of integration, and within my high school, where 70 percent of the students were black, even the most well-meaning whites were regarded with skepticism and disinterest, if not overt hostility. Though profoundly pained by this estrangement, I felt I understood its origins. A few years later, I would myself adopt a separatist stance as a lesbian, believing it the only way for women to create a new identity uncontaminated by sexism.

In the spring of 1980, the "Great American Lesbian Arts Show" was coming to culmination, nearly consuming the six of us who collectively endeavored to produce it. Although all but one of us had been previously active at the Woman's Building, members of the GALAS collective were not necessarily friends. We'd come together out of our dedication to the concept, but our meetings could be acrimonious. It was after one such meeting that the phone rang and I answered. The caller announced herself as Yolanda Retter, a renowned local activist who'd founded an organization called Lesbians of Color. She was a mainstay at lesbian events of all kinds, from dances to demonstrations, always in an orange vest handling security.

---

[37] There is much theory about the highly suspect nature of such an identification between a member of an oppressor group with the oppressed, that it's an insidious way to avoid responsibility for one's own part in perpetrating the oppression. Although I don't deny this, it may also be true that hurt seeks hurt, and that the black community's struggle to throw off the burden of brutality and injustice became the visible representation of my own struggle within my violent and alcoholic family.

I knew Yolanda by sight and by reputation, but we'd never before conversed. She was notorious for her tireless political work, her permanent scowl, and her style of confrontation, about which "blunt" is a charitable description.

She got right to the point. "I understand a group of white women is organizing a show of lesbian art, and I want to know how many lesbians of color are included."

None, I admitted, after a certain amount of hemming and hawing.

"Why is that?" she demanded to know.

My excuses sounded lame even to my own ears. "We're . . . uh . . . trying to focus on artists who've . . . achieved a certain level of . . . uh . . . national prominence." I was relieved she couldn't see me, my face blazing. "I think it's harder for . . . uh . . . artists of color . . . to be visible at all, let alone as lesbians." We had, in fact, contacted several women of color to be part of the exhibit; they'd declined, fearful that their reputations in the art world would be irreparably damaged.

She didn't bother to puncture the flimsy bubble of my argument or suggest that if our criteria made the project exclusionary, perhaps there was something racist in the criteria. She merely informed me that if lesbians of color were not included in the show, her organization was going to protest it.

A letter soon followed from a group calling itself White Women Against Racism (WWAR), who had appointed themselves to confront incidents of racism in the feminist community. The tone of this letter, shrill and self-righteous, was harder to stomach than my conversation with Yolanda. WWAR demanded our presence at a meeting.

The reaction of the women on the GALAS collective was mixed. Some felt defensive, wounded by what they perceived as an attack on their hard and well-intentioned work. We *had* made efforts, they insisted, angry that these were not being acknowledged. They wanted us to dig in our heels. Others of us, including myself, felt that the challenge had merit, however much we might not care for the tone of its delivery. We also believed that for the sake of the project, we needed to address the larger community in good faith.

A subset of us met with WWAR, a group composed primarily of lesbian feminist activists; like many politicos of the time, some of them harbored a suspicion of the arts and of the Woman's Building as an "elitist" organization. During this meeting, I found myself drawing on the lessons I'd learned working on *An Oral Herstory of Lesbianism*—to meet conflict not with opposition but to encompass it, grow bigger. We discussed our intentions for the project and recounted our difficulties involving women of color. Once we'd succeeded in demonstrating that the GALAS Collective was not a group of cross-burning, bed sheet–wearing racists, we tactfully suggested that next time they decided to confront white women on their community work, they should initiate dialogue before assuming bad faith. And we asked for their help, thus turning adversaries into allies.

It was then time to do our part. Bia, the primary curator of the Woman's Building exhibit, rededicated herself to seeking out artists of color whose work fit the criteria of this show; unsophisticated as we were, we knew that token inclusion would do more harm than good. The final roster of ten artists included Lula Mae Blocton, an African-American artist in New York City, and Gloria Longval, a Cuban-American who made her home in Los Angeles.

We also received assistance from Nancy Taylor, who'd worked with us on the Incest Awareness Project. A Native American activist, she helped us to make connections with local lesbians of color, sometimes serving as liaison, and personally worked to organize a satellite show for artists of color at a women's club in South Central L.A. called Loveland.

Later that summer, I came across an article by Elly Bulkin, "Racism and Writing: Some Implications for White Lesbian Critics"[38] which furthered my thinking about racism. Two factors had been clouding my vision: I'd felt such an identification with the liberation struggles of the black community that I'd believed I could not possibly be racist. Additionally, as a

---

[38] First published in *Sinister Wisdom,* issue 13.

feminist, I was keenly aware of being a member of an oppressed group (women); I'd failed to realize that I was simultaneously a member of an oppressor group (white people).

Bulkin's analysis altered the paradigm. It insisted that racism is so endemic to the social fabric of the United States that it would be impossible to live here and stand outside of it. Most well-meaning white people want to see themselves as nonracist, which Bulkin declared impossible. That wish to be or be seen as nonracist only served to deny the persistence of racism, and fueled the frustration of women of color toward white women. One can perpetuate racism through inaction as well as through overt intention, but one can also choose to *act* in ways that are antiracist. "I think it is essential," Bulkin states, "that as white women, as white lesbians, we break out of that silence, that inaction, that wait for the never-never day when we will be blameless enough to speak."

This essay inspired me to found an antiracism consciousness-raising group for white women, which was offered through the Woman's Building. Why only white women? Because I didn't want to put the burden of our struggle to gain awareness on women of color. Because I wanted to create a space in which we could be honest about the racist thoughts or feelings we did harbor, where we wouldn't be playing for the approval of women of color.

Initially seven women[39]—as it happened we were all lesbians—came together and contracted to meet for eight weeks. This commitment was renewed twice, each time for an additional twelve weeks. At our first meeting, women were very nervous, perhaps feeling they were going to be attacked or made to feel guilty. We noted the distinction between safety and comfort, and pledged to create ground rules that would make the group safe for its participants, even if it wasn't always comfortable. We also agreed that our weekly group meetings would be a priority commitment;

---

[39] Cindy Cleary, Mary-Linn Hughes, Ginny Kish, Bia Lowe, Tracy Moore, Patt Reise, and Terry Wolverton. In subsequent years members included: Pat Carey, Jacqueline de Angelis, Cyndi Kahn, Judith Laustea, Barbara Margolies, Louise Sherley, and Jane Thurmond.

no one would miss, and no one would leave the group before our contracted time had reached its end. We further made the decision to hold our meetings at Bia's house, which offered a more hospitable environment than the white-walled austerity of the Woman's Building.

Our very first discussion centered on how it felt to us to be talking about racism. Women reported fear, embarrassment, confusion, sadness, resentment, guilt, and anger. We talked about how those feelings had kept us silent and passive about racism. Mary-Linn Hughes shared with us a model called "Unlearning Racism" that had been developed in the Re-evaluation Counseling (RC)[40] movement. This model encouraged us to go back to our earliest memories of encountering racism and to think about the ways we had initially resisted it. One woman remembered being six, and drinking from the "Colored" water fountain at a public park in Texas. I remembered attending the funeral of a black friend even though my step-father had threatened to kill me if I did so. Such memories remind us that no one is born racist; we learn oppression as children and try to resist it, though we are frequently punished for our acts of resistance. The early experience of feeling powerless to overturn injustice is one of the things that keep us passive about racism.

We used our sessions to raise instances of racism with which we were confronted in our current lives — anything from one's aunt using the word "nigger" at a family gathering to hiring decisions at work — and asked the group to brainstorm appropriate responses. We gave one another positive affirmation for behavior that was antiracist — "Good for you for saying you were uncomfortable when your friend told that racist joke" — and tried to suggest an alternative when a group member acknowledged that she'd acted in a way she considered racist.

---

[40] Reevaluation Counseling is a theory of human behavior and a process whereby people of all ages and background learn to exchange effective help with each other in order to free themselves from past hurts and solve human problems.

We each made a list of all the people of color we could remember knowing, and the kinds of relationships we'd had with them. Then we talked about what we had learned from making the list. We also talked about different cultural groups, and the varying racist mythologies that surrounded each.

One of the most potent discussions for me was one on racism and feminism, and the different ways that men and women of color experienced racism. One woman cited the fact that women had finally achieved suffrage in this country because white men wanted to offset the vote of black men. Several women talked about the myth of the black man as rapist, and how feminist antirape strategies often inadvertently supported this myth. I raised the issue of separatism, whether it had an inadvertent effect of reinforcing racism. Women of color had long complained that feminism seemed to ask that they choose between their loyalty to women and their loyalty to their culture. If I was committed to being an ally of people of color, it would follow that this would include men. And it didn't make credible sense to me that I should maintain a separatist stance only with white men. This was the beginning of the erosion of my separatism.

It took us until our eighth month of meeting to talk about our whiteness, to be willing to examine our own cultural backgrounds. We speculated that this might be for several reasons: assuming whiteness as the norm is a symptom of racism; we see it not as a particular culture, but as *the* culture, to which everyone else is the exception. Also built into the culture of the United States is that everyone is supposed to be an individual, not like anyone else, so white-identified people seldom think of ourselves as being imprinted by culture. Finally, we all felt tremendous shame and embarrassment about white culture; many of us had spent years trying to reject those values.

This led us to the realization of our difficulty identifying with other white people, particularly if those people are behaving in a racist way. We tend to want to disassociate, believe we're not like *them*. I was reminded of the women from WWAR who'd written to the GALAS collective about their criticisms; they had not wanted to identify with us. I remembered how much more their comments had stung, had felt unjust, because of that lack of alliance. This became an important commitment we all made: that when trying to educate someone about racism, we speak from a place of compassion rather than judgment.

In the spring of 1981, we attended a weekend retreat with the members of WWAR, and jointly hired Ricky Sharover-Marcuse—the woman who had developed the Unlearning Racism model within Reevaluation Counseling—to conduct a session with us using RC techniques. After presenting her theory, she then worked with individuals to help them connect with their own pain about racism. Discharging emotion, RC postulates, leaves room for one to think more clearly about an issue. This retreat provided a dramatically different way of working with other white people about racism than the old confront-and-blame method.

In the antiracism group's second year, some of the original members continued, and we merged with a second group of women that Mary-Linn Hughes had convened. It became a challenge to replicate the necessary dialogues some of us had already undergone and still feel that we were moving forward. In 1982, a subset of the group formed an action committee and adopted various projects. Some of us taught antiracism workshops in the community, others wrote articles or participated in political actions. This emphasis on action led four of us—Bia, Mary-Linn, Jane Thurmond, and myself—to embark on an intervention at the Woman's Building.

The issue of racism had been volatile within the organization, usually surfacing only after resentments had built to the point of crisis. Attempts at discussion had been tainted with venom, the sting of personal attack, and seemed to leave all parties injured. This had occured most recently in the spring of 1980, when a staff of primarily women of color was hired through a CETA grant to produce the Woman's Building publication *Spinning Off*. These staffers chafed against predominantly white management, who in turn charged them with poor work habits and a bad attitude. I was not on staff during this confrontation, so only heard later about the facilitated staff retreat that left black and white women alike screaming accusations at one another.

The issue surfaced again in 1981 when Suzanne Shelton, an African-American woman, was hired as executive director of the Building. She soon fell into conflict with white staff members and the all-white board of directors. One early instance of this was when other staff members insisted she hire me as her administrative assistant. Shelton believed it should be within her authority to hire a person of her own choosing, not another white "insider." After meeting me, she did decide to hire me, and luckily, our working relationship was both friendly and productive. Still, Shelton felt like she was not allowed to exert leadership in her position, to place her stamp on the organization; she wanted to expand the vision of the Woman's Building beyond what she considered its white countercultural confines. Some of the board and staff members felt that she threatened to undermine the feminist values that made the Woman's Building unique.

Shelton resigned in 1981, with bad feelings on both sides. In the wake of her departure it seemed to me that the prevailing, though unspoken, attitude was, "Let's just attract people who are like us or who think like we do, and avoid the pain of difference."

Bia, Mary-Linn, Jane, and I each enjoyed long and varied associations with the Woman's Building; Jane and I were currently on staff. We hoped our "insider" status would make it easier for key members of the organization to hear our message. When we approached them, we neither accused nor demanded; instead we offered a concrete plan to improve inclusion of women of color at the levels of board, staff, and artists presented, and said, "We will help."

We made good on our word. We developed a protocol for affirmative action in hiring and in board recruitment. We generated lists of artists of color and recruited some of them to join our gallery committee. We hired Ricky Sharover-Marcuse to conduct a meeting with current board members and staff. Her work helped to reorient the group's motivations for dealing with racism: neither as a do-gooder activity (a motivation that often crumbled when met with anger or criticism by people of color) nor with the cynical motivation often driving nonprofit organizations — "We'll get more grants if we appear diverse!" — but to help ourselves, to ease the pain and devastation wrought by racism in our own lives, and to strengthen the organization.

Once this commitment was made, we never stopped trying to fulfill it. Our efforts, of course, were only partially successful. We made the strongest impact in the area of programming, exhibiting, and presenting artists of color on a scale previously unachieved. This was in some ways the easiest task: artists could come and go; they presented their work without attempting to challenge the construct of the institution that exhibited them. A few of these artists did continue with the Woman's Building, as members of the gallery committee or the advisory board, occasionally taking a position on staff or the board, or teaching in the educational program.

Perhaps the pinnacle of this achievement was represented by poet Gloria Alvarez, whose three-year residency brought more than a hundred women of Mexican or Central American heritage to learn creative writing at the Woman's Building. The women flocked to Gloria's workshop, hungry for the chance to tell their stories to others who would listen and understand. Still, when the workshops ended, these students left the building; they did not stay to blend their words and rhythms into the music of the organization. We did not speak their language.

Things were more uneasy when women of color were hired as staff, which, after Suzanne, never again included management positions. This was not an intentional policy. One truth was the Woman's Building was a small-budget nonprofit organization, relying on vision, individual initiative, and personal sacrifice. Why would a bright, highly qualified woman of color want to give that to an organization perceived as white? I personally interviewed a number of women of color with college degrees and great credentials who laughed outright when I told them the salary range of a job at the Woman's Building. Another truth was that the community was run on social networks, and we did not easily embrace women who were unknown to us.

The most spectacular representation of our failure here was an incident involving a Latina who worked on the staff of the Women's Graphic Center. She had been active as an artist at the Woman's Building since the late seventies, and had served on the board of directors in the early eighties. She and I had become friends during this time.

The Woman's Building decided to give her an award for her artistic accomplishments at our annual fund-raising banquet. Before a crowd of three hundred well-dressed supporters in a ballroom of a downtown hotel, she stepped to the podium to accept her award and delivered a blistering denunciation of the Woman's Building for its racism.

Of course, the harsh note was not what we were expecting at this otherwise celebratory occasion, but what disturbed me most was that I had never heard her voice these criticisms at a staff meeting, a board meeting, or in any private conversation.

I felt personally stung because of my own efforts to heal the problems of racism at the Building. Her choice to publicly humiliate the organization and risk endangering the support of the funders attending, and to do so not as a last resort, after all attempts at dialogue had fallen on deaf ears, but as an opening gambit—these things all felt like betrayal. They seemed like gestures of estrangement and hostility from someone whom I had considered an ally. No doubt this personal investment kept me from being more compassionate about her point of view.

To my knowledge, I was the only white woman who confronted her about her action. Although other colleagues expressed their disapproval privately, they would not hazard saying it to her face and being further branded racist. It was risky and I knew it; how dare a white woman criticize a person of color for confronting racism? Still, I felt I owed it to our friendship to be honest with her.

Our conversation took place over the telephone. I did not attempt to dispute her charges about the Building; I myself had made similar charges. But I questioned whether her method was really designed to produce positive change, or merely to cast herself in a heroic light in that public arena.

Her response was furious. "You, of all people," she accused, "I would expect you to support me."

"It's not that I don't support you," I sputtered, "I just don't understand why you did what you did."

For her, it was open and shut. If I questioned her action I was an unrepentant racist, worse than the others because I'd pretended to be her friend. From her response it was clear that she too felt betrayed. This was the end of our friendship.

In preparation for the writing of this book, I discussed this incident with another woman who was active at the Woman's Building during those years. I was still carrying the old hurt from this encounter, and voiced it as I told the story. My friend was quiet for a moment, and when she spoke, her voice was gentle. "Do you know that the women of color in this community completely celebrated what she did? It was as if she'd spoken for all of them, all the ways they'd felt shut out of the Building. *She* had the entrée; *she* had the opportunity to speak, and women of color cheered her for doing so. It created a great cohesion within that community."

There was no criticism in her tone, only the desire to show me what I had failed to see. I had made a mistake, a classic mistake of well-intentioned white people: I had taken the criticism personally. Once on the defensive, I was unable to remain an effective ally against racism. And my expectation of this woman's allegiance to the Woman's Building reflected a profound denial of the historical and contemporary circumstances that would compel women of color to maintain a deeper loyalty to one another.

The incident stung everyone at the Woman's Building. Those individuals who'd been reluctant to tackle the issue of racism in the first place felt vindicated. "See? This is what happens," they said. Not wanting the stance of the organization to harden once more into a guilty inaction, the antiracism C-R group suggested that we bring back Sharover-Marcuse for a second session with staff and the board. After hearing about what had happened at the Vesta Awards, she offered this interpretation. "Rather than see it as a measure of failure," she suggested, "you might view it as an indicator of your success."

Seeing our perplexed expressions, she went on to explain that in situations in which racism is pervasive and entrenched, those who experience its effects will rarely bring it up. "Where racism is rampant, it's too dangerous to discuss it. By your efforts to raise the issue, the Woman's Building has become a place that is safe enough for the issue to be raised." Viewed this way, I was doubly regretful that my own reaction to feeling attacked had kept me from being a better friend. Sharover-Marcuse also reminded us that our motivation to eliminate racism at the Woman's Building was not to win the approval of women of color.

Fortified by this encouragement, we recommitted ourselves to the effort to hire people of color, and to struggle to expand our visions to embrace different work styles and points of view. This endeavor was only intermittently and partially successful. The place where we experienced the most abject failure was in the recruitment of women of color as board members. At the outset of this initiative we'd received a word of caution from Dr. Maria Diaz, a member of Lesbians of Color. "Too often white organizations will overlook the issue of class when recruiting women of color to their boards. When differences arise in participation levels, funding commitments, and so on, these are perceived as racial differences when in reality they are often class differences."

Still, so much of a functioning nonprofit board revolves around the formation of a social network among its members. Despite assiduous efforts to recruit women of color to join the Woman's Building board, we never seemed able to form that crucial social bond that would have cemented their commitment to the organization or fully elicit their participation.

Throughout the years of engaging in this work I grew to believe that the efforts to elicit participation by women of color in the Woman's Building could never be more than remedial, doomed to partial success at best. The organizations that achieved true multiculturalism were those founded by people of diverse backgrounds. The Woman's Building had been founded by three white women, its vision shaped by the concerns of the predominantly white women's movement of the early seventies. Not that it was a bad vision, but it was, *de facto*, not representative of all women.

In 1984, the antiracism C-R group came to an end. As if in summary, in 1984, I developed the performance, *Me and My Shadow*. I wanted to see if I could render on stage the theories and processes that had guided our three years of work. The shadow was a potent image, a projection of the self one can never escape. In the piece I related stories of being affected by racism, my own as well as others'.

Once more, Bia agreed to assist; she shot slides of various environments that, when projected, provided the setting for each of the stories—a park, a locked door, a school hallway. As I narrated each incident, my shadow was projected onto the backdrop.

My mother used to tell this story. When I was little, she and my new stepfather took me to a drive-in movie. It must have been a hot summer night, the car windows rolled down. My stepfather made some comment like, "Look at all the jungle bunnies." Before my mother could admonish him not to talk that way in front of me, I piped up and asked brightly, "Bunnies? Where are the bunnies? I want to see them!"

In one scene in the middle of the piece I danced, backlit behind a scrim; only my shadow is visible. The music was blistering, tribal: world beat. As my shadow dances, I chant the qualities white people have projected onto people of color:

Emotion. Sexuality. Spirit. Nature. Hunger. Chaos.
Rage. Body. Animal. Rhythm. Odor. Wildness. Mystery.

These qualities, of course, are also those that patriarchal thinking projects onto women. The performance also examined the intersections of racism and sexism. The piece concludes by suggesting that we cannot effectively combat racism by denying it. We must acknowledge its existence in our collective and individual psyches; we must claim in ourselves those qualities we've projected onto others. We must embrace the shadow.

This art piece would never have been possible without the previous three years of working on the issues in a community of similarly committed women. The theory of oppression that our group adopted maintained that racism, like sexism, classism, and homophobia, are social illnesses that affect all members of society, both those who are the targets of oppression and those who are the perpetrators. The performance was an opportunity to attempt to share some of the tools of recovery.

The Twelve Steps: 1985–Present

I stopped drinking in 1978, at the age of twenty-three, through a convergence of physical breakdown and misplaced relational devotion. I had always possessed a great capacity to hold my liquor; I could drink all night long, almost never got sick, and smoking a joint the next morning took care of the hangover. I thought I was invincible. I remembered one night in Toronto when I'd reveled in being able to consume more shots of tequila than the male psych professor who was trying to pick me up. This abruptly came to an end one spring night in 1978 when I was out to dinner, consuming my usual scotch on the rocks, and suddenly found myself clutching the toilet in the tiny rest room, spewing my guts into its porcelain maw. My liver, I was to find out later, had had enough; it would no longer metabolize alcohol.

This happened to coincide with my determination that my girlfriend drank entirely too much, and I proposed to her that we both stop drinking. More than likely she agreed because she felt it would be good for *me* to stop, but quit we did, just like that.

This didn't mean I was committed to sobriety. I increased my already frequent dope smoking and continued to take other drugs that came my way, although I no longer sought them out quite as vigorously as I had in Detroit. I joked about my program of "marijuana maintenance," being high as a kind of baseline reality. I felt more fun when I was stoned, more lighthearted, more festive. Smoking dope was the only thing that eased the constant worry, the gnawing brain chatter, the anxiety that otherwise filled my head.

It was 1983, on Martin Luther King Jr.'s birthday, that I stopped doing drugs. I'd always promised myself that I would stop if I felt my health being negatively affected, but for some time I'd been ignoring the daily headaches and lethargy that had begun to plague me. Some of the Anti-Racism Group had marched in the King Day parade—L.A.'s first—and when I came home and started to pull out a joint, I just said, "Maybe not today."

Looking back, it's nice symbology that this step was taken on Martin Luther King Jr. Day, but at the time I didn't see it as any kind of decision. I'd never have lasted if I'd told myself I was quitting for good, but I just kept saying, "Not today," until weeks had accumulated, then months, then it just began to seem like something I didn't need to do anymore. Without knowing it, I was following the principle of "one day at a time."

Like many addicts, I had a bad attitude about AA. Although I paid lip service to supporting the Alcoholism Center for Women, an important institution in the lesbian community, I did not identify with the women who went there. *They* had a problem; *I* just liked to party. My denial was absolute. Because I stopped drinking and doing drugs outside of the framework of a recovery program, I simply found new outlets into which to channel my addictive tendencies: into work and into compulsive relationships.

In the fall of that year, I took up an affair with a painter. It was this action and my relative forthrightness about it that brought about the end of my six-year relationship. Astonishingly, I was stunned when my girlfriend made her final pronouncement: "I don't love you anymore." The same denial that had fueled my substance abuse had me convinced that my extracurricular romances would not damage the primary bond I had with her. It was as if there were two distinct parts of my brain—the one utterly devoted to my lover and the one compelled to follow my attractions to other women—and each was operating independently of the other.

I immediately took refuge in the new relationship. I began spending every night in the painter's rundown cottage in East L.A., using it like a cave in which to hide out and lick my wounds. But an association of a few months could in no way withstand the weight of my grief and need in the face of losing the relationship I'd thought would last a lifetime.

That summer, I allowed myself to again be drawn into an affair, this time with a businesswoman who had recently joined the board of the Woman's Building. I spent several months ricocheting between the two—the artist and the headhunter; I juggled nights of the week, fabricated excuses, weathered blistering arguments. I cried on the phone every day in my office at the Woman's Building, to the great chagrin of my assistant—a demure woman who'd grown up in the South and rarely disclosed anything personal about herself—who shared the small space with me. And all the time I continued to grieve the loss of my longtime partner. I was living on drama and adrenaline, caught in a dynamic I did not understand.

The pressure did not lessen once the painter and I finally let go of each other. I expected to ensconce myself with the businesswoman, but almost immediately she began to express ambivalence. She grew extremely critical of me—my choice of clothing, my taste in film, my food preferences, my devotion to my work. I couldn't fathom how this person who'd found me so delightful, so desirable before would now have such disdain for me. I continued to cry on the phone at work.

Miserable in this dynamic, unable to extricate myself from it, I was teaching a writing workshop one day when I ran into a woman I'd once worked with. She told me she'd been taking "this amazing workshop for Adult Children of Alcoholics."

It wasn't so much the words she used to describe it as a certain charge I felt, a tingling in my energetic field. I asked for the number for information, and phoned the next day.

The workshop was led by Jael Greenleaf, who'd coincidentally been a member of my oft-maligned C-R group during my first year in the FSW. I'd been dimly aware of her pioneering work in defining the dynamics of individuals who'd grown up in alcoholic families because the Women's Graphic Center had typeset the first edition of her first booklet on the subject, *Co-Alcoholic and Para-Alcoholic: Who's Who and What's the Difference?* Jael's history with the FSW helped me to feel comfortable in the midst of the group of more than forty women who attended the ten-week workshop.

It was Greenleaf's assertion that when a child grows up in an alcoholic family, she or he learns certain unworkable ways of thinking and behaving and fails to learn important ways of self-sustenance and relating to others. All my life I had carried the belief that I was afflicted with some terrible blight in my spirit, a dark despair, an inability to be happy. I'd been sure it was some terrible, uncorrectable flaw in me. "It's not your fault," Jael insisted, standing calmly at the podium in front of our large circle, "And it's not that you are bad. It's about what you did and didn't learn." I was not the only woman in tears before the end of the first session.

Greenleaf's strategy was to painstakingly articulate those learned behavior patterns and provide us with activities that would help us to replace them with healthier ways of thinking. One of the first assignments was deceptively simple: "Once a day, I want you to look into a mirror. *Really* look at yourself; don't just fuss with your hair or see if you have anything in your teeth. Look into your own eyes. Hold that contact for a least a minute. Then smile at yourself, really sweetly, like you're greeting someone you love. Say, 'Hi, honey.'"

When I tried it at home, I found it almost impossible to do. I was used to scrutinizing my imperfections — the eyebrows that needed tweezing, the pimple erupting on my chin, the split ends caused by the perm in my hair. But to regard myself deeply seemed intolerable; a profound sense of loathing would rise up, accompanied by a desire to escape. I couldn't stand myself!

The workshop made me aware of the constant stream of "negative self-talk" that preoccupied my mind most of the time: *you look awful today, why did you do that, you're so fucked up, no one loves you.* "These were the spoken or unspoken messages of your childhood home," Jael pointed out to us, "but now you're perpetuating those messages. You're constantly programming yourself."

There was also the habit of running "disaster films," cultivating fantasies in which the worst happens, something I'd practiced since childhood: *my parents are never coming home from the bar, they've been in a terrible car crash and hours from now the police will knock on my door and lead me to their mangled bodies splayed across the asphalt . . .*

Both the negative self-talk and the habit of imagining the worst were methods of keeping ourselves in a constant state of upset, a state that was familiar to us from our early family life. "Many children of alcoholics become adrenaline addicts," Greenleaf informed us, "and as adults we create emotional chaos in our lives to keep ourselves in that state of distress. That's the way we know we are alive." And it was true that I always seemed to have some drama going, something about which I was upset.

At the completion of the first ten weeks, I signed up for another twelve sessions. In this second group, Jael presented a model for changing behavior in slow, deliberate steps rather than the grandiose "I'll just detonate my whole life" approach that so many of us tried to employ. The gifts of these workshops were many, but perhaps most significant was the assertion that the wounds of childhood did not have to be "a life sentence," that one could heal, and there were actions one could take to do so. That it was, in fact, one's responsibility to do so.

Greenleaf also strongly encouraged participation in a twelve-step program, and as my relationship with the businesswoman continued to devolve, I was moved to join Al-Anon, the program for families of alcoholics. Of course, with my own substance history, I could have just as easily chosen AA, but I found in Al-Anon a path to emotional sobriety, which seemed for me the heart of recovery.

In 1986, I was invited to make a proposal for a second Woman's

Building exhibit about incest and I asked Catherine Stifter, with whom I'd worked on both *Oral* and *Equal Time in Equal Space,* to create a performance and an installation. We were, we both agreed, "sick of incest," and had each, in our own ways, been working on our personal recovery. We agreed to make this the focus of our collaboration.

The piece we created was called *dis•abuse.* The title referred both to the effort of undoing the effects of abuse and, as the dictionary defines it, "to free oneself from falsehood or misconception," that misconception being that one is irreparably damaged.

dis•abuse was constructed in three sections; in each, three performers[41] enact a series of movement and gestures accompanied by audiotaped text. In the first section, the recorded voice provides simple explanations of Catherine's and my experiences of incest, and the internal dynamics with which each of us deals as a result of that abuse.

Terry finds it hard to trust. She thinks she has to be responsible for everything. The voices inside Catherine keep her quiet, challenge her decisions, tell her no one will ever love her.

This is followed by a recitation of those negative messages we carry inside us, the ones that replicate the experience of abuse into adulthood.

I'm crazy.
My stomach is too big.
Nothing I do is good enough.
I want to die.

In the third section the tape repeats affirmative messages that are designed to contradict that negativity, to carve new paths in the brain.

I belong here!
I'm a good artist.
People like and respect me.
Look at how I've survived!

---

[41] Cyndi Kahn, Robin Rodolsky, and Tina Treadwell.

In addition to the performance, Catherine and I also created an installation, constructing a little room — real walls, a door that shut — in a corner of the gallery. People entered one at a time and found a chair with a soft cushion, a mirror, a small desk, a notebook, a stuffed animal, and a tape recorder. Printed instructions invited the individual to put on the headphone; on tape was a series of activities designed to promote healing.

We began by assuring people that they would be safe in the experience, that nobody was going to trick them or hurt them. We asked them to relax, to breathe, and invited them to cuddle the stuffed animal, to look in the mirror and say something sweet to themselves. Then we asked them to write in the notebook, take the opportunity to say nice things about themselves, why they are special. It was a condensed version of the kinds of processes one goes through when healing from severe abuse. From the comments recorded in the notebook, it was clear this process was meaningful to many who experienced it.

Without Jael Greenleaf's workshops, I could not have conceived of this performance; I would have had no tools of recovery to share. Her workshops and my subsequent involvement in Al-Anon brought me into a more honest relationship to myself and led me to take more responsibility for my own life and self-care than I ever had before. It launched a process of integration within myself that strengthened and brought complexity to my artistic work. It opened the door to a return to individual therapy, which shortly led me back to incest work and a more profound layer of healing.

The process of recovery is, of course, a spiral; one moves closer and closer to the core. Each step is dependent on the one before.

Art Buddies: 1986–1989

It was in 1986, after the completion of *dis•abuse,* that I made the decision to quit performance art. I was having lunch with Mary-Linn Hughes at my favorite Mexican restaurant, Barragan's in Echo Park, when I made my announcement over quesadillas and guacamole.

"I really want to concentrate on my writing," I told her. "And I'll just never do it if I keep doing performances." I crunched an ice cube from my water glass between my molars to cool the effects of the salsa. "Performance is so extroverted. I need to learn to be more introspective if I want my writing to have depth."

Mary-Linn dipped a corn chip into the salsa. Her blonde curls bobbed in enthusiastic agreement. "I think that's a courageous decision," she affirmed, then talked a little about her own struggles to make her visual art.

It wasn't even a week after that lunch when, exiting the Golden State Freeway on my way to the Woman's Building, I found myself planning my next performance. It would be called *Heart Trouble,* I decided, and its subject would be my breakup with my lover more than two years earlier. I still wasn't over it, but I thought maybe this performance could be a ritual to finally dispel it. I would dissect, stage by agonizing stage, the grieving process. By the time I'd pulled into the parking lot on Aurora Street, I'd made plans to approach a venue and was preoccupied with making musical selections for the piece.

I confided this lapse to Mary-Linn when she stopped in to see me in my crowded office at the Woman's Building a few days later. "You heard me: I swore I was going to give it up. Then, all of a sudden, there I was, planning another one. I think performance is an addiction for me!" I concluded dramatically. Still relatively new to my twelve-step program, I tended to apply this model to everything in my life.

Mary-Linn's blue eyes twinkled. "I think I have a different idea about that," she began gently. "Wanna hear it?"

Of course I did. I buzzed Pam, our receptionist, and asked her to take messages for me, then went in search of a spot where Mary-Linn and I could have a lengthy and private conversation. The assistant who shared my office had already suffered far too much of my private life, the café was always in use, and the graphics studio was bustling with a printing class for teens. I finally pulled Mary-Linn into the back stairwell, where we perched on the dusty steps.

"You want to write," she began. "But you've been a lot more rewarded for your performance work. So you have to give up that gratification to do something that's more scary for you to do, which is to be alone with yourself and put words on paper."

I contemplated what she'd said as she continued, "You know I have a lot of trouble taking myself seriously as an artist."

I nodded. Mary-Linn is a photographer and installation artist, primarily interested in social art. Through her work in Reevaluation Counseling, she explained, she'd begun to develop an understanding of artists' oppression.

"We grow up in a society that is at best indifferent and at worst hostile to art. Like other marginalized groups, we're viewed with suspicion— we're crazy, we're not productive members of society, we're going to undermine its moral fabric." Her tone remained relaxed and gentle as she spoke, not furious as mine would have been, her eyes clear and intelligent. I'd seen this calm, open quality when we'd taught antiracism workshops together; it always helped put students at ease.

"Our work is ignored or criticized, censored or exploited," she continued.

"Or it's only valued if it generates a huge income," I added. I was resonating with her words. I felt the truth of them and my molecules were shifting to accommodate this new perspective. There was a flush in my body; I was getting excited.

"Like any oppressed group, artists growing up in this society internalize those values," she went on. "We begin to limit our expression—out of the fear that we'll be criticized or that nobody wants to hear what we have to say or that we'll be ignored or rejected. And if you're a woman, a person of color, a lesbian, those oppressions get compounded with the artists' oppression."

I sighed, and shifted my body on the step. I could feel the weight of all the accumulated personal baggage that could keep me from being the artist I wanted to be. I was galvanized at recognizing them for what they were, but at the same time overwhelmed at the magnitude of their effect. "So what do we do about it?" I asked, my voice more plaintive than I'd meant it to be.

Mary-Linn laughed with empathy. "I wanted to ask you if you'd like to become my art buddy." She smiled, suddenly shy.

"What is that?"

Mary-Linn explained that she'd recently attended some workshops on a process called No Limits. This process, itself an offshoot of RC, had been developed by artist Betsy Damon specifically to address the issues of women artists. "One of the things we talked about was ending isolation, and it was suggested that we each find an art buddy to work with."

Mary-Linn proposed that we talk to each other by phone every day for a time-limited period, perhaps ten minutes. Each of us would have an equal amount of time to talk while the other listened without responding. "We can talk about what we did that day for our art, or what got in the way of what we wanted to do, and what we plan to do for the next day."

This was yet another path opening before me—I could recognize them by now—an invitation to move forward into a new phase of growth. I accepted eagerly, and we made plans to talk the next night. I returned to my office with a renewed sense of hope.

The next night I perched on my bed in my Atwater Village guesthouse to call Mary-Linn. I was oddly nervous, and asked her again to explain exactly what we were supposed to do. "Just talk about how you're feeling about your art, what you want to do," she assured me. "Do you want to go first? I'll time you."

Each of us would be timed to ensure that we both got an equal amount of attention, so that the naturally more verbose (me) wouldn't dominate the more customarily reticent (her), and so the retiring one couldn't hide out and not fully participate. The harder thing for me to adjust to, however, was just listening, not interjecting comments or questions. I saw in this how hard it was for me to just receive another person without trying to intervene or help. My work in Al-Anon had already alerted me to this tendency in myself.

What I wasn't prepared for was how powerful these phone calls were for me. I hadn't realized the degree to which I believed that no one outside of me cared whether or not I made art, or how strong was the impact of that perceived indifference. When I reported to Mary-Linn that I had written that day, she would respond with delight; if I hadn't she was genuinely concerned. Suddenly, there was someone else on the planet who cared that I was creating, and I began to feel more urgency about my work.

After a few months we began to expand the format of our nightly conversations; after each had had her five minutes, we would take additional time to offer feedback and brainstorm trouble spots. Sometimes one of us would suggest an assignment for the other person to tackle.

One of the things I fretted over was that I'd become so visible as an organizer and administrator at the Woman's Building that no one thought of me as an artist.

"When people ask you what you do," Mary-Linn queried, "what do you tell them?"

"Usually I fumble around," I admitted. "I say, 'Well, I work at the Woman's Building, and I do outside consulting, and I make performance art, and I write.'" It sounded lame, even to myself.

"Why don't you just tell people you're a writer," she proposed, "and then tell them what you're working on now. Get them excited. If you're enthusiastic, they will be too. Turn them into allies for your work."

She made me practice this with her over and over, each time instructing me to "Sound more excited about it. 'I'm working on a play!!!'" she would model with exaggerated pitch, then urge me to repeat it.

This turned out to be remarkably effective. Within a couple of months, everybody who knew me or even met me once casually knew I was a writer working on a play. When I'd run into people at parties, they'd ask me, "How's your play coming?" Many volunteered resources—a dramaturg they knew, an agent who might be interested. I suddenly had a whole community of people invested in what I was doing. Not only was I shaping the outside perception of who I was, but also solidifying an identity for myself: I was a writer.

Mary-Linn was wrestling with different issues. A visual artist working in photography, installation, and social art, she'd gone to graduate school in a department heavy with Marxist ideology, and she'd become nearly immobilized by the fear of criticism. The internal critics were, naturally, more fierce than other people could ever be. I suggested that she try to personify those critical voices, figure out from whom they were emanating, visualize the people behind them. Which was her third-grade teacher, which the teaching assistant from the University of California–San Diego? Knowing the source of the criticism helps one know how to contend with it: which person was well meaning but misguided, which one was trying to shut me down? Knowing the answers to these questions, one can figure out how to talk back to the internal critics, whether to negotiate with them or banish them.

In addition to fear of criticism, Mary-Linn also found it almost impossible to ask for help. One time I had to fight to persuade her that she couldn't possibly assemble an entire installation all by herself with one leg in a cast, especially since the gallery was on the second floor with no elevator.

"When you give someone the chance to help," I insisted to her, "they feel good about it. People like to feel needed and useful. *And* they like the opportunity to be connected to an artist and an art project. It spices up their lives."

She did eventually call several friends to help her with that project. This was even more necessary than I'd imagined; the piece incorporated several dozen cords of firewood, and we had to create an assembly line to hand each log, person to person, up the steep flight of steps. Those of us who worked with her that day had fun; we were exhilarated by the socializing, by working together to achieve a common purpose, and by the involvement in an idea become manifest. We are not meant to create in isolation.

Another discovery for me in this process was my inability to take pleasure in my accomplishments. I could strive for months or years toward a goal, but once I achieved it, I felt hollow. There were many repetitions of the night when my conversation with Mary-Linn went like this:

Me: So, anyway, I found out I got a poem accepted to a magazine today (my tone is flat, without affect).

Mary-Linn (with screaming excitement): THAT'S TERRIFIC! Congratulations, Terry, that's so cool!

Me (even more vacant than before): Yeah, I guess.

She consistently nailed me on the difficulty I had with celebrating my successes. "If there'd been a rejection in that envelope," she challenged, "you'd be down in the dumps. Why can't you be happy for yourself?"

I twisted the phone cord around and around my fingers as I wrestled with her question. Maybe because no one ever got excited for me when I was a kid. Maybe because if I was excited the triumph would be taken away. Maybe I felt I didn't deserve it.

Mary-Linn was less interested in figuring it out than she was in changing it. She asked if I would be willing to accept direction from her. When I agreed, she said, "Okay, stand up, and jump up and down and tell me the news about your poem with as much excitement as you can!"

I balked. "I don't want to." A door slammed shut in my chest; it felt like the first time Jael Greenleaf had asked me to look into a mirror.

Mary-Linn's voice on the other end of the receiver stayed upbeat, reassuring. "I know. That's why you need to do it."

With resentment and as much sarcasm as I could muster, I jumped heavily a couple of times—THUD, THUD—and spat out, "Whoopee— I got my stupid poem published."

"Hooray!" she corrected gently, modeling the lilt she wanted to elicit from me. "I got published!" She was endlessly patient, making me repeat it until she was satisfied or until I called a halt to it. Usually this effort made me want to cry.

"That's okay," she'd encourage, "Discharge those feelings."

Over time, Mary-Linn and I could see the difference our Art Buddy relationship was making to each of us. She resumed making work almost immediately, experimenting with new media and finding opportunities to exhibit. By the end of 1986, I'd finished the play I'd been trying to work on for seven years, and got a staged reading produced at Celebration Theater. I was regularly writing short stories and poems, and sending them out for publication.

In 1988, I started writing a novel, and almost immediately ran into a crisis about not having time to work on it. It was Mary-Linn who suggested that I stop waiting for the four-hour chunk of uninterrupted time that never materialized, and commit myself to writing a half an hour a day. "Even *you* can find a half an hour," she challenged me.

Like many women artists, I struggled to arrive at the belief that my work deserved to take priority over all the other demands on my time and energy—the bottomless needs of the Woman's Building, my relationship, my friends, my endless community commitments. Mary-Linn posed this question: "What are you going to do today to put your art first?"

Sometimes the answer to that question meant going into work late, or not doing the laundry, not returning a phone call, or postponing dinner with a friend. It felt deliciously transgressive to "steal" time for my creative work, and over time I got really good at it. I finished the first draft of that novel in about six months, in increments of half an hour a day.

Mary-Linn and I remained art buddies for a period of three years. Over that time, our process deepened and changed. Some of our issues were put to rest; others continue to challenge us and we still call one another for help in thinking about them. In 1988, we offered a workshop at a statewide conference for artists funded by the California Arts Council, presenting our model of being art buddies, issues of artists' oppression, and some of the exercises we'd employed over the years.

Because the societal oppression of artists still persists, part of being an artist is to constantly work to dismantle it, internally and in the world. This process is one I impart to my students as an inevitable part of the artist's task: working to improve oneself as vigorously as one works to advance one's art. "If you had a child," I tell my women students, "and someone attempted to attack that child, to snuff the life out of it, you would fight to the death to protect your creation. It is no different with your artwork. No one else will defend it. No one else will fight for it if you don't."

One of the things they say in twelve-step meetings is that "there is no 'ed' at the end of the word 'recover,'" that one is always "recover*ing*," that the process of healing is never finished but requires constant participation in its maintenance. It is not dissimilar to what I tell my students about their lives as artists: that one is always on the journey, always risking more, digging deeper, never fully arriving at the destination.

I'd begun my journey as an artist thinking of my work as an escape from the damage of my history, a way to invent a new life, a new persona with which to live it. What my sojourn at the Woman's Building gave me were the tools of excavation and of reclamation, not to create a shinier surface, but to find the authentic self within, the one who lived beneath the wreckage of the past, waiting to be set free.

Some of the staff of WGC Typesetting and Design, (l. to r. seated: Jane Thurmond, Linda Nishio, Terry Wolverton, Laurel Beckman. Standing: Sue Ann Robinson, Judith Lausten, Susan King, Linda Preuss, Anne Gauldin, Sue Maberry.)

Survival
1981–1987

We must survive, not merely in the sense of
"living on," but in the sense of living beyond.
Surviving (from the Latin super plus vivere)
I take to mean living above, through,
around the obstacles thrown in our paths.
—Mary Daly,
from *Gyn/Ecology: The Metaethics of Radical Feminism*

I WAS THIRTEEN WHEN I BEGAN TO STEAL. BEFORE THAT, THERE'D BEEN THE occasional sweep of the pockets of my stepfather's pants, tossed carelessly over a chair while he sprawled, passed out from drinking, on the living room floor. Or the plucking of an extra bill from my mother's purse when she called, "Take a dollar and run to get me some cigarettes."

Stealing from strangers was different. Standing in the makeup aisles of Cunningham's Drugs, slipping tubes of mascara and lipstick into my coat pocket, caused my armpits to dampen. I moved on to stores outside the neighborhood, stealing clothes and makeup, candy and snack foods, books, records, cheap jewelry.

Although my life of petty crime was diagnosed as adolescent acting out by the middle-aged shrink in black fishnet stockings with whom I met every other Thursday instead of going to Home Ec, my teenage rebellion was soon to acquire political significance. By the 1970s, the antiwar movement grew louder and more vehement, and private property was just one more tool of oppression by the capitalist state. So said Eldridge Cleaver. So said Abbie Hoffman. By watching news clips of demonstrations on TV and reading underground newspapers bought at the local head shop, I picked up a smattering of Marxist analysis and a big helping of live-for-today hedonism and became convinced that my "liberation" of retail goods was a revolutionary act.

Three decades later, it's easier to see that this attitude was manipulated by the very system we were determined to undermine. When the Jefferson Airplane sang, "We're all outlaws in the eyes of Amerika," we thrilled to their rebellion, but overlooked the fact that their records were marketed, recorded, distributed, and reviewed by large media conglomerates. Abbie Hoffman wrote *Steal This Book,* but still cashed his royalty checks.

We wore blue jeans and tie-dyed shirts, Yardley cosmetics and Love perfume, advertised on TV with a Donovan song. The industries of fashion, entertainment, and media were busy appropriating youth culture faster than youth could create it, then selling it back to us. Our drug use, radical politics, and shoplifting were not only tolerated but anticipated by capitalism because these actions fueled the ambience for further sales.

Few of us understood this at the time. We embraced the image of the Outlaw, the lone individual who refuses to conform to the conventions of society and thus achieves greatness. As children we had thrilled to TV images of the outlaw of the Wild West, the tough and brutal man (inevitably) who lives outside the strictures of civilization and morality. We'd flocked to theaters to see Faye Dunaway and Warren Beatty heroize bank robbers Bonnie and Clyde; their bloody, bullet-riddled end only made us love them more. The Outlaw is a romantic notion deeply embedded into the fabric of American culture, though at the time we believed we were subverting that culture.

The Outlaw also appears as an icon of revolutionary movements: the dissident rises up against oppression and is declared a criminal by the State, is thrown in jail, tortured, executed. Or escapes to a life underground to live reviled, furtive, hunted at the margins of society.

Shoplifting may seem a trivial example, but it aptly demonstrates the sense of entitlement that fueled the youth culture of the sixties and early seventies. Although the wish for social justice was fiercely held, it existed alongside a drive for individual gratification — a "get it while you can," "rip-off" mentality — that was profoundly antisocial. Although this drive was often expressed in petty acts of rebellion — refusing to wait in line, smoking dope in public places, acting out in meetings when the agenda wasn't going one's way — such behavior revealed a larger set of attitudes that shaped the cultures of both the youth-based antiwar movement and the women's movement.

Feminism's embrace of the Outlaw has complex origins. Undeniably, feminists were marginalized and demonized by the system we denounced (this was especially true in the late sixties and early seventies, before our adversaries decided it was more effective to trivialize and make us ridiculous). In being vilified as "castrating bitches," "bulldykes," and "witches," we attained the status of principled dissidents, thus confirming (in our own minds, at least) the nobility of our cause, the evil of the forces aligned against us. At the same time, because so many of us had come of age as part of the youth culture of that time, we also fell in love with the image of the Outlaw, romanticizing our own capacities for danger and effectiveness.

In addition, feminism was a rebellion against being the Good Girls into which patriarchy had tried to mold us. Outlaws were definitely Bad Girls, and Bad Girls weren't boring; Bad Girls were free. As masculinist an icon as the Outlaw was, it accurately reflected our ambivalence about whether we wanted to *overthrow* men or *become* them, to dismantle their power or acquire it for ourselves. But it also infused our community with contempt for authority, disdain for rules, and a certain ethical sloppiness that made it harder to build an institution, a movement, an alternative culture.

Throughout the sixties and seventies, the nation was torn by conflict between those who sought to break down the social order and those determined to uphold it. There were those who believed that America's military defeat in Vietnam was directly related to the students who marched and demonstrated against that war. Their America had been weakened, not only by that defeat, but by the uprising of blacks and women and gays and young people threatening to displace straight white men from their rightful position at the top of the heap. When the economy turned downward in the 1970s, the long-held bitterness burst like a boil. In 1980, this resentment fueled the election of Ronald Reagan as president, an event that presaged the gleeful dismantling of many of the social gains of the previous two decades.

Like many of my sisters in the women's movement, I was ill prepared for the social convulsion that split the seventies from the eighties, as if the ever-expanding universe had, in a sudden spasm, contracted. That countercultural lifestyle I'd been so smug about living — easy bohemianism laced with anti-Establishment politics — was revealed to be largely dependent on a climate of economic prosperity and political largesse. I'd once lived grandly in a $125-a-month duplex; by 1981 even a single apartment was quadruple the price. A War on Drugs had been declared and suddenly your dealer was more likely to be a hardcore gang member than someone who just sold a little pot on the side to support his own use. Food stamps, subsidized housing, and free health care — these things all but disappeared.

The funding sources on which the Woman's Building had relied dried up as well. The CETA IV employment program, which had subsidized most of our staff salaries, including my own, was eliminated from the federal budget. This affected every nonprofit organization I knew about. We had also relied on grants from the National Endowment for the Arts to support our exhibitions and the Women Writers Series, and to provide scholarships to our educational programs. This federal program saw its budget sliced in half, and the funding became a thing of the past.

The policies of Reaganism cut a wide swath in the social fabric of Los Angeles. In my recollection it is as if overnight the streets of the city were flooded with desperate people layered in mud-caked, urine-soaked rags, clanking shopping carts over cracked pavement. Suddenly people had no homes. Suddenly there were beggars clutching cardboard signs on freeway ramps, shaking coffee cans at intersections. Haunted-eyed refugees from the U.S.-backed death squads of Central America huddled in bus shelters. All the while newspapers featured photos of women in ball gowns and precious gems.

It was a war of rhetoric. There was no more talk of "freedom and justice." Thinly disguised racism, class contempt, woman hating, and homophobia tapped into that festering well of post-Vietnam bitterness and rallied foot soldiers to the cause. The brilliant spin put on this backlash was that those who argued for social justice were themselves responsible for their condition, as if all we needed to do to dispel our oppression was to re-envision ourselves as winners.

In this climate of rising greed and evaporating compassion, it became more dangerous to dwell on the margins of society—the very region that white progressives once believed we had been so bold in choosing. The margins were being lopped off, and there was a ferocious scramble back to the relative safety of the middle. Poor was no longer glamorous and bohemian; in the New Economy, it was grubby and miserable, desperate. The Outlaw was no longer a romantic figure but a criminal to be expunged.

Some artists gave up their work for jobs in the film industry, commercial photography, graphic design. Some lesbians renounced their alternative lifestyles; I began to receive invitations to their heterosexual weddings. A number of women of my generation began to speak publicly about the "postfeminist" era, as if the goals of the women's movement had all been attained and now we could go home and relax. These women declared in print and at cocktail parties that they no longer wanted to see themselves as "victims" or "be so angry all the time." After all, as Cyndi Lauper warbled, "Girls just wanna have fun."

In the brave new world of the 1980s, those who could afford to go to college or graduate school were no longer drawn to an alternative feminist art school. These prospective students could read the signs; they were headed into MBA programs or other avenues that would ensure their professional success. As our funding shrunk along with our applicant pool, the decision was made to close the Feminist Studio Workshop in the summer of 1981. Tuitions had once provided a significant portion of the Woman's Building's budget. The program's closure left not only a vacuum of purpose but also a serious hole in the organization's revenue stream, and it began to seem as if the Woman's Building might have to close its doors.

In the summer of 1981, the board of directors attempted a last-ditch fund-raising effort, securing a feature story in the Sunday edition of the *Los Angeles Times Calendar* about the Woman's Building's fight for survival. It was hoped that the threat of loss would rally people to come forward with offers of money. This was an unfortunate miscalculation; although crisis fund-raising works well for social causes and political campaigns, it is anathema in the arts. People give money to the arts in order to feel good; they're motivated by achievement and success, not by impending disaster. Even a hint of failure drives away support. Not only was this article ineffective at generating income, it created a public perception that the Woman's Building was in fact already defunct.

In the wake of this failed effort, the Woman's Building faced two further blows. First came the resignation of Executive Director Suzanne Shelton; this had been a long time coming; since the inception of her tenure she had clashed with the board and many of the staff over issues of vision, policy, and management. She chafed under the constrictions she experienced as an African-American woman in the predominantly white organization, her efforts to exert real leadership thwarted. That her departure came in the midst of a budget crisis meant the organization could not afford to hire a replacement.

The second blow was the disintegration of the board of directors. In the late 1970s, there had been an effort to expand and professionalize the board in an effort to broaden the audience for the organization and attract new sources of financial support. By 1980, this all-woman board included an attorney, a public relations expert, and the program officer of the Playboy Foundation, who was always trying to give us money that we always refused. There existed great tension between those members who felt the need to pull the Building closer to the mainstream, and the founders and faculty who remained rooted in a more alternative vision. When the *Los Angeles Times* fund-raising appeal proved futile, this board just stopped meeting, as if the engine propelling them had thrown a rod.

No board, no executive director, no Feminist Studio Workshop, no funding for salaries or programs or our newsletter. If the Woman's Building had closed its doors in 1981, we would have been one of any number of the nonprofit organizations and activist groups that folded in the wake of the Reagan Revolution. The saving grace of the Building was a core of committed individuals — graduates of the FSW — who stepped forward to carry the organization into the brave new decade of the eighties. Prominent among these women were Sue Maberry, Cheri Gaulke, and myself.

Sue had been on staff since she'd completed the FSW. A woman with a practical bent, she had a great ability to get things done. In 1979, the Woman's Building had applied for, and received, a grant from the federal government's Fund for the Improvement of Post-Secondary Education (FIPSE), the focus of which was to develop a professional training program for women in graphic design. Part of the grant provided for the purchase of computerized typesetting equipment, on which women were to be trained for employment. As the financial outlook for the Building grew more dismal, Sue proposed to launch a profit-making typesetting business that could subsidize our artistic activities. She became the manager of this operation, WGC Typesetting and Design.[42]

Cheri had come to the FSW the year before I did. She was an accomplished performance artist, who'd worked both solo and collaboratively in

---

[42] The initials stood for Women's Graphic Center, which continued to operate as an artistic and educational program of the nonprofit Woman's Building.

the Feminist Art Workers and Sisters of Survival. She'd come out as a lesbian when she and Sue were both in the cast of *An Oral Herstory of Lesbianism;* they'd been lovers ever since. The strength of this bond fueled the commitment of each to the Woman's Building.

In the late 1970s, artists, in search of cheap rent and large spaces, had begun to locate in the industrial pockets of downtown in enough numbers that people had begun to notice. Although we were located north of Chinatown and not in the central hub of this artists' district, the Woman's Building was close enough for us to define ourselves as part of it. In the fall of 1981, Cheri proposed that the Building should sublet some of its space to artists for studios to generate some income. She was well situated to link us with the community of working artists looking for studio space, and agreed to take charge of this program.

For the most part we were stoic when we let go the second floor that had provided the Building an immense exhibition space and been the site of so many important shows, including the "Bedtime Stories" exhibit two years before, or the "Great American Lesbian Art Show" little more than a year earlier. We felt practical, businesslike, responsible. But when it became clear we would also have to rent out the third floor, sacrificing our glorious six-thousand-square-foot performance space, complete with skylights and home to so many dances and theatrical events, we were heartsick. It was especially hard on women like Cheri and myself, who had presented works there. What space would there be now for a *FEMINA,* or *An Oral Herstory of Lesbianism?*

As Sue began to establish the typesetting business, she hired Linda Preuss, who'd worked with Judy Chicago on *The Dinner Party,*[43] as marketing manager. Sue and Linda were opposites in both appearance and temperament; Sue was tall and large, stubborn and quick to anger. Linda

---

[43] *The Dinner Party* is an art installation by Judy Chicago and over four hundred collaborators; five years in the making, the piece is a monument to women's history.

was tiny and mercurial, given to worry. Sue had no previous experience running a business; Linda had managed a health food restaurant in Cincinnati, Ohio. Still, their combined vision and energy made WGC Typesetting and Design a success. Since my CETA-funded job had become extinct and I had no wish to leave the feminist environs of the Woman's Building, I learned to typeset.

This was a disastrous employment choice for me. My brain is well suited to the big picture, but I'm impatient and careless with detailed operations. Typesetting is entirely about details — that "y" is a fraction of an inch too far from the "a" that precedes it; the line under the title should be a hairline, not a half-point rule. The proofreader was constantly returning my work with blue-pencilled corrections decorating the margins of the strips of type. This was in the days before computerized typesetting, so one started from scratch each time. I'd get one thing right only to make a mistake on something I'd done correctly the time before.

It didn't help that I came to work stoned every day, smoking a joint during my morning freeway commute, taking breaks during the day to toke in the parking lot or on the loading dock, sometimes by myself, sometimes with another staffer. I was also badly affected by the constant stress of ever-shifting deadlines: the top priority annual report that needed to be done by noon could be supplanted by three rush jobs that walked in the door at ten, ten-thirty, eleven, but the noon job still needed to be picked up on time.

Sue and Linda were, for the most part, patient with me. My longevity at the Woman's Building inspired trust. As often as possible they found non-typesetting tasks for me to perform: writing copy for client projects, developing ad campaigns, writing grants for the Woman's Building, and eventually, working to revive the membership program of the organization.

I also was put in charge of bookkeeping for the business. This meant that every Friday afternoon at about three P.M., I would sit down with the checkbook, a small pile of checks to be deposited, and a larger stack of bills to be paid. As the other staff left and the sun went down, Sue and Linda and I would remain, fretting about which bills to pay, which we could defer, and what to do about the shortfall. Sue and Linda often disagreed; "That client already gave us the check for their job; we need to pay the printing bill." "But the printer will wait another thirty days. The landlord won't." As they shouted between their two offices, I would play quietly with the keypad of my calculator, the only child of bickering parents. It was often seven-thirty or eight before we dragged ourselves, spent, to the parking lot.

As a small, undercapitalized, woman-owned business, WGC Type-setting and Design never did contribute large amounts of revenue to the nonprofit Woman's Building, but its existence allowed staff to be hired, like myself and Sue, who could also work on Woman's Building programs. It also provided free graphic design services to those programs. And the presence of those employees and clients lent energy to the Building at a time when program activities were scant.

We consolidated the Woman's Building operations onto the first floor: a thousand-square-foot combination gallery/performance space, staff offices, a conference room, a kitchenette and lunchroom, the facilities of WGC Typesetting and Design, and the letterpress studio of the Women's Graphic Center. Our rental program brought about a further shift in our way of operating, because as landlords we could not legally rent only to women artists; thus, men became tenants at the Woman's Building. Even a few years earlier this would have been the subject of intense and bitter debate; now we were too desperate for revenue to worry about ideological purity.

To supplement my meager paycheck, I began to work as a freelance consultant, drawing on my skills in grantwriting and publicity and my years of working with feminist communication processes. I began in these areas, but soon broadened my practice to include marketing, planning, budgeting, board development, and employee management. How did I know how to do these things? Without ever having been trained in business, I found I had an intuitive understanding of it and a facility for identifying problems, posing solutions, and developing strategies for implementation. My clients were other arts and social service organizations, as well as small businesses and individual artists. As I took more responsibility for the survival of the Woman's Building, I acquired skills that I could bring to my clients; in turn, the tools I learned from my consulting work made me a more valuable asset to the Woman's Building.

Early in 1982, Sue called a meeting with Cheri and Linda and myself to address the organization's need for a functioning board of directors. Frustrated and disappointed by the defection of the previous board, she had decided that this was the inevitable result of the inclusion of "outsiders," that is, women who did not share the founders' vision. She proposed to re-create a board that would be composed of women with a longtime history with the Building.

I'd been working with my anti-racism group long enough to know that xenophobia would not be in the long-term interests of the Building. I could also see that the immediate crisis required a group that would be devoted enough to see the Woman's Building through hard times, and who could serve as volunteer staff until programs could get re-funded, so I supported Sue's plan despite my reservations. We each contributed names to the list; most of them were former FSW students or women who had otherwise been active with the Building. Sue also asked each of us to join the board.

As the decade's shift had been drastic, so too was our tumultuous change. In the course of half a year, we'd gone from being hippie Outlaw artists to being landlords, business managers, and board members. I suppose one might say we grew up. For our love of the Woman's Building, our commitment to its vision of feminist art, we entered a world of balance sheets, grants*man*ship, and marketing. It was a turn of events rich with irony.

My own willingness to make this transition was rooted in the deep bond I'd formed with the institution and its vision; no other structure had been so embracing of the totality of me—woman, artist, lesbian, crackpot, seeker. No other system had been so nurturing of my development; the

Woman's Building had become my family, and I was as loyal as if my bloodline could be traced back for generations.

The women's movement in the United States was changing. Politically, the movement was reeling from backlash, most evident in the failure, after a ten-year campaign, to ratify the Equal Rights Amendment. This kind of defeat, coupled with the infighting that had always plagued the movement, had resulted in burnout. The restructuring of the economy meant that every-one needed to work more; there was less time to devote to unpaid activism. The shifts in social values put progressives on the defensive: why should one care about the plight of others, why shouldn't one just try to get as much as possible for oneself? This was the new *zeitgeist*. A younger generation of les-bians embraced the code of pleasure seeking and transgression, a new version of the Outlaw ethic. A new crop of female academics embraced postmod-ernism and poststructuralism,[44] profoundly questioning and severely cri-tiquing the tenets of seventies feminism. They were perhaps most successful in dismantling the notion that there might be any qualities held in common by women as women, a notion that was dismissed as *essentialist*.

In the face of such an altered social environment, those of us who remained at the Woman's Building needed to reenvision it, to forge new purpose and programs that would serve the needs of our audience and at the same time prove able to attract funding support. And we needed to redefine and broaden that constituency to serve more women.

We wanted to continue to present women's art in various forms — visual, performance, literary, video. But we needed to ask ourselves what services we were providing to those artists: a place to show, an audience to view it, the potential for sales, the possibility of critical review, a catalog

---

[44] Poststructuralism contests the belief in a predictable order, a ground of being, an intrinsic meaning, a stable truth. It asserts that there is no essence to the self, that one's identity is merely a construction of social habits. Poststructural feminists challenged the notion that there were inherent qualities that were common to women as women, which had been the basis of much of the seventies women's movement.

to document it? A decade after the women's art movement had begun in Los Angeles, we could no longer assume that a woman artist would be grateful just to have a wall on which to hang her work. In some ways our movement had succeeded; women artists were in galleries all over town. What could we offer? The art scene in Los Angeles was developing, and most women artists were working toward carving a place for themselves within it.

In its founding, the Woman's Building had sought to step outside the discourse of the mainstream art world from which women were largely excluded. Now we needed to rejoin the conversation. In the 1970s, we had been a women's organization about art; in the 1980s we became an arts organization about women.

The content of feminist art was changing too, no longer exclusively concentrated on women's condition. As the political landscape became more repressive, artists turned activists for a variety of causes—the increased threat of nuclear war, U.S. intervention in Central America, the environment, gay and lesbian rights. Our understanding of oppression grew more sophisticated as we began to perceive patterns and linkages between women, people of color, political exiles, immigrants, poor people, gays and lesbians. Whereas once we might have believed that ending sexism would transform the world, we now saw oppression as a web with many strands that would require alliance, not separatism, to untangle.

We rented an office in the Building to CISPES (the Committee in Solidarity with the People of El Salvador) and were placed under FBI surveillance. Through Cheri's connection, we became a sponsor of Target L.A., a citywide antinuclear arts festival. My own 1984 performance, *Me and My Shadow,* addressed racism from a feminist perspective. When an official in the Reagan administration was quoted as saying that all we needed to survive nuclear war was "enough shovels to go around" (presumably because we could dig shelters), the political cartoonist Paul Conrad published a cartoon in the *Los Angeles Times* that depicted a graveyard, the crosses made of shovels. Artist Marguerite Elliott, a former member of the FSW, re-created Conrad's shovel graveyard on the lawn of city hall to demonstrate the threat posed by the administration's dangerous policies. A group of performance artists from the Woman's Building, including Sue and Cheri, Nancy Angelo, and others, constituted themselves as the Sisters of Survival; dressed in nun's habits the colors of the rainbow (nuns used as a metaphor for sisterhood), they staged a performance in Elliott's environment and carried their antinuclear art activism to Europe.

At the Woman's Building, we were grappling with our own survival. We needed to reestablish our presence as a public institution that was addressing contemporary concerns. Like any reformed Outlaw, we suddenly felt the need to rehabilitate our image. I joined the Public Relations Committee[45] to help fashion our image and expand our visibility. One of the activities we launched was an awards ceremony to honor women artists. The Vesta Awards were named after the Roman goddess who was keeper of the flame, the woman dedicated to her work. Although later the event became our annual fund-raiser, in that first year, 1982, the event was free, and held at the Building. We awarded a group of prominent women in a variety of disciplines—among them artists Judy Baca, Betye Saar, and June Wayne—who'd had connections to the organization. In doing so we were carrying forward one of the principles of feminist education, the promotion of female role models. It was this aspect that was meaningful to those who attended year after year; artists who received the award were genuinely honored to be recognized and audiences were heartfelt in their celebration of these women.

We survived to celebrate our tenth anniversary in the fall of 1983, relieved and grateful to have reached that marker. Sue had raised funds and masterminded the renovation of the first floor to be more welcoming to the public and more suitable for its new uses. I undertook the publication of a tenth-

---

[45] Anne Gauldin, Cheri Gaulke, Eloise Klein Healy, and Michele Kort were the other founding members.

anniversary booklet to document our history and promote our continued existence. To cover the cost of printing I sold advertising, borrowing the model I'd learned from my consulting work with the *Women's Yellow Pages.*

In writing and editing this publication, I shaped a version of the Woman's Building as I wanted it to be perceived; I mastered the art of "spin." Not that the version was untruthful, but I questioned what to include, exclude, emphasize? What's for public consumption, and which public? In an upbeat version of the history of our first decade, I chose to emphasize the accomplishments, eliminate the hard times we'd undergone. Such considerations hadn't been part of the previous decade when we just *were* our outrageous, irreverent selves, and didn't worry about who might not like it.

Still, I continued to paint a version of the organization as alternative, crackpot. I included a photo from *An Oral Herstory of Lesbianism,* as well as one from a Feminist Art Worker's performance, *Heaven or Hell,* which captures performers Nancy Angelo, Cheri Gaulke, and Laurel Klick in leopard-print tunics, each with one breast exposed, in the style of the Amazons.

Though we'd made it to our anniversary, board meetings were full of Sue's anguished inducements to raise money for the organization. Nobody wanted to do it. We all had excuses; I was no exception. I didn't know anyone with money; I couldn't possibly ask for money; people with money had values antithetical to mine and to the organization's.

Women have issues with money. Ours was the first generation in which it was assumed across the board that a woman would earn her own. In the middle and upper classes, money came from fathers and husbands, and usually at the cost of dignity or autonomy. In the working and poverty classes, women know scarcity. We hadn't been trained to know about generating money or having to be responsible for it. Each board meeting became a litany of why we *couldn't possibly* raise funds.

I finally grew impatient with all the hand wringing and lack of forward motion. It wasn't premeditated, but one day in a meeting, I found myself annoyed with everybody's excuses, including my own, and raised my hand.

In a weary voice, I announced, "Okay, here's what I'll do. I will commit to raise enough money for a year's salary for a fund-raiser. Then we can hire someone and she can worry about it." There was an outbreak of applause. Sue beamed at me with satisfaction and everyone else regarded me with guilty relief; this meant they might be off the hook.

Nancy Angelo had been fund-raising for the Gay and Lesbian Center and suggested I contact the James Irvine Foundation, which employed a female program officer who she thought might be sympathetic. I called and made an appointment. This was new terrain for me; not once in my adult life had I tried to dress up and present myself in a corporate environment. The culture of philanthropy is conservative. Sitting in the posh environs of her Newport Beach office, I felt I'd landed on an alien planet. Her coifed hair, manicure, trim suit, and gold jewelry were of a different culture than my lack of make-up, my bright yellow eyeglass frames, my plastic shoes — those were years when I would not wear leather and my car, an ancient Audi, sported a bumper sticker that said "Vegetarians for Reggae." Pants hid my unshaven legs.

Still, I made a convincing case for the Woman's Building and its new mission: to provide professional opportunities to women artists, professional education to women in the arts, and an experience of women's art to a wide and diverse audience. We'd softened the edge of counterculture; no longer did we promote an alternative to the mainstream but instead claimed to provide a way for those who'd been marginalized to enter it. This was a very eighties message. The program officer worked with me to craft our grant proposal, so well that the foundation not only agreed to fund us, but gave us $10,000 above what I'd requested. I'd hit a grand slam my first time at bat.

We soon realized that, as dedicated and comforting as a board of "home-girls" had been, we were going to need to expand that network if we hoped to raise significant money. As I quipped at a meeting, "We all know the same ten people, and they're all poor." Though it made Sue uneasy, fearing that "outsiders" would threaten what we were working so hard to rebuild, we began to recruit more professional women to the board again, non-artists, in some cases women who might not have identified with the word "feminist." As new members came aboard we asked them to recommend their associates, and slowly built a board that could move the organization to the next step.

This was how we happened to recruit a powerhouse of a woman named Hermine Harman, who not only joined the board but became its president. She had been a social worker and had lived in Vienna with her husband, but returned to the States when he was in poor health. Hermine was restless, seeking a vehicle into which to pour her considerable energy, and the dual cause of women and art captured her imagination.

Hermine was ultra in all things. She was exuberant in her passions and intractable in her opinions. Her long hair was professionally tinted, her makeup elaborate. She wore shocking pink silk sequined jogging suits and lots of jewelry. Although she represented a different style and class than most of us at the Building, she was the dream board president; she treated it like a full-time job and personally identified with the organization's success. Hermine's involvement in the Woman's Building unleashed her own desire to express her creativity, which gave her a personal stake. She was a gracious hostess and a marvelous cook, and she frequently invited the board to gatherings in her home.

In 1984, in the midst of helping Sue to draft a job description for the newly funded position of development director, I realized that when someone was hired for the job she would become my boss. I bristled at the thought of taking direction from someone whose job I'd made possible, and I finally gave in to Sue's request that I take the position.

On Nancy Angelo's advice, I made it a condition of my contract that Hermine and I both be sent for a weeklong training at The Fundraising School, then based in San Francisco. There we spent five days immersed in the theory and practice of fund-raising, absorbing everything from what you say on the envelope of a direct mail appeal to how to get someone to remember your organization in his or her will. At night we sampled some of San Francisco's finest cuisine; next to art, Hermine loved food. During this week we shared a hotel room, kept an intense schedule of classes; I teased her about how she'd packed far more luggage than she could carry, and confided in her about the latest ups and downs of my turbulent love life. This served not only to bond us personally, but also provided me with an ally who understood what the board needed to do to support the Woman's Building. We made a good team; in the years between 1985 and 1988, the organization doubled its annual budget to $300,000.

Though I had no lack of resistance to it, I found the process of asking for money to be one of the most empowering things I had ever done. It involved strategy, to consider the personality of a prospective donor and find the motivation that would make her likely to want to give to the Building. It called on my social skills, my ability to find commonality and forge a bond with someone quite different from myself. It required me to confront all of my feelings of worth or lack thereof, all of my sense of deserving or not deserving, in order to look a prospect in the eye and ask her to write a check. A big check. When someone did so, I was thrilled, but even when she said no, I came away exhilarated that I'd been gutsy enough to ask.

Performing my job well, however, required holding my nose and taking positions that were sometimes personally repugnant to me for the good of the institution. "People can embrace the concept of women's art much more easily than they can feminism," I found myself arguing to the board. "And 'feminist' is such an ambiguous term—can't we just say 'women's art' in our promotional material?" The more mainstream members of the board were nodding enthusiastically, wanting to reach a broader audience, attract more donors; the more radical members stared at me as if I were Judas.

Although no one ever made the suggestion that lesbians at the Woman's Building should go into the closet, and while lesbian artists continued to present their work in our space, overt lesbian content disappeared from the public presentations of our history.

There were women who accused us of selling out, but I believed that the survival of the institution was more important that political purity. More, perhaps, than other women on the staff, I was interacting with the mainstream on a daily basis. I was the one schmoozing the media to give us coverage. That was me, riding in the limos of prospective donors, or in one case, on her yacht, despite my extreme seasickness. And trying to maintain my calm while arguing our case to granting organizations. I couldn't forget the woman in one corporate giving program who pointed her finger at a photograph printed in the tenth-anniversary booklet. It was the photo of the "WILL YOU HELP?" poster—seven naked women, from youth to middle age, with regular bodies, lumpy or zaftig or scrawny. The flyer was made to solicit donations of clothing to our thrift store, and our nakedness demonstrated how badly we needed them. I was praying the program officer would not recognize me as one of the models. Still, the funder's lip curled in disgust as her index finger thumped the printed page. "Do you really expect us to support *that?*"

My wardrobe changed. I never did adopt the formal navy blue suit (peach linen with a *very* short skirt was as close as I ever came), but I did refamiliarize myself with nylons and pumps. Polka-dot pumps, to be sure, fuschia suede high heels. It was a new world to me. After a decade of lesbian feminism, I had to be pulled aside by a board member and counseled that one should really wear a bra when meeting a prospective funder. And, presumably, underwear. And then I shaved my legs.

The whole construction of my seventies persona and politics began to give way. I rationalized my inner conflict by assuring myself that such steps were necessary to ensure the continued existence of the Woman's Building.

These transformations were abetted by the woman I was seeing at the time, an executive recruiter named Vicki Yerman, whom I'd met when she joined the board. Vicki was a lifelong lesbian and a confirmed butch. She'd bypassed both the hippie and the feminist eras, which she considered travesties for the cause of femininity. She took on the project of trying to recivilize me, but with only partial success. A Jewish woman, Vicki's personal motto was "speak Yiddish, but dress British," and it frustrated her no end that I disdained the polo shirts and khakis she tried to press on me.

"No way," I told her, when she'd bring home these purchases; granted, I might need to appear more professional, but I was not about to go preppy. I was still an artist.

I was considerably more receptive to her efforts to cultivate my femme persona. It was she who bought me a black slip. For her I bleached my hair platinum and adopted red, red lipstick. Although I hungered for the attention these steps elicited from her, the Svengali aspect of our relationship was a source of ceaseless conflict; I grew defensive, worn out by her constant effort to change me.

However, her cultivation did serve to prepare me for the day I paid a visit to the city councilman who represented the Woman's Building's district; the city was trying to disallow parking on Aurora Street, the only available parking for blocks. We knew we would never get the public to attend our programs if they had to park at a distance away in this desolate neighborhood. I'd been advised that "The councilman"—a gentleman in his nineties—"rarely says no to cleavage." It's for the Woman's Building, I told myself as I hooked my push-up bra and wore a dress with a plunging neckline to the meeting. I made sure to lean over as I shook his hand at the beginning and end of the meeting. He smiled and told his aide, "Take care of this young lady." We heard no more about not parking on Aurora Street.

"Good job!" Vicki beamed when I reported the outcome of the meeting.

"Fund-raising," I grumbled in response. "The world's oldest profession."

These were not the only changes required of me. Vicki and other board members introduced me to a number of people with the capacity to give significant money to the organization. It was my job to socialize with them, introduce them to the Building, establish a relationship with them. I found myself attending banquets in hotels where a suite cost more than my monthly salary. Sometimes I would park blocks away rather than face the disdain of the valet for my battered vehicle. I visited designer houses in which the bathroom was bigger than my entire guest cottage.

I could remember feeling "less than" in grade school and high school. I knew kids whose Barbies had whole wardrobes, kids who had bikes, whose families took trips to Europe or Disneyland. My mother had told me a story about attending a Parents' Night at my school when I was in the fifth grade. When introduced to a neighbor, my mother was regarded with, "Oh, yes, your husband works at the *garage,* doesn't he?" in a tone of amused scorn. There was no place for these memories when I needed to woo a donor. The lumpy girl from Detroit needed to be put away; in her place was constructed someone who could appear at home stepping out of a limo.

It also provided me the opportunity to get to know some people with wealth, to witness their human struggles, to stop viewing them as "the other." They were like everybody else I knew — some enlightened, some self-deluded, some callous, others kind. For some, it seemed their wealth was a kind of restriction: I felt sorry for the woman who was afraid to take the subway in New York, for the woman who'd never held a job and thus had no faith in her own competence. My interactions with these privileged women began to drain my class resentment; I grew more satisfied with my own self-sufficiency.

I also helped the organization to redefine its relationship to men. In the seventies the Woman's Building had been a separatist organization, to the point that women who brought men to events had sometimes been treated rudely, and I had no doubt had a hand in perpetuating this. But survival in the political climate of the eighties called for coalition, not isolation. In a 180-degree reversal of my previous sentiments, I argued strenuously that we needed to build connections to men who might support our mission. I made a case for putting men on the board, but was voted down. I did get permission to appoint men to the Advisory Committee, and include their names on our letterhead. In the latter part of the decade, I even spearheaded an exhibition called "Gentlemen's Choice," in which prominent male curators and collectors were invited to select a woman artist to include in the show. The resulting exhibit was not in itself extraordinary; the artists chosen were for the most part already known to us. But it was the first time men had had direct input into a program of the Woman's Building, and not everyone was thrilled with this.

"Maybe it's not worth surviving if we have to sell our souls," Sondra Hale, one of our board members, suggested to me. She had been chair of a progressive women's studies program at California State University–Long Beach; she and several of her colleagues had been fired when the Religious Right decided to challenge feminism at a state-funded university. The ensuing lawsuit had dragged on for years, but Sondra had not lost her rigorous commitment to radical politics. She was often appalled by the assimilationist stances I took, but luckily, she also liked and respected me. Although we frequently clashed in meetings, I was grateful for her presence on the board, reminding us of our core values.

But I fervently believed it *was* worth surviving, even if we had to change the packaging — the language we used to talk about our mission, the fashion we adopted, the company we kept. The Woman's Building seemed to me now less a utopia and more an icon, *the* institution that symbolized the vision of women's art. What would become of that vision if the Woman's Building failed? I felt the weight of personal responsibility to make sure this did not happen.

The success of our programs convinced me that I was right. Our exhibitions, workshops, and events were well and enthusiastically attended. We had begun to attract a more culturally diverse community of artists, and our audiences reflected this as well. Sue had begun to develop funding to commission artists to produce new works. The first such project, "Madre Tierra," funded twelve Chicana artists and writers, under the direction of artist Linda Vallejo, to produce broadsides that were printed in the Women's Graphic Center studio. In the 1983 project, "Private Conversations / Public Announcements," ten artists—including Betye Saar, Alexis Smith, and Qris Yamashita—were chosen to produce a limited edition print reflecting the artist's personal connection to a public site in Los Angeles. This theme—the links between personal and public life and women's relationship to each sphere—had been an important source of exploration since the early days of the Woman's Building. These posters were exhibited at the Bridge Gallery in Los Angeles City Hall. Almost twenty years later, I still display artist Robin Valle's whimsical, shocking pink rendition of the La Brea Tar Pits, with its rendering of prehistoric bones, on the wall of my writing center.

I held a special enthusiasm for those projects that encouraged the production of new works of art. In 1986, the project "Cross Pollination" commissioned twenty-two artists to produce posters addressing issues of their cultural heritage. Artist Patssi Valdez created a glorious tribute to Latinas in her photographic portrait of writer Sylvia Delgado, ringed by gladiolus blossoms. Artist Cyndi Kahn and poet Michelle T. Clinton created and illustrated a tapestry exploring the state of relations between the Jewish and African-American communities. Suzan Ocona combined image and text in a moving statement about her own experience of homelessness. As part of our commitment to help artists expand their audiences, complete sets of posters were distributed free to eighty arts and community organizations across the United States, along with information about how to purchase posters from the artists.

In our efforts to cultivate a mainstream audience for women's art, we didn't limit ourselves to gallery exhibitions. We also engaged in literary publication projects, including *Manteniendo El Espiritu,* edited by Aleida Rodríguez, and *Women for All Seasons,* edited by Wanda Coleman and Joanne Leedom-Ackerman. In 1987, we launched a show on local public access cable stations, "The Woman's Building Presents," which screened women's video art, both tapes created by artists directly connected to the Woman's Building and other tapes submitted to us by artists.

To engage in the critical dialogue about art, we also sponsored two conferences, "The Way We Look/The Way We See: Art Criticism for Women in the Nineties," which explored the various critical theories in use at the time (1988) and their implications for women's art. In 1989, "Three Generations of Black Women Writers" presented the evolution of concerns and literary styles in the work of African-American women writers. Both projects were cosponsored with other institutions in an effort to broaden their impact.

Hundreds of exhibitions, workshops, performances, and arts projects were fostered and presented at the Woman's Building during the 1980s. With the exception of helping to secure the funding, I was responsible for only a handful of them, although I was frequently called on to troubleshoot or brainstorm; every activity at the Woman's Building was collaborative.

In addition to these programs, there were a number of special events designed to promote the Woman's Building as a whole, and I was primarily responsible for these. Perhaps the most visible was the Vesta Awards, which by mid-decade was drawing more than 500 attendees and netting in excess of $20,000. This event gave us the opportunity to reach into many communities and across numerous disciplines; among the awards given to distinguished women artists were those to surrealist and ceramicist Beatrice Wood, WPA photographer Marion Post Wolcott, designer Ray Eames, and actress Beah Richards. We also gave awards to numerous women who were renowned within a particular community, culture, or arts discipline, and it was thrilling to shine a brighter spotlight on these unsung heroines. When a woman received her award, she was handed a tropical flower, a four-foot stalk of scarlet ginger or a tumescent proteus. This had been originally been Bia Lowe's inspired notion, and for years it was our ritual to meet at four A.M., haggard and morning-breathed, at the flower mart on the day before the event to carefully select the perfect bloom for each winner.

Although everyone loved the Vesta Awards, some were uneasy that the event was geared to a wealthy audience. When a board member suggested we should cut the ticket price, I resisted vigorously; it was already the lowest priced banquet event I knew about. When it was suggested that we make some tickets available for free to low-income women, I countered that the board should donate money to subsidize tickets. Built into the culture of the organization was a deep ambivalence about money and in trying to do my job I often ran up against it.

In 1986, Hermine suggested a different sort of fund-raiser, one that would involve the many prominent women chefs of Los Angeles. Hermine was a food enthusiast and knew that many moneyed people in Los Angeles shared her passion; I fretted that the event was too far outside the mission of the Woman's Building. With the board president having her heart set on it and willing to commit the energy to make it happen, "Food Is Art/Art Is Food" was launched, a combination tasting party and art exhibit. This event was controversial for some of the more politicized members of the board, so clearly was it geared to privileged interests. But the organization needed to attract the attention and support of wealthy donors; we could not make it on the annual $25 contributions of the devoutly radical.

"Food Is Art" captured the imagination of another board member, Betty Ann Brown, an art historian who was at the time married to the food critic for the *Los Angeles Herald Examiner.* She and her husband had recently completed a book about women chefs, and Betty was instrumental in enlisting a number of them in the event.

Betty had a passion for art and a profound commitment to feminism; although she was relatively new to Los Angeles, she intuitively understood the culture and mission of the Building. It was she who proposed that the Woman's Building sponsor art tours to other cities and make these available only to donors. This would, in theory, induce more people to become major donors and would reward those who had already given significant contributions. She proposed to design and lead an inaugural trip to Santa Fe, combining tours of museums and private collections with fine dining in the area. This fostered further dialogue among board members about the ethics of sponsoring an event that was *only* open to people who'd given large donations, though it should be said that within the funding structure of the Woman's Building, a "donor" was anyone who'd given $100 or more. The majority of the board, however, was enthusiastic about the idea, and five of them actually came on the tour.

Vicky was one of them and I, as development director, naturally had to come along to court donors. We bickered through most of the trip. She could not seem to contain her criticism of me in public as well as private settings, and I was especially humiliated by it in front of the rest of the group. I was there as a representative of the Building and I needed to present a professional face to the group, even if that face was blotchy with weeping. We'd skirmished all afternoon before the night we went to the Santa Fe Opera; I cried through the entire production of *Madame Butterfly,* and tried to pass it off as having been affected by the performance. During the mid-eighties, I spent much of my time trying to present a convincing front while falling apart inside, a stance that seems emblematic of the times. It's ironic that during this time I was engaged in recovery processes to gain greater authenticity, but my chosen professional life required me to cultivate a more impenetrable façade.

Within myself, I struggled to balance my artistic soul with my administrative brain, my alternative vision with the *realpolitic* of the times, the competence of my work with the emotional wreckage of my personal life. The Woman's Building wrestled with its countercultural roots and the mandate to build itself into an institution, its mission to serve the marginalized and the concurrent need to court the privileged. The decade of the eighties seemed to heighten those contradictions. And always, there was the challenge to create a context in which any women could imagine herself.

Cofounder Sheila de Bretteville had always envisioned the Woman's Building as a crossroads, a place in which women from different sectors of society could gather and meet. Heterosexual and lesbian, trust fund babies and welfare mothers, academics and politicos and artists—ironically, perhaps it was in the eighties that this vision came closest to being fulfilled. The Hmong weavers were exhibiting in the gallery while poet Gloria Alvarez coaxed Central American refugee women to write their stories in their native language. Later that night, a champagne donor reception would fill the pot-holed Aurora Street with Porsches and BMWs. And no, these groups did not necessarily rub elbows in the small café, or chat while standing in line for the bathroom, but they did walk through a common door, stand under the same roof.

The Woman's Building was not the same organization it had been in the seventies, but neither was the society that contained it. By mid-decade, the Building was thriving, thanks to its dedicated board and to the extraordinary commitment of its staff—Sue, Linda, Cheri, myself, and others. Artists, outlaws, insurgents—in reshaping the institution we'd had to reinvent ourselves into glossier, more competent, less reckless versions of who we'd been. I'd changed my wardrobe, reconstituted my rhetoric, and replaced my substance abuse with workaholism, the socially acceptable addiction of the new era.

The redistribution of wealth caused by Reagan's policies and the flush of prosperity it brought to some fostered a new vigor in the art world. During the 1980s, the art community of Los Angeles came into its own. The 1984 Olympic Arts Festival lent a new international focus to the scene; new galleries opened and nonprofit arts organizations proliferated. The Community Redevelopment Agency funded a few high-profile projects to locate artists and arts venues in the downtown area, and the city developed a Master Plan for the Arts. When I wasn't courting donations I was trying to build connections between the Woman's Building and this newly invigorated art world. I served on grant panels for the city and county arts agencies, attended both local and national arts meetings and receptions, and was invited to join the public policy committee of the

California Confederation of the Arts and the board of the Los Angeles Fringe Festival. I was opinionated and not afraid to speak an unpopular viewpoint, a quality my colleagues grew to appreciate. I began to be looked to for leadership; my opinions were respected.

I was surprised by this not because I thought myself incapable, but because a decade earlier I'd pledged to place myself beyond the pale of influencing the mainstream — except, of course, by subversion or revolution. Now I found myself with a working knowledge of Robert's Rules of Order, and local journalists kept my number in their Rolodexes to call for commentary on cultural issues. Who had I become? I scarcely recognized myself.

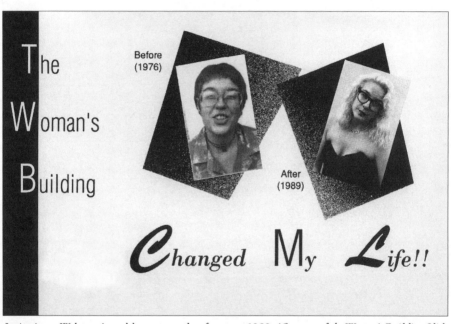

The Woman's Building

Before (1976)

After (1989)

Changed My Life!!

Invitation to Wolverton's good-bye party and performance, 1989. (Courtesy of the Woman's Building Slide Archive)

The Vortex
1987–1991

*That world! These days it's all been erased
and they've rolled it up like a scroll and put it
away somewhere. Yes, I can touch it with my
fingers. But where is it?*
—Denis Johnson,
from "Emergency, " in *Jesus' Son*

MAYBE THE BURDEN OF ALL THAT RESPECTABILITY WAS TOO MUCH FOR ME TO contain. Maybe I'd sunk my high heels into too much plush carpeting, squeezed my thighs into too many pairs of pantyhose, or taken one too many donor lunches.

Or maybe I knew I'd reached the end of what could be accomplished through dedication, seduction, cunning, and a fourteen-hour workday. How else to explain why I was receptive to Kamaka Restivo?

Kamaka was in her early forties, tall and big-boned, red-complected. She lacked the gloss of L.A. eighties' style, her wardrobe containing neither the hard-edged black uniform of the art world nor the eye-searing neon colors that underscored just how much *fun* we were having here in California in the Reagan years. She wore simple pastels that seemed beyond the reach of fashion. She could have easily passed for a housewife from Des Moines until you noticed her eyes, which almost glowed with focused intensity. Her simple, unassuming manner belied the fervor with which she approached her spiritual work.

I first met Kamaka when she enrolled in one of the writing workshops I was teaching at Connexxus Women's Center/Centro de Mujeres. I wasn't sure about her sexual orientation; she may have signed up for a workshop at the lesbian center simply because it was free. I'm usually open with my students about other aspects of my life, so it wasn't surprising that she knew about my work at the Woman's Building. It's likely that she over-heard me complaining in class about some aspect of my job. Not long after that, I received a letter from her, a proposal really, about a metaphysical technique in which she was trained and with which she believed she could help the Woman's Building and me.

In many respects, by the fall of 1985, the Woman's Building was more successful than it had ever been — our budget was healthy, our board ded-icated, our programs flourishing, and our reputation solid. We knew, how-ever, that these victories could not be sustained and that we could not fully attain the recognition and stability we sought without making a move from our present location. North Spring Street was too remote, perceived as inhospitable, too isolated from other arts activities. One would never just *be* in that part of town, never drop in at the Woman's Building on a whim. Although there was now a thriving downtown arts scene that drew the normally timid westsiders to the loft district, our location isolated us even from that. Some people got as far as Alameda Street, but turned back once they crossed the railroad tracks.

Since 1982 we'd declared our intention to move, even publishing a spe-cial fund-raising appeal that pictured two dozen women carrying the red brick building on our shoulders. Still, we'd known that we needed to rebuild our infrastructure before we could take that step. All of my fund-raising work, my corporate contacts, my efforts to build a base of donor support, was conducted with an eye to this larger goal. Sue, Cheri, and I spent a lot of time shopping for real estate.

We'd toured the abandoned bank buildings of South Spring Street, vast palaces of architectural grandeur full of dust and stale, dead air from their twenty-year vacancies. We'd stepped over bloody syringes and human feces in loft spaces occupied by squatters. We'd shone flashlights into darkened spaces just in time to see a rat's tail streak by. We'd traveled in shuddering freight elevators, measured the square footage of enormous rooms into which sunlight strained through dingy panes of glass. We'd participated in countless meetings where we fantasized the uses to which we'd put a particular building: "We could have a café in this courtyard"; "That could be our video screening room"; "We could even have childcare in that ground floor space!" Sue had gotten particularly adept at drawing space plans.

Sue also kept abreast of every method used by other organizations to solve their space dilemmas: SPARC[46] had a lease on a city-owned building for $1 a year—did we have the political connections to get a deal like that? The Community Redevelopment Agency (CRA) had helped LACE[47] buy a building—would they provide that kind of low-cost loan to us? One of the members of our Advisory Committee, Linda Griego, had turned a run-down firehouse into one of downtown's trendiest restaurants—maybe there was another historic building that needed renovating.

We tracked down every option, examined every angle. I huddled with the guardians of *The Dinner Party;* Judy Chicago was seeking a permanent home in which to exhibit her monumental artwork, and wouldn't the Woman's Building be an ideal place? Or maybe some developer would like to incorporate us as his "Percent for Art" contribution?[48] Or could we pur-

---

[46] Social and Public Art Resource Center, an organization founded by muralist Judy Baca.

[47] Los Angeles Contemporary Exhibitions

[48] In the mid-eighties, the City of Los Angeles enacted an ordnance that 1 percent of the budget of all new development projects needed to be devoted to the arts. The sum could be paid into a fund administered by the CRA or the art could be built into the project (for example, a mural or sculpture commissioned for the building or space allocated for a small theater or other arts facility).

chase a building and then sell the air rights to fund our costs?[49] We even considered leaving downtown, an action favored by many of our board members and vigorously opposed by the artists on staff; "The Building was downtown when nobody else was here," I was heard to argue frequently, "Now that downtown *has* an arts scene, we're going to leave?"

Each of these options, so energetically pursued with such hope, led us to a dead end. The world of development is not much different from the entertainment industry: so much more is speculated than ever comes to fruition. The fact we were women was a disadvantage; we had fewer resources, fewer inroads to power, and our cause was no longer trendy.

Worse, we were facing a deadline because the city was finally enforcing the retrofitting of old buildings to bring them up to earthquake standards. Our landlord had warned us that this construction was imminent and might shut us down for months. We also feared it would render the space much less aesthetically desirable; did we want gallery or classroom space with all the windows bricked up? With the real estate boom of the 1980s, rents had skyrocketed; we could never afford to duplicate the square footage we currently had.

By the spring of 1986, Sue had conceded that our only option was to try to buy a building. She had one in mind: the Neptune Building (so-called because the structure was ornamented with carvings of the Roman god) on Alameda Street. Still located in the industrial part of downtown, it was close to a number of other arts organizations, galleries, and artist loft spaces, and adjacent to Little Tokyo. It would house our programs with room for expansion, and allow us to continue to rent studio spaces. "With the down payment and renovations," she informed me, "we'll need to raise about $3 million."

---

[49] This bizarre legal machination was a strategy to circumvent the city ordinance forbidding new construction to exceed a given height. A developer could, however, purchase "air rights" from the owner of a shorter building and add the additional height to his development — as if a thirty-story building next to a ten-story building would be the equivalent to two twenty-story buildings.

Ten times more than our current annual budget. I tried not to pale. I attempted to picture myself leading this effort, to imagine that there existed $3 million worth of support for the Woman's Building that I could access. I tried to envision our board being able to conjure this money out of their network of contacts. It was impossible; my mind collapsed under the weight of it.

Sue and I were already each working eighty-hour weeks. My head ached every day; my stomach was inflamed. The skin of my face had erupted with acne and my hands were weeping with eczema. Vicki and I fought almost every day. I was exhausted and not writing. A year earlier, Sue had brought in a consultant to administer a written test to measure stress among the staff. The lengthy questionnaire explored the myriad sources of stress, both positive and negative. New job? New responsibilities? Divorce? New relationship? Change in residence? A score of more than two hundred, the consultant had told us, indicated a life-threatening level of stress. Between my work and personal life, my score had topped three hundred and fifty, and nothing had calmed appreciably since.

Yet, if not me, who would do it? The Woman's Building needed me, and I needed the Woman's Building to survive. Thus far, I'd manage to grow to accommodate each new challenge in the life of the organization. Maybe I could do it again.

"Okay," I told Sue, with a sick feeling in the pit of my stomach. "Okay, but once we're in this new building, I'm done. Then I get to hand it off to somebody else, okay?" I saw myself presiding over the opening festivities of the new building, then walking away, the surface of my desk spotless, uncluttered. I needed my escape plan to endure what I knew the next few years would entail.

The board approved our plan to purchase the Neptune Building. They were energized by the chance to leave this kind of legacy. We began to interview capital campaign consultants, although I privately told Vicki that I feared each board member was thinking it was all the *other* members who were going to pull this off, and she did not disagree.

Perhaps this is why I was so receptive to Kamaka's proposal.

In the seventies I'd practiced Wicca, feminist witchcraft: burning candles and incense, scrawling my intentions on parchment in dove's blood ink. I'd read astrological charts for money and huddled on mountaintops with women chanting under the full moon. Arlene and I had used tarot cards to guide our work on the Lesbian Art Project. I was no stranger to the metaphysical, but in the eighties I'd returned to the earth plane, bound by my job responsibilities and influenced by Vicki's determined materialism. Now, I thought, a little help from the unseen realms would not be unwelcome.

So Kamaka came to the Woman's Building and asked me to show her around. She explained that her work involved a Hawaiian practice called *Ho'oponopono*,[50] which she described as a method of clearing and neutralizing energy and removing the blockages that kept at bay what we desired — prosperity, success, increased visibility, and effectiveness.

As we moved from room to room, floor to floor in the old building, she nodded gravely, sensing the vibrations of each space. Her eyes would widen whenever she perceived energy she thought disruptive. "See how this room is much cooler?" she asked, gesturing to the air. I'd always thought it had to do with the fact that it had no windows, but Kamaka demurred.

Near the end of the tour, she asked me to show her a storage space under the stairs; I'd overlooked it the first time through. She shivered as she stuck her head in. "There's been a lot of death here," she announced in a solemn voice. "I see skeletons, piles of bones and skulls." She noted something on the checklist she'd been keeping. "This building needs a clearing."

Disruptive energies, she explained once we were back in my office — which she pronounced "pretty clear"— could come from the people in the

---

[50] Defined in *They Have a Word for It: A Lighthearted Lexicon of Untranslatable Words and Phrases* by Howard Rheingold as "a social gathering and healing process that combines the function of a religious ceremony, group therapy, family counseling session, town-hall meeting, and small claims court. It is a method of solving problems by talking them out."

building or from anyone who'd ever related to those people. They could come from objects or from anything that had come into contact with those objects, in the present or historically. It seemed a little conveniently all encompassing, but I kept that opinion to myself. *Ho'oponopono* was the way to disperse these energies, and for a few hundred dollars, she would do this for the Woman's Building and for all of the people in it.

It is some measure of my influence at the time that I was able to talk the board into this scheme. It helped that the amount of money was relatively modest, of course, but I think the board members also realized we were going to need a miracle. Although many of them joked about it ("Kamaka the *Schtarker*," Vicki frequently quipped in Yiddish), each board member completed the form Kamaka provided, detailing her view of the Woman's Building's current situation as well as her own personal problems; Kamaka had promised that every person who participated would also receive a personal clearing. These forms were mailed directly to Kamaka, who presumably went to work.

I wasn't entirely sure what that work was; she'd only shared with me a small piece of the process. She had instructed me to meditate on whatever was troubling me, all the people connected to that trouble, all the people connected to those people, and anyone who had ever been in contact with them. She told me to consider all the places, objects, and situations connected to that trouble ("Your board meetings happen in a particular room, but who built that room, where did the materials come from? Who painted it, where was the paint mixed? Where did the chemicals in the paint come from?"), everything and everyone linked to those places, objects, and situations. The immensity of it was dizzying to me as I would lie sleepless in my bed at night, all the stresses of the day tumbling in my mind like a load of clothing in a hot dryer. Once I'd gathered all these things into my awareness, Kamaka had instructed, I should imagine loading them into an enormous mail sack—I always envisioned the kind I used for the ubiquitous Woman's Building bulk mailings—and dropping

that sack into the crater of Mount Haleakala, one of Hawaii's dormant vol-
canoes. Each night I repeated this process, my skepticism at war with a
desperate hope.

At the end of 1986, Linda Preuss left her position at WGC Typesetting
and Design. She was burnt out on sales and marketing and from the stress of
the business never having quite enough money to make ends meet. Perhaps
she, more than the rest of us, anticipated the revolution that was about to
shake the typesetting industry; she began to learn everything she could
about personal computers and went on to become one of the region's fore-
most Macintosh consultants. The staff held a big party for her going away —
even the normally earnest Sondra Hale performed a ventriloquist act — and
presented her with diamond earrings. This gift would have been unthinkable
in the previous decade; we would have spurned its traditionalism and its
commodification. We would have cited the political plight of South African
miners. Although the gift reflected the esteem in which we held Linda, the
wish to give her something of "real value," as a gesture it was pure eighties.

I would especially miss her quick and sardonic wit. Linda had brought
to the Building a vast network of connections to other segments of the
feminist community; I believed we'd be poorer for the loss of it. It didn't
occur to me that this transition might be the result of Kamaka's work; it
was not the kind of change I'd had in mind when I engaged *Ho'oponopono*.

Linda's departure left Sue to manage the business alone, in addition to
overseeing the programs of the Woman's Building. She hired a replacement
to handle outside sales and supervised a staff that had grown to include not
only typesetters and designers but proofreaders, a production manager,
receptionists, and even a delivery person.

To the outside eye, the Woman's Building of 1987 appeared to be thriving. We hosted a tribute to author May Sarton that was attended by over four
hundred people. Exhibitions included an homage to Frida Kahlo by contemporary artists and an important presentation of the traditional textile arts
of Hmong immigrant women. Sondra Hale presented a challenging series of

evening discussions about current feminist theory; she was determined to make us confront the poststructuralist theories that were currently dominating feminist discourse. News of our impending move was rippling through the community, creating a sense of excitement and expectation.

I could no longer perceive where the boundaries of my job ended and the boundaries of my life began. If I wasn't having breakfast with a prospective donor, attending a networking lunch with other arts organizations, or in an evening meeting to plan an event, I was writing a grant proposal late into the night or on the phone at seven A.M. to counsel a board member on whatever was troubling her. My phone rang all day long.

Not unreasonably, Vicki hated my schedule, and hated the way stress distorted my personality. She seemed to find fault with so much about me by this time; several times a month she would threaten to break it off. Despite the insight I was working to gain in Al-Anon, those threats produced the same reaction in me every time: terror at the prospect of being abandoned.

"Why can't I just let her go?" I would ask in my Sunday night Al-Anon meeting, which took place in the fluorescent-lit community meeting room of the Glendale Federal Bank.

Each time I asked, someone would remind me, "Things happen in God's time."

As a feminist and a lesbian, I was having a lot of trouble with the concept of "God" in general. I was especially impatient with "God's time."

God apparently did not think it was time for the Woman's Building to accumulate $3 million. Sue was trying to work out the scenario of whether we could even afford to operate the Neptune Building once we were able to purchase it, and I kept meeting with prospective donors and funders trying to generate enthusiasm about the project. They all thought it was a great thing for the Woman's Building to move, but were decidedly cautious about whether and what they might contribute toward making that happen.

Most nights I would lie awake and imagine dumping everything—my job, the Woman's Building's money pressures, my frustrated career as a writer, Vicki and our whole relationship—into the crater of Mount Haleakala, but this never seemed to bring me relief.

In the late summer of 1987, I met with Kamaka again in the conference room of the Woman's Building. It was one of the rare afternoons that no letterpress class was being offered in the adjacent graphics studio, and we enjoyed the relative quiet without the clang of type against platen. Outside the window on Aurora Street, a group of men unloaded cartons from a refrigerator truck. I studied the Chinese characters on the boxes but these yielded no meaning as to their contents.

"Kamaka," I whined, "I'm frustrated. We've done everything you suggested but things aren't shifting! I feel like I'm pushing against some invisible weight."

She regarded me for a long moment and then said, "There's one other thing we can do."

"What?" I demanded, eager for any solution.

"The Vortex," she replied. She explained that we would create a pattern of swirling energy that would inevitably alter everything that needed to change, reveal what had been hidden, and clear away whatever did not serve the universal plan. "It's very potent energy," she concluded in a slightly ominous tone.

I ignored the implied warning. With a combination of bravado and naïveté, I answered immediately, "Let's do it." It wasn't that I had no sense of the gravity of the undertaking; I was simply at the point where *any* change seemed better than the stasis I felt.

This time there was no list making, no compulsive enumerating of causes. Kamaka instructed me to close my eyes; if she said any other words, I don't remember them. As I stared at the inside of my eyelids, my perception of reality altered, and I felt myself surrounded suddenly by a spiraling current of energy that seemed to be both within and outside me at the same time. My molecules seemed to stir and churn, as if the force that held them together as an entity—me—might release its hold, spinning me off to far-flung corners of the universe. Throughout it all, Kamaka remained a calm presence beside me, her midwestern housewife demeanor making it all seem oddly pedestrian, ordinary.

After a time—ten minutes? thirty?—the movement subsided; the room was restored to its normal dimensions, my body reassumed its customary parameters. Out on Aurora Street, one man barked orders to another man who stood, bored, a cigarette drooping from his mouth. I opened my eyes, soothed by the presence of the scarred worktable in front of me, the battered folding chairs.

"What happens now?" I wondered.

"Wait and see," was Kamaka's advice.

All my doubts had been suspended. The experience had been unmistakably potent; I was convinced that finally the obstacles would lift and our intentions would come to fulfillment.

In August 1987 I turned thirty-three. I was already in the thick of producing that year's Vesta Awards, which always consumed the better part of August and September. That year our celebrity awardees were writer Jane Wagner, comedian Lily Tomlin's partner and collaborator, and progressive singer/songwriter Holly Near. We'd sold more tickets than in any previous year, but two days before the event was Black Friday, so-called because the stock market lost 30 percent of its value in a single afternoon. This occurrence signaled the beginning of the end of Reagan Era prosperity, but we didn't yet realize it.

Nor did we realize that the Woman's Building was about to be threatened with an altogether different crisis. A week after the Vestas, Sue appeared in the doorway of my office. "Ter, I need to talk to you."

This in itself was unremarkable, but something about the urgency of her voice made me stop typing the final report on the event and pay attention.

"Not here," she insisted, and gestured to me to follow her. She led me into the stairwell, where privacy could be more assured.

Then she handed me a letter from the Internal Revenue Service. I had to read it a few times before I understood even its basic message, let alone its implications. The letter stated that the Woman's Building owed $40,000 in taxes; if this amount wasn't paid within three weeks, IRS agents would close down the facility. The top of the letter stated that this was the third and final notice.

I started to feel a swirl of energy, a riptide inside of me, the dizzying vertigo of fear.

"Wh- what is this? What does it mean?" I sputtered. I knew very little about the IRS but it was clear to me that this was very bad news. "How long have you known about this?"

Tears began to spurt from the corners of her eyes as she explained that for the past three quarters, she had not paid the business's payroll taxes to the IRS. Instead she had used the money to shore up the cash flow at WGC Typesetting and Design.

"Linda left and business went down," she defended herself. "I just kept thinking things would pick up and I could make up the money."

She had been carrying this all by herself for over nine months. Horrified as I was, I couldn't bring myself to chastise her. She was ordinarily a rock of certitude, and to see her so panicked made me concerned for her.

I took a deep breath and tried to calm myself. "We can't solve this by ourselves," I said to her in the most reassuring tone I could muster. "We need to tell the board."

"NO!" Sue shot back, "They won't do anything except blame me."

She'd had conflicts with Hermine in the past, had neither forgotten nor forgiven the time our board president had taken the side of a disgruntled employee over Sue's in a grievance procedure.

I saw then that, to Sue, this board who had helped to bring the Woman's Building so far was still a group of "outsiders." I thought I glimpsed the child part of her who'd felt betrayed by people in authority—they didn't understand, they wouldn't help, and they would punish her. It was, I understood, this mistrust, this unwillingness to ask for help, that had allowed the situation to reach this crisis point.

I reminded her that there were businesswomen on the board, women who had a far better understanding of tax law than we did. I reminded her that there were women who liked and supported her.

"Besides," I concluded, "We have to let them know. They're liable."

The vortex had begun to spin, and our course would never be the same. The board was, not surprisingly, outraged. They did blame Sue. They also blamed me. And they blamed one another for failing to exercise proper oversight. The board had regularly received quarterly financial statements for the nonprofit Woman's Building, though they were never given to scrupulous study of these documents. Their eyes tended to glaze over whenever I presented budget reports during board meetings. But they had never asked to see the books on the typesetting business, and Sue hadn't offered them; the board had "trusted" or had "neglected their duties," depending on which version you subscribed to.

Board member Julia Gibson, who managed the creation of special effects for films, located an attorney, an angel named Carolyn Dye, who agreed to take us on pro bono. A group of us met with her one Saturday morning in her Century City office. A sandy-haired woman in pressed chinos and a button-down shirt, Carolyn haled from Kentucky and peppered her legalisms with plenty of bluegrass. "That's a two-beer story," she said when I asked her how she'd come to Los Angeles.

In that first meeting, Carolyn outlined our situation, confirming that the board was indeed liable for the funds (as were all authorized check signers—Sue, Cheri, and myself), and that the IRS could and would confiscate personal property until their debt was satisfied. She also warned that they could impose penalties and interest that could compound the amount of debt several times over.

This motivated several board members to make significant contributions to the organization. Women who'd never given more than a few hundred dollars wrote checks for $1,500, $3,000. One member with a family foundation had earlier that year given us $10,000 to publish a book from the proceedings of our upcoming conference, "The Way We Look/The Way We See." She agreed to let us borrow those funds to help pay the debt on the condition that I would raise additional monies to still publish the book. Altogether we accumulated $32,000.

Carolyn went with me to the IRS to plead our case and get them to revoke the 100 percent penalty. We managed to draw a sympathetic case manager who agreed to this, and to accept our $32,000 good faith payment and allow us pay off the remaining $8,000 over the next year with no further penalties or interest. We were, on the whole, very lucky. Then I had to make a similar arrangement with the State Board of Equalization, because state withholdings had not been paid either.

Although we'd saved the Woman's Building from immediate padlocking, without the business funding we were going to be in serious trouble. WGC Typesetting and Design had outstanding debts to printers and other vendors. I became determined to sell the business, and persuaded the board to let me try.

Through a referral from one of my consulting clients, I engaged a business broker who guided me in writing a business plan. I'd expected Sue to be eager to help in this effort, this chance to redeem the situation from utter cataclysm, but she was numb, sleepwalking through her days, concentrating mostly on the upcoming "The Way We Look/The Way We See" conference and exhibition. I spent one day struggling with a budget projection while she glued photos onto the covers of a thousand copies of an exhibition catalog. She seemed to have a limited capacity to engage the events that were whirling around her.

I didn't exactly blame her. We'd both endured inquisitions by a panel of board members, some of whom had a hard time believing that I hadn't known about the financial situation of the business.

"You were there every day," one challenged me. "Did you never hear Sue speak of the tax situation? You must have known that business was poor."

"I would overhear some worried comments about the cash flow," I admitted, "but I was too busy with my own job to inquire into what was being done about it."

"And when you found out, why didn't you call us immediately?" I had never before heard such a tone of mistrust directed toward me from this group of people. It was as if they believed I had somehow benefited from the situation. No one had done this for gain. Sue had mistakenly assumed that the Graphics Center was undergoing a temporary ebb; once business picked up, she figured, she could make late payments to the tax entities for a small penalty. But business had never improved; no one had foreseen that the revolution in personal computers would forever change the typesetting industry.

"The truth is," I attempted to explain, "I didn't fully understand the implications. I needed to know more about what the problem was exactly before I brought it to the board."

"And you never had occasion to see the financial statements for the business?"

As unpleasant as my interview had been, Sue's had surely been worse.

Despite her lack of participation, I kept pressing forward, meeting with prospective buyers. It was a tough sell; our assets were few — the typesetting equipment was leased, the office space rented. Some prospects were shrewd enough to see what we had not: that the typesetting industry was on the verge of extinction as more and more people acquired personal computers. Others perceived, not incorrectly, that our business was based on personal relationships with our clients, their allegiance to the Woman's Building.

Eventually, though, we attracted a serious buyer, and negotiated terms that, while not ideal, would allow us to pay off our debts and walk away with a little money. I wanted so much for this deal to transpire, to save us from catastrophe. The prospective buyer had one condition: that our sales manager would agree to come to work for him for at least a year to provide continuity for the clients. Pam Ward had replaced Linda Preuss; she was much beloved by the staff of the Building for her sunny temperament and sense of humor. She knew how urgently we needed this sale to happen, and agreed to meet the buyer.

When she came back from that meeting, everyone crowded around her the minute she walked in the door.

"So, how'd it go?" I tried to sound casual, but I'm sure she could smell the desperation exuding from my pores.

Pam slowly shook her head. "I like this job because of all of you," she told us, "because this is a women's business and it's a special environment. It wouldn't be like that with him, not at all like that." She looked at us with a steady gaze. "I'm not a slave. I can't be sold or transferred along with the typesetting lease. I'm sorry. I know what this means to you. I just don't want to work for him."

I couldn't blame her. Hearing her words, I felt guilty for even putting her in that position, making her feel like we saw her that way. I instructed our broker to tell the client of Pam's decision.

And so we began to prepare for bankruptcy.

We worked hard to keep these events secret from the public; it was critical to maintain the image of forward motion. The spin we put on the dissolution of WGC Typesetting and Design was that it was closing because typesetting was no longer profitable, computers having rendered us obsolete. In January 1988, several hundred people attended "The Way We Look/The Way We See," our conference on art criticism in the nineties.

This was the Building's first foray into the brave new world of postmodernist and poststructuralist theory, and it produced a generational clash. I found myself livid at the language used by some of the presenters, which seemed designed to deliberately obfuscate rather than clarify, and to make self-evident premises appear profound. Such objections tended to be dismissed as "anti-intellectual," but it seemed to me that the ostentatious pedantry was calculated to erect an elite club; only those who knew the secret code were entitled to enter. Still, I recognized the necessity for the

Woman's Building to learn this language, to be part of the dialogue. We needed to be seen as engaged in the ideas of the future, not bound to the ideologies of the past, however unjustly those might have been discredited.

I was deeply invested in everything appearing to be fine; the law of the eighties was that of shark-infested waters: you couldn't let them smell blood on you. I'd fought too hard for the Building to see it all slip through my fingers.

Maybe it was this determination that caused the board to decide to keep me on and let Sue go. Without the business revenue, there wasn't enough money for two salaries. Maybe the board decided fund-raising skills were more necessary than program management. Or maybe they couldn't forgive Sue's error in judgment.

I suppose I could have fought harder for her. I could have refused the job of acting executive director, could have insisted we split one position. I did neither. What I cared about, beyond anything, was the Woman's Building's survival, and I was not certain that Sue was any longer the best one to safeguard that. Not because of her decision to withhold the payroll taxes; I could understand that as a well-intentioned lapse in judgment. It was more the numbness that enveloped her, the hunch of her shoulders, as if to ward off blows. The vortex was in motion and it was not over yet. We needed to remain afloat in the eddying waters. It seemed kinder, ultimately, to let her get away from having to witness daily the consequences of her actions: laying off employees, hauling away the big typesetting machines, the awful hush that fell on the business's former offices.

Perhaps she thought I was the lucky one; I know it broke her heart to leave behind all she had worked so hard to build. But there was no great advantage to what I inherited: two eighty-hour-a-week jobs instead of one, the task of trying to configure a viable budget for the Woman's Building, negotiations with the IRS, initiating bankruptcy proceedings for the business. When I was growing up, my parents always spoke in whispered tones about the threat of personal bankruptcy; it carried the taint of scandal, something to be avoided at all costs. I had so much shame testifying at the bankruptcy hearing, at calling printers we'd worked with for years to say, "I'm sorry, we are never going to be able to pay you."

The board allowed her to resign. The staff threw a party for her like we had honored Linda's exit; we bought her diamond earrings. Still, as brave a face as we all tried to put on, no one more so than Sue, her leaving was like cutting out a necessary organ of the body, the lungs or the liver, something vital and irreplaceable.

Sue's departure seemed epic to me, containing the elements of Greek tragedy. The Woman's Building had only continued to exist into the eighties because of the strength of her vision and dedication. It was because she stepped forward in 1981 that the rest of us did too. Yet, like all tragic heroes, Sue possessed a fatal flaw. She chose to do it her way, not perceiving the limits of her capacity, unable to reverse her commitment to that path, not willing to trust enough to ask for help.

To be sure, that approach was deeply woven into the fabric of feminist culture—outside the mainstream, beyond the laws of men. That Outlaw spirit, though severely muted in the eighties, was never entirely expunged from our consciousness.

Many years later, Sue would say to me, "I never felt more alone in my life than during that last year at the Graphics Center." Her comment causes me to think about the limits of sisterhood. Although I would have sworn she could have come to me before the tax problem spiraled out of control, I also know I was constantly giving out messages that I was burdened, overwhelmed. I had even told her I was preparing to leave once we had a new building; why would she have relied on me? We had in the past seen boards disperse in the face of hard times; how could she trust that this one would not do so as well? As much as we paid lip service to community, it seems we were not able to engage the deeper levels of commitment the term requires.

Not long after Sue left, my relationship with Vicki suffered its last gasp and expired once and for all, the next casualty of the maelstrom that had been set in motion. One day on the phone when she, as was her constant habit, announced, "This doesn't work for me. I need to let this go," I didn't argue or plead. I simply said, "Okay," and put down the receiver. I didn't call her back, and when she, inevitably, called, I did not respond. The pressure of events at the Building had exhausted my capacity for drama. I had finally had enough.

The last time I saw Kamaka, she showed up unannounced at my office door. I was reeling from all of the losses, straining to accomplish eighty-seven tasks in that particular hour, and my greeting was laced with irritation. "What do you need?" I snapped.

"I just wanted to see how everything was going," she said hesitantly, already sensing the answer.

"Well," I began my list, "The graphics business is bankrupt, Vicki broke up with me" (a slightly skewed view of the truth), "Sue got fired, and now I'm left to pick up all the pieces." My tone was accusatory, as if this were all *her* fault.

Kamaka's round face fell. She looked both helpless and distraught. No doubt she'd imagined being the one who would rescue me with her *Ho'oponopono* and her faith. In this moment those illusions were torn away in the same swirling current that now surrounded the Building and she stood, naked and half-drowned like the rest of us. I saw this, but I had no comfort left to offer. I was long past the capacity for sentiment, living on nerves and determination.

I sublimated my grief in dedication to the Building. My insomnia was now full-blown; I was at my desk at seven in the morning, padlocking the security gates after ten each night.

I was grateful and relieved that Cheri did not seem to blame me for Sue's departure. I can only imagine the pulls on her loyalty, but she stayed on at the Building, continuing to manage the space rentals and tend to the finances. We soon realized we would need to sublet even more of our space to make ends meet. During the painful quest for a balanced budget—a process that took months—we would call each other on the intercom whenever one of us had a new brainstorm.

"Ter," Cheri's voice filtered through the speaker into my office. "I figured out we could get another $200 a month if we rent out the conference room."

I steeled myself against another loss. "So where would we hold our classes and our meetings?"

"We can use the big table in the graphics studio." Ever resourceful. The Woman's Building had certainly taught us the art of problem solving.

"Okay, let's do it."

Then we'd total up the numbers again and still find a shortfall. Then a few days later I buzzed her extension. "Cher, how much do you think we can get for my office?" My corner office with the tall windows.

"Are you sure you want to do that?"

"We have to, don't we?"

"Yeah."

We had to find the formula that would allow us to cover our expenses, keep our programs going, pay our staff, and eke out our monthly payments to the IRS.

We held onto our gallery and performance space, and the studio of the Woman's Graphic Center. We retained our kitchen and the small lunch-room space. Then we moved all of our other operations into the area that had previously housed the typesetting business. The possibility of moving to a new building was, of course, now out of the question, our dreams of a capital campaign and the Neptune Building swirling away in the gurge.

Our staff was shrunk to a bare minimum to maintain our operations, everyone part-time. Even as acting executive director, I was paid three-quarter time. I had an administrative assistant; there was also a reception-ist, a gallery coordinator, an education coordinator, slide librarian, and Cheri as building manager. We all worked more than the hours for which we were paid, and now everyone was receiving new assignments as Sue's duties were parceled out.

To shore up morale, I instituted weekly staff meetings and took responsibility for trying to keep spirits high. This was a new role for me; I was not known at the time as a cheerful person. I'm habitually the one who sees the dark side to every situation, the potential problem lurking in every scheme; it's a valuable function, but not always appreciated. I was conscious of asking the women on staff to carry on in the face of incredible loss and hardship; these women had worked closely with Sue and they not only missed her, but felt she had been treated unfairly. I was asking them to do more work in the same number of hours, to continue to create top-quality programming despite slashed budgets. Perceiving the threat to the institution they too held precious, the staff responded like champions.

The only way I could reward them was by honoring who they were and what they did. At every staff meeting we devoted some time to allow each woman to talk about her own creative work—what she was working on, what obstacles she was confronting, what successes she'd had recently. One of my own difficulties with working at the Building had been the feeling that I was draining my energy serving other artists while my own work was neglected. I wanted each woman on staff to know that she was recognized and valued as an artist, part of the constituency the organization existed to serve.

One day, before our bankruptcy was final, I was on the phone calling people who owed money to the business, clients who'd gotten behind in their bills. I dialed the number of a designer named Susan Silton, who'd come to us for typesetting almost since the beginning. She was a lithe brunette with a dancer's body and a cocky attitude. She had occasionally flirted with me when she came in to drop off a job, but I'd been involved with Vicki and chose not to respond.

Still, I felt embarrassed to be calling, more so than I had with the others whose accounts were in arrears. "Susan, this is Terry over at WGC Type," I began the conversation. "Uh, this is a little awkward, but you have a couple of past due invoices . . ."

She immediately apologized, and launched into an explanation. "I'm sorry, I just haven't really been able to deal with my work lately . . ." She told me how a good friend, a woman with whom she'd been close, had died recently of AIDS, and how she, Susan, had been grief-stricken and lethargic.

"You poor thing!' Suddenly I felt like the bad one, pestering her over something as mundane as money in the middle of her bereavement. I wanted to do something for her. "Would it help if I took you to lunch?"

There was the briefest pause. She seemed surprised, but not displeased. "Well, yes, it might," her tone warming.

That lunch, at the elegantly spare L.A. Nicola, led a few weeks later to a movie. The movie led to plans for the theater a few weeks after that. One night I came home from a late-night coffee shop date and realized that I was exhilarated in her presence, something I hadn't felt in a long time. The night I wore my blue leather miniskirt to dinner, I knew I was in trouble. That was the first night we kissed. It made me very nervous; my history of relationships had been so bruising. Still, this was my first evidence that the vortex might restore and renew, might add something to my life, not just strip away.

The other thing that came to me during this period was an idea for a novel. For a while the concept had for been tugging at my sleeve, but I kept pushing it away, convinced I had no time. Then with the help of my art buddy, Mary-Linn, I committed to give myself a half an hour a day to work on the first draft.

Amazingly, I did. Some mornings I would get up a little earlier, or go in to work a little late. More frequently, I'd take a break for lunch and scribble on a yellow pad while eating vegetarian Vietnamese potstickers at a little dive not far from the Building. My pages began to multiply. Being absorbed in my own work nurtured and grounded me. Both the novel and my new relationship were deepening my inner life, made me better able to face the daily onslaught of running a nonprofit organization.

As the summer of 1988 slid into fall I was once more planning for the Vesta Awards, an extra special event this year; on November 5 we would be celebrating our fifteenth anniversary. Using Cheri as intermediary, I enlisted Sue to create a costume for me to wear at the awards ceremony. I was touched and delighted when she agreed; she'd taken a job as education director at the Armory Center for the Arts, and I hoped she was healing from all that had happened at the Building.

A skilled seamstress, Sue concocted an elaborate three-tiered birthday cake in pink sateen, complete with a headdress of fifteen Styrofoam candles. My appearance on stage at the awards in this regalia must be considered a major slip in my performance art recovery program, but I felt it was crucial that the Building convey a festive and celebratory image. We were not going to dazzle the public with our new building and roster of big-name supporters, but we could still deliver the most artfully crackpot event in town. The banquet attendees responded with hoots and howls of delight when I sang "Happy Birthday" to the Woman's Building in the style of Marilyn Monroe serenading President Kennedy.

Other anniversary activities had been planned as well. I'd managed to produce a new anniversary booklet, taking the opportunity to update and reformulate the history and public image of the organization, and I persuaded Susan to design the cover. This document was slicker than its predecessor five years earlier; it reflected a further trend toward mainstreaming the organization. It was, again, funded by advertising; this time I enlisted Jennifer Lockwood, the Building receptionist, to handle the ad sales.

Working with Cheri, Ruth Ann Anderson, our gallery coordinator, and some members of the board, a group of artists was invited to participate in a special anniversary exhibition, "Having Our Cake." These artists created original art pieces using the theme of birthday cakes, which we auctioned off to benefit the Building. Beatrice Wood contributed a ceramic cake, resplendent with her trademark luster glazing. Folk singer and artist Phranc provided a whimsical drawing of a punked-out cake.

I'd also planned a special two-day celebration on the anniversary weekend, and enlisted the sponsorship of the city's Cultural Affairs Department.

On Saturday night would be a special reception for "Having Our Cake" and "Members' Salon," a juried exhibition of the art of Woman's Building members. This evening would include the presentation of a special proclamation from the city by councilwoman Joy Picus.

Sunday night there was to be a special fifteenth-anniversary reading by writers who'd been prominent at the Woman's Building over the years, an event planned by our Writing Committee and in which I was included. Our supporters would enjoy the chance to celebrate this anniversary, I knew, but for me the weekend had additional meaning. It was a benchmark, hard evidence that we had survived the tumult of the previous year, that our sacrifice had paid off, and I, for one, planned to revel in it.

On Tuesday, I came down with a severe case of flu—102-degree fever, glands the size of Ping-Pong balls, profound laryngitis. Was this the body's final protest of the nervous exhaustion on which I'd been running for the past twelve months, or a deeper psychological reaction to all the stresses that year had contained? Of course I kept working, bundled in sweaters, shaking with chills—I had a grant deadline, calls to make to the media about Saturday night—until Friday morning when the staff insisted I go home.

All Saturday, I drove Susan crazy, maintaining that I *would* still attend the big event that night. "Look at you," she demanded, "Your eyes are glassy, your forehead's burning up, and your voice sounds like an accordion being squashed by an elephant's foot."

"I'll be fine," I whispered with vehemence.

She raised an open palm in my direction as if to say, "I rest my case."

At five that afternoon my fever began to spike, and I finally relented. I called Cheri to croak, "I need you to run the event tonight. I'm just too sick." Then I collapsed in bed to sulk—my moment of triumph would be happening without me.

"I *am* going tomorrow night," I warned Susan.

She shook her head. "You are so damn stubborn," she complained as she fed me soup.

That I am. The next day I dispatched Susan to buy lemons and honey, and to track down a vial of phosphorous, a homeopathic remedy that might restore my voice long enough to read ten minutes worth of poems. "I'll get well much faster if I'm not depressed," I wheedled in a whisper, trying to mollify her anger at me.

"Don't talk," she chided me. Even though she disapproved, she still helped me.

Come evening, I rose and showered; dressed in black velvet and toting a thermos of hot tea and a bag of lozenges, I made my way to the Woman's Building. Susan drove, stealing worried glances at me as she steered her VW Rabbit in the direction of downtown. I was shivering with fever as she pulled in beside the dumpster.

We entered the gallery, hung with the paintings and drawings of Woman's Building members; my glazed eyes could take in none of it. "Ter, you made it!" Cheri greeted me. She assured me that the night before had been a great success. "Though you were really missed," she added sweetly.

Every chair in the gallery was full as the program began. Deena Metzger and Eloise Klein Healy had been my teachers; Bia Lowe and Jacqueline de Angelis and Michelle T. Clinton had been my cherished colleagues over the years. When my name was announced, I rose to stand at the podium, clutching my thermos cup of "Throat Coat" tea. My eyes swept over the room, taking in my audience, and I opened my mouth, unsure of what would come out.

Amazingly, I found a register through which sound would pass, a kind of throaty cigarette-and-whiskey Lauren Bacall tone. This was the perfect voice with which to read "Black Slip," a poem I'd written in the wake of Vicki's departure.

I read a group of new works that night, poems I'd never before read in public, and from the enthusiasm of audience response I saw I'd broken through to a new level in my work. After my reading, I had to slip upstairs and cough my brains out, but I knew I'd made the right decision to come. At the end of the evening Deena came up to me and commented on one poem, "That one about the cement dress? That's the best thing I've ever heard you do." I warmed under her praise.

Things had fallen apart, but they were coming together too. The doors of the Woman's Building were still open. I was close to landing a new grant from the Irvine Foundation that would give us a stable basis from which to regather our financial footing. I had installed a new board of directors, the president of which was Carolyn Dye. I was starting to feel pretty head-over-heels about Ms. Susan Silton, and I had finished a first draft of my first novel. Perhaps we were finally emerging from the vortex, transformed.

Still, the severity of my illness had been a warning signal: I could not continue to work at the pace and level of stress that I had for the past year. I was exhausted and depleted. And, if I looked honestly at my novel, it was not yet very good. Oh, the idea held promise, and I deserved to be proud of having written a first draft at all, especially under the circumstances. But it was skeletal and crude, riddled with flaws. It had been written in increments of half an hour a day over a six-month period, and that was evident. It wasn't only that the narrative was fragmentary, but it betrayed the lack of depth that was the inevitable result of a short attention span and scattered energy. I had to face the fact that Deena had been right, more than ten years earlier: I would never be the kind of writer I wished to be if I kept giving everything away to the community.

I had dedicated thirteen years of my life to the Woman's Building; twice I had helped to save it from extinction. Mary-Linn said to me, "Maybe it's time to do that for your own work. Maybe it's time to put your art first."

What had been unthinkable now was suddenly inescapable: I would have to leave. Perhaps this was the final spin of the vortex.

Of course, the Woman's Building was not only my devotion; it was also the source of a major portion of my income. How was I going to manage to live if I quit my job? The answer came from Ginger Lapid-Bogda, an organization development consultant who was volunteering her services to help me establish the new board.

"You've given so much to the community," she reasoned. "The community should support you to write this book."

I wasn't sure "the community" would see it this way, but the idea eventually evolved into positioning the novel as an investment opportunity; people could buy shares that would support the rewriting process, then share in the returns once it became a blockbuster. This was still the 1980s—Donna Tartt had received a $3 million advance on her first novel, *Dying Young;* why not me?

Through friends I connected with a New York agent who was enthusiastic about the project. The broker who'd worked on the sale of the business was willing to give me advice. Carolyn Dye helped structure the proposal, and Susan designed an impressive presentation.

Sometimes we do things in life and only later do we understand why. I'd never known what had possessed me to become a fund-raiser until I realized that without that experience, I would never have had the courage to ask a group of people to financially support my work. Nine women bought shares totaling $32,500. This would give me at least a year to complete my book.

I announced my resignation over a greasy breakfast at the Crest Coffeeshop with two of the board officers; they were distressed but not surprised by my decision. Ever the negotiator, Carolyn asked, "What would it take to keep you on?"

"A raise to $45,000 a year," an amount more than double my current salary, "and a six-month paid sabbatical." I knew they could meet neither condition, but nothing less would have persuaded me.

"I'm glad to hear you say that," Carolyn quipped, "I was beginning to think you were downwardly mobile."

I gave six months' notice. I had the idea that if I could organize it well enough, the transition would be seamless. I began to work with some members of the board on a search committee to find my replacement. I had secured funding from the Irvine Foundation so there would be a salary in place for two years. That money had to be matched by a two-to-one ratio, which would result in a solid revenue stream for the Building. The debt to the IRS was fully paid. The budget was stabilized and, although growth would be restricted for a while, we had achieved a balance that would allow us to maintain the current levels of staffing and programs. Grants were pending that would fund future activities. I needed to convince myself that I wasn't abandoning the organization.

I began working even more closely with the staff, getting them used to the idea of my leaving, and informing donors and funders, as well as my colleagues in the arts community, of my imminent departure. I was so happy that I could present it with a positive spin: "I'm leaving to work full-time on my novel." In the value system of the Woman's Building, and indeed of the larger art world, this was a celebratory thing: after years of community service, the artist returns to her art.

I wanted my leaving to be a festive occasion, one that could strengthen the Building, so my next step was to plan an elaborate good-bye party for myself. It would be part performance, part ritual, and it would be a public event, not only for the immediate staff and board. It was also to be a rite of passage, since extricating myself from the Woman's Building was not going to be easy. It was leaving home, a home that had sheltered, nurtured, and challenged me, the place where, in very real ways, I'd grown up.

"The Woman's Building Changed My Life" was the banner headline on the invitation I sent out. On the front were two photos: one, a reproduction of the snapshot from my first FSW student ID. At twenty-two, I was a raw girl with cropped hair, no makeup, aviator glasses, and a stoned expression on my face. Juxtaposed with this image was a photo of my current persona thirteen years later: long platinum blonde curls and severe black-framed glasses, bare shoulders visible in a black velvet dress.

Once more I enlisted the indefatigable Bia Lowe to help me stage the event. She took photos of me and pulled a series of slide images from the archives. She recorded a music tape with songs about work, including

"Take This Job and Shove It," "Car Wash," and "Got Me Workin' Day and Night." She helped me to glue my entire collection of plastic shoes (about twenty-five pair) leading down the hallway of the Building and out the front door.

On the night of the performance I had myself tied with rope to one of the pillars in the main gallery. As the audience entered, the music played and people mingled, my friends coming over to chat with me or have their pictures taken with me bound to the pole.

At a cue, the performance officially began. Six of my dearest friends — Susan, Bia, Mary-Linn, Linda Preuss, Jere Van Syoc, and Vicky Helton — emerged from the hallway wearing blonde wigs and black-framed glasses, holding aloft a giant six-foot-long pencil (created from Styrofoam by artist Ruth Ann Anderson). They'd come to liberate me; wielding the pencil, they freed me from my bondage and conveyed me to a small stage, where I donned a sandwich board with a rendering of the Woman's Building.

The first slide documented a performance done by Feminist Art Workers (Cheri Gaulke, Nancy Angelo, and Laurel Klick) in 1978 in which the artists married the Woman's Building. The three women wear flowing white bridal gowns, pledging their devotion. The next slide shows me in a short black dress, tied to my desk with multiple phone cords, several receivers in each ear. "While the Feminist Art Workers married the Woman's Building," I told the crowd, "*I* was its love slave."

Several women came onstage to tell stories of their memories of me at the Building — among them Sue Maberry and Sondra Hale. The board and staff presented me with — what else? — diamond earrings. At the end I removed the sandwich board from my neck, called to the stage the newly appointed executive director, and placed the burden of the Woman's Building around her neck. I had passed the torch; I was home free. The vortex would at last, I thought, shudder to a stop.

Of course, it wasn't that simple. I was still involved in Building projects that had not yet reached their conclusions: another donor art tour, this time to Chicago; the "Three Generations of Black Women Writers" conference; a three-week symposium about the ethics of representation. I was also contracted to produce the 1989 Vesta Awards.

Through this continued contact with the Building over the next few months, I gained the distinct impression that things were not quite working out with my successor. It seemed a bad sign that she'd moved her office into the most interior space of the building, a closetlike space into which she appeared to retreat from both her staff and the public. Many times I extended myself to her and offered to help, but she seemed to take this as a rebuke. I believed she felt she was working in my shadow and resented it. The Building had needed someone who could hit the ground running; although the director's salary was covered by the Irvine grant, those monies needed to be matched, and she needed to be fund-raising from day one. Instead, she appeared to be overwhelmed by the job, and never succeeded in gaining the confidence of the staff or board. Within nine months, the executive director was asked to resign, and the board did not commit the funds to replace her.

During this time, the arts were undergoing a fierce attack by the U.S. Congress. Certain right-wing congressmen and senators were working to dismantle the National Endowment for the Arts. By publicizing and misrepresenting grants made to artists whose work might be considered controversial in the mainstream, they developed a mandate to severely cut the agency's budget and restrict its mission. They focused on grants to four performance artists—Karen Finley, John Fleck, Holly Hughes, and Tim Miller—and used the sexual content of their work to discredit the NEA. These artists later sued the Endowment for violation of First Amendment rights and became known as the NEA Four.

This affected the Woman's Building on two levels: the funding cuts in the NEA meant less money for the organizations it supported, including ours, and the Woman's Building was of course supporting artists whose work fell outside the mainstream. This came very close to home when

Cheri's performance work[51] was cited in congressional testimony as an example of indecent art. Suddenly the arts, especially the alternative arts, faced a chilling threat of censorship.

Without the leadership of a strong executive director, the relatively new board of the Woman's Building did not engage in fund-raising, and the financial prospects of the organization began to dim. Staff cutbacks became necessary, programs began to be restricted. Several board members did not renew their terms of office in 1990, and a new board president was elected, Sandra Golvin, a lawyer who had recently retired from her career to pursue art full-time.

Eddies were still churning in my own life. I was teaching writing at the Gay and Lesbian Center, including a workshop for people with HIV and AIDS; I was still consulting with other organizations. In the fall of 1989, Susan and I moved in together and bought a beautiful Spanish-style house in Atwater Village, my first real home. The yard contained nineteen fruit trees—lemons and tangerines, plum and pear and apricot—and I felt such abundance. I made a garden for the first time in my life, learning the patience of soil and light. And I—once the fervent nonmonogamist—found it incredibly satisfying to commit to my relationship to Susan. I loved to sit at my desk in the breakfast nook of the kitchen and look out the window to see Susan in her studio in the back, flashing a smile at me as she talked on the phone.

The swirling current did not bring only good news, however. The second draft of my novel, which I'd submitted so proudly and with great hope, was rejected by the New York agent, who advised me that I needed to "put a murder in it." This stung and outraged me; how could a feminist agent advise me to turn my book into a thriller? How could I face my investors with this failure? Humbled but determined, I began my third draft.

---

[51] In 1982, Cheri Gaulke had created *This Is My Body,* a performance that juxtaposed her religious upbringing—her father is a minister—with her explorations of sexuality. In 1987, she created a work, *Virgin,* about being a lesbian trying to get pregnant.

I was deeply worried about the Woman's Building, and night after night would dream I was still working there. In conversations with Sandra Golvin, I began to offer alternative strategies to the organization's dilemma, even volunteering to come back and reinvolve myself. I developed a proposal for a new vision for the Woman's Building, a model of operations that would allow programming to continue without maintaining a permanent site. I'm not sure why these overtures were rebuffed, whether the members of the board didn't have the will to gear up to lead another effort or if my guiding spirits were protecting me from reimmersion.

I wasn't there in those final months; I cannot begin to know what obstacles were looming, what constraints were tightening, what prospects were dashed. One afternoon I was at my desk, watching the late afternoon light filter into the garden. My cat Keppie was rolling on the driveway, near a potted columbine. The phone jangled, and the caller turned out to be Eloise Klein Healy.

Eloise had been my writing teacher in the early eighties, when I was part of a women's writing group she'd conducted at her Echo Park home. I'd been part of a small network of women who'd helped support her through the process of leaving her marriage and coming out as a lesbian. Eloise had herself received encouragement to pursue her writing when she'd attended the Women's Words Conference at the Woman's Building in 1975. She'd been part of the board of the early eighties, then rotated off to concentrate on her career as a poet. She'd returned to the board after I'd left my staff position.

Her voice in the receiver sounded tired and sad. "Terry, I have bad news. The board has voted to close the Woman's Building. We just can't do it anymore."

A heaviness engulfed me, as if the pull of gravity had increased tenfold. In the space of my silence, I heard Eloise say, "I'm sorry." She apologized as though she'd let me down, but guilt was roiling inside me: *I never should have left. This is all my fault.*

Right alongside this emotion was its twin: anger. *How could the board take this unilateral action? How could they give up? How could they not take me up on my offer to come back?* Part of my brain was already formulating a plan: whom I would approach for money, whom I could cajole to be on my new board, how the new Woman's Building should be structured.

I wanted to cry out, to protest. I wanted to argue, to throw myself into the fray and try to stop this course of events. But the heaviness was so pervasive I could scarcely draw breath. I could scarcely lift my arm to hold the receiver against the weight of the inevitable, the awful relief of death.

In the rooms of twelve-step meetings, I'd heard them say, "Let go and let God." I'd heard, "Acceptance is the answer to all my problems today." I'd heard, "*Thy* will, not *my* will be done."

I had asked for change, begged for it, prayed for it. I had been willing to set the vortex in motion—albeit with neither full consciousness of nor proper respect for its consequences. It was futile to now imagine I could throw my body in front of that force, could stopper the energy that had been set loose. Acceptance *was* my only answer, though it would take me years to embrace it.

The women on the board had carefully planned for the Building's dissolution. The printing presses of the Women's Graphic Center were bequeathed to the Armory Center for the Arts. Katherine Ng, a book artist who'd worked in our studio, would head up a program there so artists would continue to have access to producing multiple works.

The slide library, more than ten thousand slides of work by women artists and documentation of Woman's Building history, would be donated to the Otis Art Institute, where Sue was now working as librarian. The video archives were dispatched to the Long Beach Museum of Art, which operated a premiere program for video art. In addition, eighty-eight boxes of files and paper records were shipped to the Archives of American Art in Washington, D.C.

In July 1991 there was a giant garage sale at the Building. I went down

to the Building a few days before the sale and wandered, numb and disbe-
lieving, through stacks of office supplies, art books, posters and prints, old
typewriters, pots and pans, and mismatched dishes. I couldn't imagine how
they were going to dispose of all that was before me: eighteen years of history and art production, accumulated evidence of the effort to make a
home for women artists.

Here was a sheaf of posters from the "Cross Pollination" project.

Boxes of postcards celebrating women. Cheri had conducted a three-
year project teaching letterpress skills by having students create postcards
about their heroines. Mine had celebrated playwright Lorraine Hansberry.
I remembered Hermine had made one honoring Barbra Streisand and had
been determined to get a copy to her idol, convinced the star would make
a large donation to the Building.

Here was the Lucite box I'd had constructed for *Excavations;* for years I'd
stored it here, having no other place to keep it.

I wandered away from the sale area, deciding to take a last tour of the
space that had housed thirteen years of my life. I climbed up the back stairwell to the third floor; I'd seldom ventured up there once the area had been
subdivided into studios ten years earlier, but now I circled the narrow cor-
ridor, recalling that this had been the launching pad for the women who
left for *FEMINA.*

I made my way to the second floor, recalling the early days of meeting
in the FSW room, lounging on the fire escape between classes. I summoned a vision of the performance Betsy Damon staged for the opening
night of the Great American Lesbian Art Show, *What Do You Think About
Knives,* and the particular vision of a nude woman dancing with a shining
blade while another chopped meat with a cleaver.

I went all the way to the scary basement where Mary-Linn and I once
found and rescued a litter of kittens, then made my way back to the first
floor, to the room that was wall-to-wall with desks. I found mine, ran my
fingers lightly over its familiar surface.

"Take anything you want," offered Kathy Clark, now the sole staff person and the one authorized to preside over this wake. "I mean it, anything," she repeated. "You earned it."

Part of me wanted nothing to do with it; I didn't want to pick through the disarticulated bones of this institution I had loved. At the same time I wanted it all, wanted to rent a huge truck to haul every bit of it away and keep it safe, convinced I could stir the bones, resurrect the life that had once animated them.

In the end, I took some art books and some artists' books, a few posters, the electric skillet in which I'd cooked my special tofu and mushrooms for years of staff lunches. I could hardly carry these items to my car for the weight of sadness.

That was the last time I set foot in the Woman's Building. I didn't go back for the public sale, couldn't bear to watch the organization being taken apart, poster by poster, desk by desk. I didn't want to witness the final swirl of the vortex.

When someone asks me now whether I really believe it was *Ho'oponopono* that brought about the end of the Woman's Building, I can only shrug. There were so many reasons. The vision of feminism had shifted so drastically. The funding climate for the arts had grown brutal. We'd all wearied of keeping the organization alive with our own blood. The new decade required a different model and we no longer had the adaptability to mutate. Still, there were always two Woman's Buildings: the material structure of brick and plaster and the energetic presence, the vision, the dream. We had always dwelt in both the seen and the unseen. The gyration of the vortex could not create the conditions of our destruction nor could it alleviate them; that swirling energy could only remove obstacles to realizing the consequences of our actions, could only propel us forward to confront what had already been set in motion.

The board did organize a Vesta Awards in 1991, and they did so without my assistance: they had decided to give me an award for literary arts.

It was apparent to all that this would be our last event. I was too sick with grief at the loss of the Building to be able to properly appreciate the tribute I was being paid.

The event was held in a new location — the Beverly Wilshire Hotel — not the Bonaventure where for so many years I'd produced the event. Perhaps the neutrality of the space was a blessing. Still, I missed the familiarity: the ballroom where I was well acquainted with the sound system, and the lighting grid; the tables on which we'd assembled so many centerpieces; the stage on which I'd stood as a birthday cake and from which I'd dispensed tropical blooms to so many vibrant women. This room was empty of history.

Yet the touch of the performative that always surrounded each aspect of the Woman's Building, a quality that infused the richness of myth into everything that took place under its auspices, was still present that afternoon. At the close of the program, after the awards were given, after the audience had been profusely thanked for its support over many years, and we were all beginning to swipe the tears from our cheeks, Sandra Golvin beckoned everyone to stand.

And from the PA system of this staid, elegant ballroom came the rise and raucous swell of none other than Aretha Franklin, her glorious full-throated tones still demanding "R-E-S-P-E-C-T." Sandra exhorted us to dance and we did, hips shaking, arms thrown to the ceiling. After all these years, the old anthem stirred us still.

We have such an organization as has never before existed of women for women.

Women's thought and sympathy have traveled to us along the slender, imperishable line of the thought railway. Our building is like the terminal station of a vast city, where the iron rails come together from the north, south, east, and west. The freight that our railway has brought is very precious. The Exposition will thus benefit women, not alone by means of the material objects brought together, but there will be a more lasting and permanent result through the interchange of thought and sympathy among women of all countries, now for the first time working together with a common purpose and an established means of communication.

on the occasion of the opening of the Woman's Building.

May 1, 1893

Quote from the original Woman's Building, painted on the wall of the Woman's Building in Los Angeles for the "Woman's Building 1893 Historical Handicrafts Exhibition," which opened in 1976. This quote remained on the wall for many years as a permanent acknowledgment of the connection between the two.

Medicine
2001

Believe the medicine of your own hand.
Believe that emptiness is the full dance between us . . .
—Linda Hogan,
from "Partings" in *The Book of Medicines*

AS VITAL AS IT WAS, PROVIDING A SITE, A HOME, A ROOM OF ONE'S OWN FOR feminist art, the red brick building on North Spring Street was always only a shell. The carapace of a dream. Does the spirit die with the skeleton, or is it released into ether to continue its work? Does the dream expire when the alarm shrills, or does it live on, unseen in daylight?

You believe it is your mission to keep that dream alive. You live now in Diaspora, carry the memory of a tribe dispersed, charged with the duty to preserve its language, customs, history. Its medicine.

It was medicine, that vision of art and community. A balm to the undernourished spirits of women, who could not then imagine all they might become. Cooperation, a tonic. Support, a restorative. Validation, a remedy. Mythmaking, a cure. To live mythically is to become more than who one has been allowed to be, to enact the fulfillment of a dream, to stir the energies and conjure one's own existence. This medicine is needed still, perhaps more than ever—and not only by women—as the world of commerce vies to eradicate the world of meaning. Are we not all seeking agency, creative power over our destinies, in a world that twists our needs and desires according to what it wishes us to buy?

It's a waste of time to idle here on North Spring Street, in the unclaimed territory between Chinatown and Lincoln Heights. Even the trains don't come this way anymore, tracks overgrown with weeds, railroad yards fenced off. It makes no more sense to stare at the padlocked door than to probe the beached conch for an evening meal; all you'll gain is an echo of what has passed.

~

TO KEEP THE DREAM ALIVE, I have to weave it into waking, threading its visions through each breath, every gesture. I am a teacher, and I see in my students' eyes their need for this medicine, this vision of art and community.

I saw it in the eyes of men with HIV and AIDS, whom I taught for nine years after leaving the Woman's Building, the last vestiges of separatism dissolving in the face of that terrible plague. Some of those men came to the weekly sessions at the Gay and Lesbian Center, to the room with the stained carpet and mismatched furniture, for communion, for the chance to be with and talk with others who shared a common experience. Others who spoke the language of blood and T cells, of opportunistic infections, of social service bureaucracies. Some came to wrestle back control of their destinies from the virus that stalked their cells. Some came to create in the face of destruction: their ravaged immune systems, their withering physiques, their lesioned skin. Some came to bear witness.

For those nine years, I brought them the medicine of the word, its power to summon the sacred. I brought them the medicine of listening, of being received. I brought them faith that their reviled stories were things of beauty, of resonance and meaning. One of these men lived eight years beyond his doctors' predictions; he lived long enough to create and to publish a magnificent book. He gave credit to this medicine—his creativity—for keeping him alive.

I have seen the need for this medicine again and again in the eyes of marginalized people—lesbians and gay men, people of color, people raised poor and working class, those abused as children, and always in the eyes of women—everyone who's been told that they do not exist, they have no right to their stories, that no one will hear what they have to say. This medicine has the power to dispel those lies, and I work with my students to dismantle them one by one, layer by layer, as they were once dismantled for me.

From the Woman's Building I learned the necessity of space, having territory one can claim, ground in which community can take root. So in 1997 I rented a space with enormous windows that look out onto trees and sky to claim as a space for writers. Warm yellow walls invite and sustain; I want a place for writers to build connection, a laboratory for invention and risk. How can I live in a world without such a place? I am only too aware of my impulse to re-create the Woman's Building, albeit on a much more modest scale. So Spring Street has become Fountain Avenue, but those same waters still feed the creative spirit. A sign on the door announces, "STOP AND REALIZE YOU ARE ENTERING INTO A SPACE FOR THE IMAGINATION."

In the classes, taught by myself and other colleagues, we dispense the medicine of encouragement, yes, but more: We tender craft, tools to empower the word; the expectation of excellence and someone to applaud when a student achieves it; processes to negotiate the terrain of doubt, defeat, and terror at attempting more than they were ever allowed to dare.

Healing happens in tiny moments that reverberate throughout a life.

Trish has survived cancer but imagines no one wants to hear about it. Still, she is coaxed to read her words aloud. When she finishes the room erupts in applause, everyone so moved to be entrusted with her words. Her eyes glisten, some piece of her restored.

Pat's whole face brightens when I tell her she's finally mastered the element of plot. She raises her hands in delight; her classmates cheer with her.

Eric cannot seem to write his novel, until he remembers the experience of being molested as a child. Now he writes about a monster and the world does not explode.

Anne and Carole make a pact: to rise at six A.M. each morning, call one another and thus provide support for each to write before leaving for work. "My whole day goes better," Carole reports gratefully, "when it begins with writing."

The members of the Saturday afternoon poetry workshop dub themselves "The Club for the Too-Intense," claiming pride in a way of being for which they have long been criticized. They are so relieved to find at last the tribe that does not disparage their sensitivity, all that they refuse to not feel and see.

This is the medicine of the Woman's Building at work in the world. And in extending it to others, I can keep it alive for myself.

~

OF COURSE, I am not the only one who carries this medicine to the world. Cheri teaches at a private high school, where she exhorts her students to use the medium of video to address social issues—teen pregnancy, homophobia. Sue is the librarian at Otis College of Art and Design; she's recently launched a web site with vast selections from the Woman's Building slide archive. Vicki Yerman has become a public school teacher, enticing fifth- and sixth-grade students to fall in love with poetry. Sondra Hale is on the faculty of the Women's Studies Program at UCLA; Betty Ann Brown is a professor of art history at California State University–Northridge. Eloise Klein Healy founded an MFA writing program at Antioch College in Los Angeles, where she infuses the spirit of feminist process into graduate study. Sheila de Bretteville heads the Design Department at Yale, and receives commissions for public art projects that honor the lives of women.

Suzanne Lacy has founded the Center for Art and Public Life at the

California College of Arts and Crafts; this program serves as an umbrella for collaborative projects between artists, CCAC students, and schools and organizations in the community. Linda Vallejo offers sweat lodges and other ceremonial activities for women in prison. Deena Metzger has delved deeper into shamanism as a foundation for her private teaching. Arlene Raven continues to carve out a new voice for art history, insisting on the resonance between personal, social, and aesthetic meanings of art.

And there are countless others, both known and unknown to me, in disparate locations across the country and around the world. Perhaps the Woman's Building was at one time like a seedpod where we clustered together, enclosed and safe, as we gathered our potential; then the pod burst open and we were scattered in the wind to sow ourselves in far-flung gardens.

~

THESE DAYS, researchers call; they e-mail, they come to my door. They are curating an exhibit of lesbian art; they are writing theses on feminist art of the seventies, dissertations on the Woman's Building. Can they talk to me? Can they paw through my files? Can they borrow my slides?

I make time for them, even when I have no time. I serve them water or tea while they sift through ancient typed documents (yes, products of another technological age, before the advent of the personal computer, pages still pocked with the imprint of the keys and daubs of Wite-Out), and squint at slides whose labels have unglued themselves and drift to the floor. They ask me questions to which I dutifully respond into their micro-cassette recorders. I am grateful to them for proving that the work we once performed, the vision to which we dedicated ourselves, is seen, is recognized, valued still. Grateful that we will not yet be written out of history.

Every once in a while I have the impulse to clear out my crowded office, where the records of the past jostle for scant space with the projects unfolding toward the future. I should, I think to myself, clean out my cabinets, donate all these records to an archive. But then I realize I would miss the chance to encounter these researchers, inevitably women, almost inevitably younger than myself. I would miss their curiosity, the moment of discovery, the insights they summon that reflect on my experience in a way I never could. I would miss the young woman who says to me plaintively, "I really wish I'd been part of it; there's nothing like that now."

I make time for these young women because they are the answer to the question that has plagued me: did we, by embracing an alternative path and unconventional methods and a decidedly crackpot vision, marginalize ourselves into oblivion? No, they tell me, the signals sent are resounding still, vibrating underneath the culture, seeds erupting unseen in fertile ground, inside the pulse of consciousness.

~

A QUARTER CENTURY AGO I left behind the Great Lakes and the greenery of Michigan, journeyed, like so many, across the continent to make a home with other women, a home rooted in art. Within those red brick walls we learned that art flourishes not in isolation, but in community. On a strip of dirt bounded by railroad tracks and the cement-lined L.A. river, we gained permission to explore our authenticity, to unseal the locked rooms inside ourselves, fill them with light and air. In the shadow of Dodger Stadium, we discovered the mythic, the sacred, and savored the richness of life that comes from planting oneself in that ground.

Now we carry that home inside, alive in every cell, pulsing with each breath. Freed of the weight of bricks and mortar, we are each the embodiment of that second building, that grand mansion of our dream. Now we throw open the doors and enter the future.

About the Author

TERRY WOLVERTON is the author of *Bailey's Beads,* a novel, and two collections of poetry: *Black Slip* and *Mystery Bruise.* Her fiction, poetry, essays, and drama have been published in periodicals internationally and widely anthologized. A novel in poems, *Embers,* will be published by Red Hen Press in 2003. She has also edited twelve literary compilations, including the award-winning *His: Brilliant New Fiction by Gay Men* and *Hers: Brilliant New Fiction by Lesbians.* Additionally, Terry collaborates with choreographer Heidi Duckler and Collage Dance Theater on site-specific performances including *subVersions* in Los Angeles and *Under Eden* in Miami.

Since 1976 Terry Wolverton has lived in Los Angeles, where she provides management consultation and coaching to arts organizations, small businesses, and individual artists. Terry has taught creative writing for over twenty years; in 1997, she founded Writers At Work, a center for creative writing in Los Angeles, where she offers several weekly workshops in fiction and poetry. She is the recipient of numerous awards for her artistic and community contributions, and is a certified instructor of Kundalini Yoga.